Scotland's
SPLENDID THEATRES

Scotland's
SPLENDID THEATRES

*Architecture and Social History from the
Reformation to the Present Day*

BRUCE PETER

Polygon

Polygon
An imprint of Edinburgh University Press Ltd
22 George Square, Edinburgh

Typeset in Sabon
by Pioneer Associates, Perthshire, and
printed and bound in Great Britain by
The Cromwell Press, Trowbridge

A CIP record for this book is available
from the British Library

ISBN 0 7486 6261 8 (paperback)

The Publisher acknowledges subsidy from

towards the publication of this volume.

CONTENTS

ACKNOWLEDGEMENTS

The research for this book was completed thanks to the assistance of an award from The Carnegie Trust for the Universities of Scotland.

Many thanks are also given to: Aberdeen Central Library, The Architectural Heritage Society of Scotland, Bob Bain, Johnny Beattie, Professor Dugald Cameron, Sheila Campbell, Graeme Cruikshank, Michael Davis, John Duddy, John Earl, Staff of Edinburgh Central Library, Allen Eyles, John Fairley, Elizabeth Ferguson, Archie Foley, Stephen Fraser, Martin Frutin, Vincent Gillen, Glasgow City Archives, Ann Glen, Carol Goodfellow, Ian Gordon and colleagues at the Mitchell Library, Ian Gordon of the Glasgow Pavilion, Richard Gray, Xandra Harper, *The Herald*, Paul Iles, Billy Jardine, George Lane, Christine Lang, Jimmy Logan, Janet McBain, Scott McCutcheon, Murdo MacDonald, Donald McKenzie, Ray McKenzie, John J. McKillop, Irene McMillan, Frank Manders, Memories of Hendon, Ann Menzies, Tony Moss, Christopher Neale, John Peter, Pitlochry Festival Theatre, Eddie Poole, David Roberts, Teresa Roby, Colin Ross, Gaylie Runciman, The Scottish Music Hall Society, Adrienne Scullion, Moira D. Sim, Ronald Singleton, Mrs M. Stephen, Derek Sugden, The Theatre Museum, The Theatres Trust, Gertie and Trixie Thomson, David Trevor-Jones, The Winter Gardens Trust, Andrew Young, and the enthusiastic management and staff of all the theatres who received me so courteously.

Special thanks go to David Cheshire and Bill Findlay for their friendly advice and editorial skills and to Jackie Jones and Alison Bowden for their continuing assistance with the publication.

INTRODUCTION

EARLY HISTORY

Prior to the Reformation, the theatre had been popular in Scotland. Strolling players travelled from town to town but gradually the power of the Roman Catholic Church came to be challenged. As the fifteenth century drew to a close, Scotland became ever more ready for rebellion against its clerical oppressors. Many nobles were alarmed that the Church owned almost half the total wealth of the country. Scots saw that the most fertile land, which had once belonged to their forebears, was now attached to the cathedrals and abbeys. The common people had to pay the Church taxes to work this land. The clergy were greedy and lived extravagantly. Much seditious literature was then being printed denouncing the priesthood, but as most folk were illiterate, such protests made little impact outside the nobility.

Sir David Lindsay, a playwright and former Lyon King at Arms to King James IV, became one of the most outspoken critics of the Church. Lindsay was a close friend of James IV and became an influential adviser to his son, James V. Most of Lindsay's writing was devoted to forceful and well-argued attacks on the vices and impositions of the clergy. His most famous drama, *A Satyre of the Three Estaites*, portrayed the avarice of the prelates so accurately that they wanted Lindsay killed, indeed it was only the protection of the King that saved him. For the Church, the worst feature of the drama was that it could be understood and relished even by illiterate folk. They could stand around the open stage on which it was performed and eagerly follow every word and action by which it ridiculed or denounced the priesthood's excesses. Lindsay did not want to destroy the Roman Catholic Church, merely to reform it, but across northern Europe events took on their own momentum.

Ironically, after the Reformation the theatre was harshly persecuted in Scotland. A phase of Puritanism arrived, during which the arts were repressed as decadent and popish. The Reformed Church took the lead in the suppression of staged performances. Glasgow ministers were even more outspoken than their Edinburgh counterparts in denouncing frequenters of 'the Devil's play-house'.[1] Those who attended plays were excommunicated from the Church and congregations were encouraged to persecute actors. On 24 April 1595 the Kirk Session of Glasgow directed the town's drummer to forbid 'all persons from going to Ruglen to see vain plays on Sundays'. On 20 May 1624 the Session announced that all 'resetters of comedians would be severely punished'. As a result of pressure from the Kirk, on 20 July 1670, the Glasgow Magistrates decided to prevent 'strolling stage players from running in the street and per-forming plays in private houses', claiming their tough stance was supported by 'The Wisdom of Solomon'.

Writing in 1830, the historian Hugo Arnot commented that 'the Presbytery were possessed with the most violent and most illiberal animosity against the stage. The writings of their most popular divines represented the playhouse as the actual temple of the devil, where he frequently appeared clothed in corporeal substance and possessed the spectators whom he held as his wor-shippers.'[2] In seventeenth-century Scotland belief in demonology and witchcraft was widespread, and raging against theatrical entertainment found popular support. In England a more liberal theology prevailed, so the theatre made faster progress there than north of the Border.

But as in every case of intolerance and persecution, in Scotland the van-quisher was bringing nearer his own defeat. A few of the privileged and wealthy employed itinerant actors as servants, who could both entertain their masters and do the housework, thus escaping the attention of the Kirk. By the eighteenth century, Edinburgh in particular was experiencing the Scottish Enlightenment with an astonishing upsurge in activity in all the arts, including theatre. This interest spread throughout the country and although the Kirk used its consid-erable power and influence to persuade magistrates all over Scotland to ban the theatrical performances, they rarely succeeded as the lawmakers were themselves some of the most avid theatre-goers.

The first theatres were simple wooden booths, often built outside the boundaries of the towns they served and thus escaping local anti-theatre bylaws. Sometimes the audience stood outdoors on a piece of common ground with a raised platform at one end acting as the stage. Occasionally the theatre was fully enclosed, being either a purpose-built timber structure, or a conversion of a barn or warehouse with wooden fittings. Either way, lit as they were by candles, these first illegal playhouses were fire-traps. Many that did burn down were set on fire by arsonists who thought they were carrying out God's will, as preached by the Kirk. Spurred on by loud-mouthed preachers like the notorious Reverend George Whitefield, who appeared in Glasgow and Edinburgh, many less well-educated Scots thought that attacking theatres was somehow waging war against the devil.

The Theatres Licensing Act of 1737 gave the Lord Chamberlain power to grant licences for the performance of drama, comedy and opera. All scripts had to be sent to his office in London to be vetted. This was to prevent anything satirical or subversive reaching a wide audience at a time of political instability. On paying £300, a theatre manager had the legitimate right to present the drama in a particular town (hence the phrase 'legitimate theatre') and to name his premises with the Letters Patent, Theatre Royal. In Scotland various pieces of local legislation kept theatres officially illegal until 1767 when the Act of Parliament to allow the building of the New Town was passed. This legislation enabled Edinburgh magistrates to grant licences and Letters Patent for twenty-one-year terms to the highest bidder. It was not until 1803 that Glasgow followed suit. These Acts precipitated the construction of the first stone theatres, which were essentially sheds with forms and rows of wooden boxes along the sides of the auditorium. In front, a Doric order was then the height of fashion in theatre architecture and, with their unadorned capitals, these caused much controversy in architectural circles. Some thought that the fact that they sat on the ground, without bases, made them exceedingly vulgar! In this day and age, when we take modernism for granted, such obsession with designs of classical antiquity seems very strange indeed, but the accurate replication of the form and proportion of classical designs was then a sign of advanced culture and civilisation.

If the early Theatres Royal had pretensions as temples of culture, their audiences were, for the most part, somewhat uncivilised. Actors were often surrounded, for if the house was full, more space for patrons was made on the stage behind the performers. Behaviour could be drunken and disorderly and audience participation was more akin to that at a football match with wild cheers for the hero, or for a particularly dramatic performance. There were occasional riots when the audience felt short-changed, or when republicans and monarchists clashed around the period of the French Revolution.

In 1843 the regulation of theatres by Letters Patent was abolished. Ever more prosperous theatres were erected and, by the early Victorian phase, many of Scotland's larger cities had several, each vying for patrons. The Theatres Royal were still the most respectable places to see a play, with good resident companies and occasional visits by 'big name' actors from the London stage (London then, as now, was thought the be-all and end-all of distinction and prestige in the theatre). Alongside these 'legitimate' playhouses, a shoddy collection of 'minor' theatres sprang up. They were badly built, in fact often dangerous fire-traps, but they served new audiences of folk off the land as the process of urbanisation gathered momentum in the early years of the industrial revolution. The streets around Glasgow Cross were notorious for their unplanned rows of wooden theatres and open booths (known as 'geggies'), showing illegitimate drama and causing congestion in the streets. Their managers would visit the legitimate Theatre Royal, note down the script of whatever was being performed, and produce their own uncensored version a few days later at a fraction of the cost.

By offering entertainment pubs could attract more drinkers, so the first music halls were essentially glorified drinking dens in which men sat at long tables at right angles to the stage to be entertained by singers and comics while they drank cheap whisky. Trongate in Glasgow and the streets around Kirkgate in Leith were infamous for their shebeens, brothels and music halls (the three invariably co-existed) for the entertainment especially of sailors on leave. As competition increased, music halls quickly became more comfortable and chairmen were introduced to present the acts and maintain some semblance of order. It was only a small step to the birth of variety theatre in the form we understand it today.

In the mid-Victorian era, the growth of railways made travel much easier, and this in turn led to the disbanding of the 'stock' theatre companies resident at the various Theatres Royal. In these companies, young actors were trained with practical experience in minor roles by following the example of older performers. The system was hit or miss as the success of a theatre depended entirely on the calibre of its actor-manager and bad leadership would mean at least a season of poor performances which could ruin a theatre's reputation. Companies were able to take the train from town to town, so there was a much greater choice and a higher quality of performance overall. At the same time interest in the theatre increased and a theatre-building boom began.

When Edward Moss opened the first of his sumptuous Empire Palace theatres in Edinburgh in 1892, celebration was in order. The variety business had gone through revolutionary changes. The old-style, chairman-conducted, male-dominated music halls with drinking in the auditorium were closing by the score, victims of tougher licensing controls and the changing tastes of an increasingly affluent public. To all outward appearances, buildings like the Moss Empires were regular theatres, rather than music halls. They had fixed seating facing the stage; their bars and drinking areas were strictly separated from the auditorium; they lowered their house lights during performances. They were gorgeously enriched yet determinedly respectable. They aimed to attract a cross section of the population rather than a class, although their audiences were clearly segregated by ticket price and, consequently, the level of comfort of their surroundings. The best seats were reached through marble-clad foyers and ante-rooms, swathed in gilt and plush. Pit and balcony customers went in a separate door round the side, up stone stairs with disinfected tiled walls to reach wooden benches. They were solidly built with much thought given to minimising the ever-present risk of fire. Many theatres burned down due to the proximity of drapes, wooden scenery and upholstery to gas lighting.

Iron safety curtains, numerous fire exits and electric house lights made these new theatres much safer.

British theatres of the Victorian period were very different from those in Europe. On the continent, the major theatre or opera house in each town was usually a grand municipal building on a very prominent central site, either occupying an entire block by a square with imposing show facades on every side, or standing in its own grounds. No time or expense was spared on these grand European opera houses, whose foyer spaces were sometimes larger and more opulent than the auditorium itself and some took years to build. In Britain, neither the government, city authorities nor the aristocracy has traditionally been interested in theatre as an art form (least of all in Scotland, where even at the turn of the century, theatres were still regarded with disdain by sections of the public). Instead, every theatre in Britain was built strictly for commercial reasons.

Late Victorian theatres are perhaps the most iconic buildings of their era. Their architecture combined the latest structural technology of steel framing, fireproofing and cantilevers to support thousands of seats with all that was ripest and fruitiest in decoration. The sources of inspiration for their adornment were legion; painted scenes from Greek and Roman mythology or the muses of comedy and tragedy were familiar themes, combined with fibrous plaster representations of the architectural styles of Second Empire France, the Italian Renaissance and the most exotic styles from the corners of the burgeoning British Empire. Lively, swirling, gilded French baroque was thought an ideal style for theatre interiors. Baroque is identified with movement and sensuality and so it was a perfect complement for staged performances. Often, especially in variety theatres, many styles were juxtaposed. The richness of architectural readings offered by such apparently random mixtures of baroque, Indian or Italianate decoration allowed patrons to escape from the toils of industry and fantasise in an environment of sumptuous comfort where location and chronology were suspended. It also excited expectancy in audiences for the strange diversity of acts in their variety bills.[4]

Late Victorian theatres represented a marked departure from what had gone before. The most radical and noticeable change was structural. The use of steel (in place of timber and cast iron) to carry deep balconies across the full width of the auditorium eliminated the short spans and regularly spaced columns which had governed the design of early auditoria and given some sense of inevitability to their architectural treatment. The new freedom produced a generation of extravagantly modelled theatres whose uninhibited eclecticism looked suspiciously like fancy dress to many later architectural historians. Structural freedom, it has since been argued, should produce a movement away from unnecessary ornament towards a purer 'functional' style. Seen in this light, a richly decorated Victorian theatre is an aberration verging on the immoral. Such pedantic views have clouded much twentieth-century architectural thought and ignore completely the achievement and complexity of these astonishing theatres.

THE ARCHITECTS

In Britain not only did theatre architects need to be technically proficient in designing the complex structures of cantilevers to support the massive spans of balcony tiers and backstage equipment but they also had to devise ravishing interior decoration (a task only occasionally left to the imagination of the plasterer). On the other hand, theatres in Britain had to be constructed relatively inexpensively, quickly and within budget. The skill of their architects was further tested as developers often bought some exceedingly awkward sites on which to have their theatres built. The Edinburgh Empire Palace was behind a row of shops, the Olympia in Glasgow was fitted into a Y-fork between two roads and His Majesty's in Aberdeen was built over a river. It is therefore no wonder that a small, but distinguished, group of specialist theatre architects emerged who could be relied on to provide exactly what owners and audiences wanted. Although these talented Englishmen did some of their finest work north of the Border, their Scottish theatres cannot be examined in isolation. Apart from the obvious use of native stone dressings for facades and the need to satisfy local fire regulations, inevitably there were few obvious differences between Scottish theatres of the period and their English cousins.

The first theatre specialist to emerge was Charles John Phipps, born near Bath in 1835. Phipps's most prolific years preceded the flowering of music halls in the 1890s and so his buildings tended to be more seriously classical in tone and well suited for drama. Although always built on a more modest scale, his designs were apparently influenced by the great continental theatres of the eighteenth and nineteenth centuries. His Royal Lyceum in Edinburgh, for example, had a solid civic dignity absent in most British theatres of its period. Decoration in a Phipps theatre was always applied in low relief. Some of his work, such as his rebuilding of the Theatre Royal Glasgow, was criticised because it was executed in great haste and underneath the elegant veneer of plaster, the design was rather shoddy. An unfortunate blemish on his career was the burning of his Theatre Royal, Exeter, where 140 patrons were asphyxiated by smoke. At the inquiry, Phipps claimed that while he had considered fire when designing the theatre, he had not thought about smoke. He was ridiculed for a time in the architectural profession, but by the time of his death in 1897, he was once again a respected architect with over forty theatres to his credit, including four in Scotland. The Theatre Royal in Glasgow and Royal Lyceum in Edinburgh are among the best survivors of his work.

Bertie Crewe was one of the most dynamic architects of the 1890s and 1900s, designing mainly variety theatres of wildly florid splendour. He trained in London and later in Paris at the Atelier Laloux and his facades and interiors were heavily influenced by contemporary French fashion. Crewe's earliest theatres were designed in collaboration with W. G. R. Sprague, who also became a distinguished theatre architect based in London. Their first joint efforts, like the Paisley Theatre of 1890, were tepid in comparison with what was to follow. By the Edwardian era, Crewe was in his stride, producing in Scotland the ravishing Palace, the Pavilion and Bostock's enormous Scottish Zoo and Circus complex in Glasgow. His large variety theatres typically had horizontal balconies tied to stacks of stage boxes, with stunning three dimensional decoration; giant papier-mâché elephant heads, seated gods and caryatids making a gorgeous and elaborate frontispiece for the stage.

Frank Matcham was arguably the greatest of British theatre architects.[5] Born in 1854 in Newton Abbot in Devon, he trained as an apprentice to a local architect. He moved to London in the 1870s, marrying the daughter of Jethro T. Robinson, a well-known theatre specialist, and taking over his practice. Between 1879 and 1912 Matcham designed about 150 theatres, or over twice as many as his nearest rival, and nearly a quarter of all the theatres built in this period. Some, such as the London Palladium and the London Coliseum, are internationally famous, while others only ever entertained local audiences. All show Matcham's genius and vision in creating luxuriously opulent pleasure palaces for the enjoyment of everything from circuses to four-hour-long operas. Despite his enormous output, he developed a very personal style, which is instantly recognisable but no two buildings are identical. He was the supreme example of an unacademic architect who became a master of his craft and could always be relied upon to deliver a lively, sensuous building, inexpensively yet solidly constructed. He was acutely aware of the technical difficulties of sight lines, acoustics, fire escapes and ventilation. He even took out a patent for the design of cantilevers.

Matcham was at his best and most fanciful in the 1890s with an incredible grasp of the three-dimensional possibilities of auditorium design, using every trick to maximum effect: dipping balconies, stage boxes twisted and set forward or back to better the sight lines and the whole composition swathed in luscious decoration and drapery. Architectural critics have, until recently, savaged Matcham for being 'architecturally illiterate', that is to say, appearing to mix and match various periods of classical architecture without reverence for their origins or correct proportions. Perhaps chastened by this onslaught, or maybe simply responding to changing taste, after the turn of the century, Matcham's designs became more restrained. In Scotland Matcham produced theatres in every combination of styles he favoured. His three vibrant variety theatres – for Moss in Glasgow and Edinburgh plus the Tivoli in Aberdeen – contrast with the more restrained opulence of touring venues like the King's and Royalty, both in Glasgow. He also designed a circus for Hengler. Lastly, His Majesty's in Aberdeen had one of his most subdued and dignified interiors. During the 1960s ignorance of the value of these buildings led to many being destroyed, but nowadays his astonishing theatrical flair has been recognised as near genius and any city with an intact Matcham theatre can consider itself very fortunate.

In Scotland several local architects rose to the challenge of designing provincial theatres with a finesse and quality which often matched that of the London experts. The finest, and so far unsung, group of home-produced theatres was designed by Alexander Cullen, an outstanding architect from Hamilton, who was one of Scotland's leading exponents of art nouveau. Perhaps because he did not work in the city, his buildings have not attained the prominence of contemporaries like Mackintosh or Burnet. Cullen, born in 1857, was a partner in Cullen, Lochead and Brown. From 1902 to 1904 he not only designed but also invested in three important theatres for the Edinburgh councillor Robert C. Buchanan; the Motherwell New Century theatre was the first and most interesting of the group. These suffered terribly in the battle for survival as they were first adapted and then demolished to make way for cinemas. Cullen was a superbly adaptable and prolific architect who could also design houses, churches, municipal buildings and hospitals with equal quality and conviction.[6]

The Kirkcaldy architect and town councillor John D. Swanston, born in 1875, produced designs for several fine Edwardian theatres, such as the King's Theatres in Edinburgh and Kirkcaldy (both with sumptuous Viennese baroque interiors of operatic proportions), the Gaiety in Methil, the Palace in Kirkcaldy, the Alexandra in Belfast and a new interior for the Dunfermline Opera House.[7] Many other small Scottish firms produced one-off theatres, such as James Thomson's exceptional King's in Dundee and Boston, Menzies and Morton whose imposing Alexandra was a well-loved Greenock landmark for nearly seventy years.

Shortly after the turn of the century, a new fashion for more refined classicism, known as the Georgian revival, eclipsed the eclectic taste of the Victorian period. With their fruity, gilded excess, many theatres came in for the sharpest criticism. During the remainder of the twentieth century, theatres have tended to be ever more plainly decorated, the theory being that ornament is an unnecessary distraction which comes between the audience and the action on-stage.

THE OWNERS

The majority of these new provincial theatres were financed by syndicates of local businessmen, or occasionally by public subscription. R. C. Buchanan became the acknowledged Scottish theatre entrepreneur and acted as managing director for many of these syndicates. As a young man, Buchanan was a teacher of elocution in the Glasgow Athenaeum. For a time he was managing director of the Grand Theatre in Glasgow and enthusiastically organised many notable pantomimes there. Touring theatre companies and variety acts were becoming a significant feature of the entertainment life of Scotland in the late Victorian period. With remarkable initiative and foresight, Buchanan was one of the first impresarios to realise the economies of scale of having a large chain of 'touring' theatres in smaller towns which alternated between offering grand opera, drama, light entertainment and variety shows. In the 1890s he set up an office in London to book acts from the prestigious West End theatres to send on tour in Scotland. While in the south, he attended the first British cinema shows at the Polytecnic Hall in Regent Street and quickly realised the potential of cinema as a supplement to variety bills. As films improved in quality, he opened several full-time cinemas of a standard similar to that of his theatres. Inevitably, as the new craze became much more popular and profitable than live entertainment, Buchanan's venues in towns like Motherwell, Falkirk and Kirkcaldy all became cinemas during the First World War. These theatres were all sold to John Maxwell's Scottish Cinema and Variety Theatres for reconstruction.

The Edinburgh King's, which Buchanan controlled until his death in 1935, was absorbed by Howard and Wyndham, another highly successful Scottish theatre chain. Founded by two enthusiastic Edinburgh-based actor-managers, James B. Howard and Frederick W. P. Wyndham, who had opened the Royal Lyceum Theatre in 1883, the two started a limited company two years later to run their new acquisitions, the Theatres Royal in Edinburgh and Glasgow and the Royalty also in Glasgow. Howard died in May 1885 shortly after the company was launched, but by 1928, when Wyndham retired, it owned theatres in Dundee and Aberdeen as well as six across the north of England. A. Stewart Cruikshank then became managing director and expanded the business with nationwide tours of musicals, plays, revues and pantomimes. Not only were Howard and Wyndham renowned for the size and magnificence of their theatres, but also for the high quality of their magnificently costumed and choreo-graphed productions. In 1949 Stewart Cruikshank Jnr succeeded his father when the latter was killed in a car accident. He moved the company's office to London, but from the late 1960s, the slow demise of variety shows and the sale or closure of its theatres inevitably led to Howard and Wyndham ceasing operations in 1979.

The name of Moss Empires is synonymous with the variety business. Edward Moss was born in Edinburgh in 1852. He was the son of an enter-tainer, James Moss, who toured Scotland with singers, an Irish dancing troupe and a diorama show. Moss was determined to make variety as respectable as legitimate theatre. In 1877 he took over the failing Gaiety Music Hall in

Edinburgh and successfully revived its fortunes by booking the best of the new generation of variety stars from London. Thereafter, Moss opened variety theatres in almost every major city in Britain, creating a nationwide touring circuit. To play the so-called 'Moss Route' was to have 'made it' as a variety artiste. Moss was knighted for his services to entertainment in 1905 and his theatres soon enjoyed royal patronage but after fire destroyed the stage of his Edinburgh Empire Palace in 1911, his health declined and he died in 1912. The business, however, survived and expanded. Many of the Victorian Empires were enlarged and modernised to compete with a new threat – the luxury super cinema. In 1932 Moss Empires Ltd owned thirty-eight theatres and merged with the General Theatre Corporation, with George Black as managing director and Val Parnell as general manager. Parnell imported top American performers (including many film stars) to the London Palladium during the 1950s and their subsequent tours of Moss's provincial theatres gave them added glamour as people flocked to see their idols in person. In 1960 Moss Empires was taken over by the rival Stoll circuit. By then the advent of television, coupled with changing tastes in entertainment and the allure of easy profits by selling valuable theatre sites to property developers led to the closure and destruction of many fine theatres across Britain. Today, the Stoll–Moss company has adapted from a vast variety enterprise to the owners and lessees of a dozen of the best-known theatres in London's West End.

Moss Empires countered the threat of cinema by building theatres whose appointments equalled the best picture houses and by booking expensive acts from around the world. Smaller variety chains in Scotland, such as the Fred Collins and William Galt Circuit, succeeded by offering patrons what the American-dominated cinema could never match – acts with a Scottishness and obvious local flavour which directly involved folks, work places and homes.[8]

The glory days of commercial variety and touring productions were not to last. Increased fees for performers, costume hire and transport meant that theatres could no longer survive without subsidy and some of the finest venues passed into municipal ownership. During the 1960s and 1970s, accustomed ways of life in our cities were increasingly disrupted by destructive modernisation, redevelopment and social upheaval. Glasgow, which already had mounting social problems, was one of the most radically affected. Densely packed inner-city communities were split up and thinned out as whole tracts were comprehensively redeveloped. The tramway systems that brought patrons into city centres for entertainment were abandoned and urban motorways drove wedges through the cityscape. Many Victorian and Edwardian theatres were destroyed, but, despite these changes, the theatre in Scotland has remained progressive.

RECENT DEVELOPMENTS

The very nature of theatre, and consequently theatre buildings, has also changed. Modern productions can be 'in the round' with an audience seated all around the stage, in 'promenade' format with a standing audience following the actors around the performance space, or on 'open stage' in attempts to provoke a greater intensity of audience involvement by dispensing with curtains and the proscenium arch. Then there are the so-called 'found' spaces. Recent epics like *The Ship*, a drama about life in a Clydeside shipyard starring Jimmy Logan, took place all over the abandoned Harland and Wolff engine works at Govan. The Tramway, in Glasgow's former transport museum and tram works, and the Cottier, in an old church, show the diversity of buildings which have been used as theatres.

Sadly, most modern purpose-built theatres in Scotland have been very dull and undistinguished with a few notable exceptions. The Pitlochry Festival Theatre, designed by James Dunbar-Naismith and opened in 1981, nestles discreetly in woodland on the bank of the River Tummel with an entirely glazed front elevation overlooking the water.[9] The modern Traverse Theatre in Edinburgh, by locally based Nicholas Groves Raines, was completed in 1992. It makes a fine landmark off Lothian Road, appearing as a tall, cylindrical edifice, tied tight by a large cornice. Its crisp foyer spaces and comfortable auditorium have a metropolitan smartness which complements the innovative productions of its resident company.

In parallel with these developments, there has been a long-overdue re-evaluation of our Victorian and Edwardian theatre heritage after decades of neglect and countless unopposed demolitions. The architectural community finally discovered what theatre folk had known all along: that the prosperous and inviting facades and warmly coloured, elaborately gilded interiors set a feeling of well-being in audiences. It is thrilling to sit in such vast and boldly modelled spaces, with wide sweeping balconies and a sea of plum plush seats stretching away in all directions. When the house lights dim and the thick, embroidered velvet curtains close and open, the bulging plaster and gilt glows in the reflected light from the stage, looking rich and mysterious. The decor and the proximity of the audience to the stage makes for a wonderful ambience and soon everybody joins in the singing, laughter and tears, absorbed in the fantastic experience that is theatre.

NOTES

1. Walter Bayham, *The Glasgow Stage*, pp. 2–12.
2. Hugo Arnot, *The History of Edinburgh*, p. 48.
3. Charles Oakley, *The Second City*, p. 63.

4. Interview with David Cheshire, theatre historian.
5. See Brian Walker (ed.), *Frank Matcham: Theatre Architect*.
6. Interview with Christine Lang of Cullen, Lochead and Brown.
7. Obituary in the *Fife Free Press*.
8. Interview with Donald Mckenzie.
9. The Pitlochry Festival Theatre was built to host the highly acclaimed Pitlochry Festival, a season of plays and music attracting famous actors and often showcasing new writing. Started in 1951, it was initially housed in various tented or temporary structures. Information on Law and Dunbar-Naismith theatre projects provided by Colin Ross of the firm.

EDINBURGH

When the poet Allan Ramsay converted a hall in Carrubber's Close into the first full-time drama theatre anywhere in Scotland in 1736, the *Mercury* reported that it was 'as complete and finished with good taste as any one of its size in the three kingdoms'.[1] It opened on 8 November when *The Recruiting Officer* and *The Virgin Unmask'd* were performed but not before Mrs Bridges had recited a prologue (presumably by Ramsay himself) which reflected the current conflict between the Church and the Enlightenment.

> Long has it been the business of the stage
> To mend manners and reform the age.
> This task the muse by nature was assign'd,
> Ere Christian light shone in upon the mind;
> Ev'n since these glorious truths to men appear'd
> Her moral precepts still have been rever'd
> And when the sacred monitors have fail'd,
> Just satyre from the stage has oft prevailed.
> Tho' some sour critics full of phlegm and spleen
> Condemn her use as hellish and obscene;
> And from their gloomy thoughts and want of sense
> Think what diverts the mind gives Heav'n offence.
> Would such from truth and reason form their sample
> They'll find what's meant for precept, what example,
> Nor think when vice and folly shall appear
> The characters were drawn for them to wear!
> Fools in their native folly shall be shewn,
> And vice must have its language to be known.
> To such this lesson then we recommend
> Let each mend one the stage will have its end,
> Good sense shall flourish, Reason triumphant reign,

And hypocrites no more their power maintain,
The muse shall once again resume her throne,
And our stage vie with Athens or with Rome.
Long in those realms she held her rapid flight,
Filling their minds with profit and delight!

Despite opening with such an eloquent plea for tolerance of the drama, public opinion was still against the venture and Ramsay's theatre closed for good after only six months.[2]

It was not until November 1747 that another new theatre opened in Edinburgh, the Canongate Playhouse. It was a simple stone hall with a small entrance portico, fashionably embellished with Doric columns. In its early years, the Playhouse suffered from bad management and quickly fell into decay. In the summer of 1752, John Lee, a former manager of the Theatre Royal in London's Drury Lane was brought in to improve matters. Results soon showed that Lee was a wise choice, being a good administrator and a talented Shakespearean actor. He stayed for three seasons, being replaced by West Digges, also a fine actor famous for his 'persuasive tongue, good looks and loose standard of morality'.

The 1761–2 season introduced John Jackson to the Edinburgh public. Jackson, who was later to play a significant role in the development of theatres in Scotland, was the son of an English clergyman. He was a moderate yet ambitious actor with a fractious temper, which reputedly brought him into conflict with almost everyone.

In May 1762 the Edinburgh play-goers had a greater treat in store than either the acting of Digges or Jackson. It was the first performance of *Provoked Husband* 'in which a gentlewoman will appear for the first time on the stage of this kingdom'. The 'gentlewoman' was none other than the beautiful Mrs Bellamy, a first-rank actress in London whose shrill voice, extravagant lifestyle and vivacious personality had become infamous.[3] Audiences were predominantly male, so glamorous Mrs Bellany must have been quite an attraction. Her extravagant taste in clothes, jewellery and her many romances put her in debt and so to avoid creditors, she escaped to Edinburgh. True to form, she immediately had a torrid affair with Digges, the theatre's promiscuous manager.

The Playhouse continued to make headlines, often for the wrong reasons. On 7 January 1765 it was inspected by the Dean of Guild Court after reports that it was 'in a hazardous and crazy condition'. It passed, but two years later was making news again after a riot. The audience was protesting against the expulsion of Mr Stanley, their favourite actor, from the company after a fracas with Digges. A large group of fans stayed behind after the show, throwing stones, sticks, coins and lighted candles at the building. To prevent further trouble, the theatre was closed for a fortnight. When it re-opened with *Romeo and Juliet*, Stanley had still not been reinstated, so after the ladies had been asked to leave, his fans proceeded to wreck the interior. Benches were torn up, candles were thrown about, scenes smashed and every fixture and fitting destroyed. The actors tried to keep the rioters off the stage, defending their stronghold with stage weapons. The musicians joined in, battering the rioters with their instruments. Several were pushed down a trap door in the stage. The City Guard was despatched to restore order, but even they were beaten back. Hastily a detachment of soldiers was sent from Edinburgh Castle. By the time they arrived, the Canongate Playhouse had been stripped to its bare walls. Mr Stanley, the seemingly innocent cause of the trouble, abandoned the stage to live in Edinburgh as an elocution teacher. The theatre was declared illegal by the city magistrates and forcibly closed.

Prior to 1767, theatres in Scotland were unlicensed and any play performed for profit was therefore illegal. This was an attempt to prevent the performance of anything seditious, rather than out of concern for public safety. To evade the law, concerts were advertised, the play being given under the pretence of free entertainment between the first and second movements. This was a ridiculous situation as the magistrates, who were required to enforce the law, were often the most enthusiastic patrons of the 'illegal' theatres. To preserve their reputations, they devised a theatre patent which was leased for twenty-one years to the highest bidder. A Mr Ross was successful, and responding to a growing demand for the drama, he repaired the vandalised Canongate Playhouse. In an attempt to bury its old image, he renamed it the Theatre Royal but soon realised that a more substantially constructed theatre was required. Moreover it was obvious that many patrons would be moving soon from the squalid Old Town to the new developments on the former green fields beyond the Nor' Loch.

THEATRE ROYAL, SHAKESPEARE SQUARE

In a far-sighted move, Shakespeare Square, near the corner of North Bridge and Prince's Street, was chosen as the location for the new **Theatre Royal**. Although there were only a few houses in that area in 1767, the architect James Craig was shortly to produce a grand master plan for the fine terraces and gardens of the New Town still standing today.

Since 1737 in England the Lord Chamberlain alone had the power to grant general theatre licences, which permitted a theatre to present drama and use the name 'Theatre Royal', a privilege known as the Letters Patent. To finance the new theatre, the owner followed the example of 'patent' houses in England, issuing £100 shares which entitled the holders to free admission and 3 per cent of profits. Twenty-five were sold, although the building actually cost over £7,000 including £300 for the patent itself. Despite a protracted construction

The Old Theatre Royal. Princes St, Edinburgh.

Figure 2.1 *Theatre Royal, Shakespeare Square* (author collection).

process and the collapse of part of the North Bridge, linking the old and new
towns in November 1768, the Theatre Royal duly opened on 9 January 1769,
managed by Mr Ross. Externally, it was a handsome building with a grand
Doric-columned portico but the auditorium was rudimentary, with two horse-
shoe-shaped balconies supported by wooden frames. The first performance
was *Conscious Lovers*, followed on 11 January by the *Beaux Stratagem*, performed at the request of the Freemasons. Although there were several such
'bespoke' nights, business was sluggish and the season was a flop. The actor
John Jackson, who later took over the management, remarked 'Depending too
much upon the novelty of new walls, new scenery and new decorations [Ross]
had neglected providing a company of performers that ought to have kept
pace with the splendour of the house.' Ironically, Jackson was one of the most
criticised members of the company. Ross soon went bankrupt and fled to
London, pursued by the scheming Jackson with a warrant for unpaid wages.
There, Jackson probably used his warrant to blackmail Ross into leasing the
building for only £150 per annum in November 1781. Back in Edinburgh,
much delayed maintenance had to be carried out. According to Jackson '. . .
There were neither scenes, wardrobe, or any other appendage suitable to a
Theatre Royal. There was not even a roof; the thing so called was like a sieve,

which let the rain through in a million places.' Although prone to a showman's penchant for exaggeration, Jackson seems to have considerably improved the theatre's fortunes as £1,000 was spent on repairs and new scenery. It re-opened on 1 December 1781 with *The Suspicious Husband*, but it seems to have closed temporarily until mid-January while its ambitious lessee opened another Theatre Royal in Glasgow. To run the Edinburgh and Glasgow houses simultaneously at a time when the only means of communication was by horse, showed great determination on Jackson's part. To save money, he even got some members of his company to perform at both venues. This was possible because the Edinburgh theatre was open at most four nights, while only two were allowed by the Glasgow magistrates. Although Jackson was obviously no slouch, such draconian curbs on the theatre's openings made it a poor business. When the royal patent expired in 1788, Jackson moved permanently to Glasgow, leaving subsequent Edinburgh lessees with thousands of pounds of debt to be settled.

The young Walter Scott, an upwardly-mobile solicitor and staunch Loyalist, made his first recorded visit to see a revival of *The Royal Martyr, or Life and Death of Charles I* on 7 April 1793. That particular performance became notorious as a party of Irish students in the pit, who were supporters of the French Revolution then at its height, started hissing. Immediately, some of the Loyalist portion ordered the band to play 'God Save The King'. The Loyalists used the seat-backs to beat the Democrats and both sides suffered many fractures. Scott watched the fight from the safety of the balcony and gleefully recounted the event later.

On 14 April the Lord Provost of Edinburgh offered a £50 reward for the apprehension of the ringleaders and peace officers were sent to the theatre to deal with any more trouble but fortunately the officers were never needed.

For the 1802 season, expectations were raised when John Jackson resumed control with the assistance of a Liverpudlian actor, Mr Aickin. An anonymous writer, under the pseudonym 'Candidus', described the opening night:

> We crowded to the house to mark the necessary alterations upon it; but what did they amount to? The outside was whitened like a pie-shop, the inside loaded with unnecessary gilding; permanent boxes were erected upon the stage. The stage was diminished by adding some few seats to the pit; the scenery most deficient, broken crystals patched with tin plates.

Thus, the Theatre Royal began a brief phase of financial stability. Apart from the short opening times imposed, the greatest hindrance to the development of the business had been a lack of innovative plays to attract regular audiences. Luckily, Walter Scott's plays began to arouse great interest and enthusiasm for drama began to rub off on his contemporaries. Now an influential figure in Edinburgh society and a shareholder at the theatre, he realised that a complete change of management was also necessary. Actors such as Ross and Jackson were more interested in their own success than the cohesive running of the Theatre Royal.

THEATRE ROYAL, BROUGHTON STREET

Scott subsequently persuaded his friend Henry Siddons to apply for the patent and although there was a rival application, Siddons was undoubtedly assisted by Scott's backing. The eldest child of Sarah Siddons, the greatest actress of the Georgian era, he was born in 1774 and had already become a successful London manager.

Siddons thought he could exploit the monopoly position his patent gave him by opening a second theatre, and so a former circus, then used as a concert hall called Corri's Rooms dating from 1793, on the corner of Leith Walk and Broughton Street, was leased. Shareholders at the existing Theatre Royal were shocked when their new tenant moved the valued Royal Letters Patent to the Broughton Street site and a court case was narrowly avoided.

The New Theatre Royal in Broughton Street opened on 14 November 1809 with the comedy *Honeymoon*; the lead roles were played by Mr Siddons and his wife, Harriet. The *Courant* gave a glowing account of the opening:

> The house, in a few minutes after opening, overflowed in every part. Public expectation had been greatly raised by the reported elegance and accommodation of the Theatre, and it was almost taken for granted that the union of Mr Nasmyth's talents in design, and Mr Williams' [a London-based decorator and mechanist] in execution, could scarcely fail of producing a happy and successful effect.[4] The theatre is indeed very beautiful and extremely commodious, yet we are compelled to admit that the Gothic effect of the ornaments excites rather a sombre than a cheerful impression, and that this effect was aided last night by a deficiency of light everywhere except on the stage . . . the scenery is equal in beauty and design and execution to any we have witnessed.

Despite Siddons's hard work, the new theatre was actually far from ideal. The *Monthly Mirror* noted 'A house which was formerly a Circus and subsequently Concert rooms, has been fitted up with tolerable neatness, although somewhat in the *gingerbread-work* style, and the access is extremely bad, for you must make a complete circle of the house, and ascend one or two flights of steps before you arrive at the box lobby.' After two years' struggle, Siddons found the new Theatre Royal so unsatisfactory that he moved his company back to the empty Theatre Royal in Shakespeare Square. Using money he could ill afford, he leased it for £300 a year. The short-lived Leith Walk venture was easily converted back to a concert hall, later known as the Pantheon and, subsequently, the Caledonian.

Siddons worked extremely hard to recoup the costs, but now faced with a hefty debt, his health slowly declined and he died in April 1815. The success of the theatre seems to date from this time. The Edinburgh public awoke to the fact that they had lost an outstanding manager who had sacrificed health, fortune and even life to expand the theatre business and they had repaid him with poor patronage and indifference. Siddons's successor, William Henry Murray was about twenty-five years old. Immediately, he placed notices in the newspapers announcing that he was prepared to continue Siddons's good work – but only if properly supported. A 1s levy on tickets successfully cleared Siddons's debt and he arranged a special benefit for Mrs Siddons when a packed house raised £420 – the largest sum yet taken in Scotland.

On 27 August 1822, the most memorable event ever at the Theatre Royal took place – the performance of Sir Walter Scott's *Rob Roy* for King George IV. The production had previously filled the house for forty-one consecutive nights and was repeated many times every season during Murray's period of management, becoming a classic of the Scottish stage. During the weeks leading up to the royal visit, Edinburgh's population swelled as crowds of country folk converged on the capital, hoping to catch a glimpse of the King. On 14 August, the *Royal George* brought the King to Leith. The first man to go aboard was Sir Walter Scott. When he heard who the visitor was, the King reportedly said 'What? Sir Walter Scott? The man in Scotland I most wish to see.'

Special preparations were made for the royal visit to the theatre. A handsome carved wooden portico was erected over the entrance with crimson cloth for the King to walk on. The box office was transformed into a sumptuous and brilliantly lit apartment, causing one guardsman to remark 'Cor! This beats Lunnun yet.' The event was deeply significant for some Scots; in the theatre they would have been closer to their sovereign than officialdom had previously permitted. It was a gracious and politic gesture to command the performance of *Rob Roy* – a compliment to both Scott and Scotland.

The audience queued for hours in the rain and then endured the packed, steamy theatre in their wet clothes. The King was given a loud cheer as he sat in the royal box. After the play, the audience sang 'God Save The King' 'amid the wildest enthusiasm'.

The royal visit greatly enhanced the theatre's social status. The biggest stars from London became regular performers – such as Fanny Kemble, who taking the lead in *Romeo and Juliet*, in 1829 'astonished [Edinburgh] playgoers with her wonderful genius'.

The twenty-one-year patent expired once again in 1830 when Mrs Siddons bought the theatre as an investment for £42,000. Not only did Murray secure a new lease, but he also took control of a second theatre, the Caledonian. It was actually the short-lived New Theatre Royal in Leith Walk and until 1823 a concert hall called the Pantheon. Murray renamed it the Adelphi. As the holder of the patent, only Murray could legally present drama and so had a monopoly over Edinburgh theatre-goers. He cleverly avoided rivalry between his theatres by having popular entertainment at the Adelphi, while the Theatre Royal went upmarket. Indeed, the latter had been partially demolished in 1828, and rebuilt with a handsome new facade of dressed grey sandstone, designed by William Burn, with statues of Shakespeare and Garrick set in niches at either end. The auditorium was extended with an entirely new stage behind the original and delicately gilded plaster latticework on the two balcony fronts. Seasons of opera were introduced as the rebuilt Theatre Royal was not only well appointed but had superb acoustics.

The early 1830s brought a severe recession, nevertheless both theatres remained open and by 1836 Murray was sufficiently confident to rebuild the old Adelphi. To improve safety, new lobbies and emergency staircases were built and new seats fitted throughout. Typical prices were orchestra stalls 4s, circle and boxes 3s, gallery 6s and pit 2s. In the following 96-night season, some 36 new plays were premiered and many new actors were introduced. Morris Barnett, said to be an excellent impersonator of Frenchmen, starred in the farce *Monsieur Jacques*, which was so successful it enjoyed an eighteen-night run.

In November, the Theatre Royal re-opened, freshly painted and with a new wider proscenium. The public must have liked what they saw for 1836–7 was a record season. Throughout the 1840s Murray guided his theatre companies to new successes, occasionally substituting drama with the exhibition of novelties, such as a display of lions and tigers or a lecture about railways – a foretaste of the coming variety era. William Murray could be described as Scotland's first successful impresario. Besides his abilities as an actor and man-ager, he was a fine dramatist, adapting *Cramond Brig*, *Mary Queen of Scots*, *Gilderoy* and *Oliver Twist* for the stage. He was a good speaker, known for his witty prologues and farewell addresses. After retiring from the theatre business in 1849, he moved to St. Andrews, where he died in May 1852. During his forty-two years on the stage, Edinburgh had changed dramatically into a sprawling industrial and financial city with a busy port. The Victorian era had arrived and theatre was at last flourishing as the favourite pastime of urban Scots from all social classes.

The 1851–2 season brought a new theatrical era to Edinburgh. Murray's long monopoly was broken up as were the 'stock' theatre companies. In the absence of drama schools, these enabled the training of professional actors –

Figure 2.2   Theatre Royal, Shakespeare Square after 1828 rebuild
(author collection).

students learned by working with a few experienced professionals. Murray's company must have been particularly efficient, since two of the most distinguished Victorian actors, Henry Irving and John Laurence Toole, trained there. With the advent of railways, actors were at last able to move speedily from city to city as required and a few drama schools were developed. Rather than being an isolated centre, Edinburgh, as with other provincial cities, became more reliant on London. This was particularly true of the theatres which joined national circuits, whose headquarters were often in London. This reduced costs considerably as a large chain could employ its own centralised administration plus costume and scenery departments.

The Adelphi's new manager, Robert H. Wyndham, was to become one of the most successful actor-managers in Victorian Scotland. He first performed there in the 1830s at the Theatre Royal under William Murray. On the evening of 24 May 1853 a workman, dismantling scenery, saw flames coming from one of the lower boxes beside the stage of the Adelphi and raised the alarm. Only an hour later the building was in ruins. Four days beforehand, Mrs Wyndham (who stayed in a flat above the theatre) had given birth and mother and son had to be carried to safety. This first burning of an Edinburgh theatre was actually a mixed blessing, for despite its numerous rebuilds the venue was basically still a dangerous wooden structure dating from 1793 with insufficient fire exits. If the fire had occurred at night when the house was full, no more than a few people could have escaped, the passages being long and narrow. Wyndham was reportedly so concerned that he planned to demolish it anyway, when the fire saved him the trouble.

Luckily, the Theatre Royal was lying empty. Wyndham took over the lease and his company moved in, opening on 11 June 1853 with *Simpson & Co*, but the Theatre Royal's days were also numbered. Doubtless conscious of an alarming rise in serious theatre fires throughout Britain, the city magistrates were tightening their regulations. The site between Prince's Street and Shakespeare Square was sold to the government for the General Post Office and the old theatre closed on 25 May 1859.

The charred ruins of the Adelphi lay for a long time before the site was finally cleared in 1854 and a new theatre erected, known as the Queen's and designed by David Bryce. The long rectangular auditorium was commodious with space for 150 patrons in the stalls, 350 in the pit, 300 in the boxes and 1,000 in a huge balcony. Even the stage was big, measuring 58 by 62 feet with a 32-foot proscenium opening.

The new theatre was let to James Black, a merchant in Leith, who was a major shareholder in the building. Black first came to the notice of the theatre-going fraternity by publishing letters complaining that William Murray had not been fulfilling his contractual obligations in leasing the Adelphi, where Black was a minor shareholder. Murray was supposed to play a quota of nights there, but for years the trustees had ignored his failure to do so. When Wyndham took control of the Adelphi, there was no cause for complaint. Even so, Black seems to have nursed the belief that, given the chance, he would make a more efficient manager than either Murray or Wyndham.

Sadly, the vain Black was disastrous as a manager. The Queen's opened on 19 December 1855 and throughout the following summer season, Black brought in the best available companies, presenting a wide repertoire – ranging from Scott's *Guy Mannering* to Tom Taylor's *Still Waters Run Deep*. An elaborate production of the pantomime *Puss in Boots* was staged during the 1856–7 winter season, but despite good attendances, profits were marginal.

Black was fast discovering why Murray did not open the old Adelphi unless he was certain of big audiences. After a farewell benefit night on 26 June 1857, Black left, perhaps a wiser – and certainly a poorer – man.

At the same time, R. H. Wyndham was looking for a new challenge now that the Theatre Royal was to be redeveloped as the Post Office. The Queen's was empty and its owners were delighted to find a lessee of Wyndham's skill and experience. He opened the Queen's Theatre and Opera House on 23 November 1857 with a speech, followed by *The Love Chase* starring himself and Mrs Wyndham in the lead roles. Subsequent seasons were an outstanding success – the 1858 summer featured no fewer than twenty-three new artists making their Edinburgh debuts. Wyndham was so encouraged that he bought the Royal Letters Patent for the 1859 summer season. With the opening of so many railways, companies were no longer tied to a particular theatre, and travelling companies soon predominated. Edinburgh's fourth Theatre Royal prospered as a number one 'touring' house. It was unfortunately cursed by repeated fires – in 1863, 1875 and 1884. After the 1875 blaze, Wyndham decided that he had had enough and retired from the stage, handing over the management to his younger colleague, J. B. Howard. At the age of thirty-three years, he already had a successful stage career, both in Edinburgh and London. Howard was born in Ireland. Fed up with being a stockbroker's clerk, he joined the local stock drama company, first coming to Edinburgh in 1866 to appear at the Theatre Royal in an Irish play. The year after, he played what became his most popular part, Rob Roy. Because of his small stature and broad Irish accent, as can be imagined, this role was not an immediate hit. Between 1869 and 1872 he gained experience with the Drury Lane company in London, playing the title role in *Ivanhoe* and Tom Burrowes in Boucicault's *Formosa*, before spending the rest of his career in Edinburgh. As a manager he was highly regarded, the Theatre Royal being noted for its spectacular and entertaining pantomimes.

Frederick Wyndham, R. H. Wyndham's son became Howard's junior partner. The 21-year-old Wyndham had been born in a flat above the old Adelphi Theatre a week before the fire and for the rest of his life he quite simply lived for the theatre. As with Howard, he was a good actor who had played all over Britain. He was more interested in the administrative side of theatre, however, and in the years which lay ahead his ability and showmanship would make Howard and Wyndham one of the country's leading theatre chains.

The Theatre Royal was completely rebuilt and opened once more on 13 January 1876. The design was by Charles J. Phipps. *The Era* reported:

The new theatre, although erected within the external walls of the old . . . Is otherwise an entirely new building . . . specially designed for comfort and convenience of its patrons.

The entrances are numerous and every division of the audience has its
own distinct entrance . . . The circle and stalls are fitted up with comfortable armchairs. The upper circle and pit stalls have well upholstered
seats with backs. The private boxes, of which there are fourteen, are
well fitted and hung with crimson drapery.

Even so in 1883 the Theatre Royal was outclassed when Howard and
Wyndham opened their magnificent new Royal Lyceum Theatre. The older
theatre was then let to a Mr Heslop, but the stage was burned out by a devastating fire on 30 June 1884. Mr Cecil Beryl, of the Royal Princess's, Glasgow
obtained the lease and the repaired theatre was opened by him on 29
December the same year. During 1887 Mr William Hatton became co-lessee
and a variety policy was introduced.

Howard and Wyndham obviously appreciated the potential of variety
entertainment as they leased the Theatre Royal from 1895 to present variety,
light opera and pantomime seasons. There, *Peter Pan* was performed in
Edinburgh for the first time.

In 1923 it was leased to Edinburgh Varieties Ltd, whose managing director,
Fred Collins was based in an office in Glasgow above Lauder's Bar, a hostelry

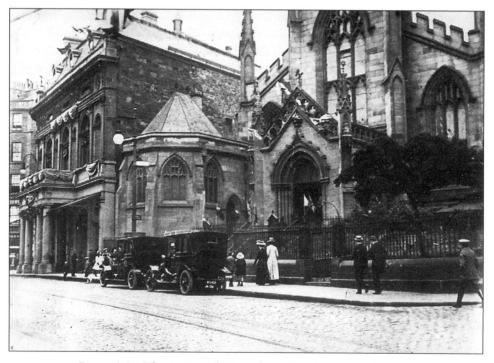

Figure 2.3   Theatre Royal, Broughton Street (author collection).

well patronised by the theatrical fraternity. Collins eventually ran a circuit of five famous variety theatres, including the Aberdeen Tivoli. When he died in 1931 his son, Horace, took charge. Horace Collins wanted to emulate the upmarket, though less cosy, Moss and Stoll theatres and so the old Theatre Royal was thoroughly renovated during the summer holidays in 1935. He had a knack for spotting new talent and succession of brilliant Scottish comedians headed the bills in the 1930s – Jack Anthony, Jack Radcliffe and Alec Finlay. In addition Dave Willis and Sir Harry Lauder paid regular visits to the theatre.

Alas, some hours after the last performance of *Hail Caledonia*, starring the great comedian Tommy Morgan, in October 1946 the Theatre Royal caught fire again. The fire brigade was soon in attendance, but could not find a working hydrant. The fire began in the gallery, possibly caused by hot ash falling from the carbon-arc spotlights. On hearing of the blaze, the cast rushed from their digs to rescue their costumes and props, making a daring entrance through the stage door. Fortunately, the iron curtain was down, so while the auditorium was burned to the bare walls, the stage was spared. Because of wartime building restrictions, it was not possible to obtain permission to rebuild. The gaunt, charred walls stood for another fifteen years before the site was finally redeveloped.

THE PRINCESS'S

The entertainment tradition at 19 Nicholson Street can be traced back to 1820 when a simple circular wooden amphitheatre was built. Circuses run by Ducrow, Astley, Sanger and Cooke all had their turn there. In the 1830s it was known as the Royal Amphitheatre. Within a decade a stage was added and in the winter of 1853–4, Wyndham's Company occupied it while the Italian Opera Company was in residence at the Theatre Royal. In 1857 it became the Dunedin Hall, a venue for classical music concerts. It was severely damaged by a fire in 1860.

On 6 April 1861 William Paterson, a stockbroker who had once been property master at the Shakespeare Square Theatre Royal, took over. He erected a new proscenium and stage, reportedly of 'unsurpassable splendour for the purposes of novel and diversified entertainment' and renamed it the Alhambra Music Hall and Gallery of Illustration, but only very briefly. After forty-two years and several fires, the Alhambra was closed in 1862 in the interests of public safety.

When Paterson realised that his lease was not to be renewed, he had a proper new theatre quickly built opposite at 50 Nicolson Street, opening it in September 1862, a mere week after the former Dunedin Hall shut. The New Royal Alhambra, as it was known, was far more successful – not least because it was a sturdy stone building with two tiers, decorated in shades of blue with a panelled ceiling studded with golden stars.

In time, Paterson decided to go upmarket and introduced a drama policy, renaming the theatre the Princess's. Whilst the plays may have attracted good audiences, they were more expensive to stage and so in 1867 the theatre reverted to a variety policy as the Royal Princess's Theatre.

In the following year A. D. McNeill took it over, and featured plays and operatic works. McNeill (born in 1829) was highly regarded by Edinburgh theatre-goers for 'his great talent, excellent management and good citizenship'. Unusually for an actor, his father was a solicitor and he had been to Edinburgh University. McNeill toured to London, Birmingham and Glasgow before becoming manager of the Theatre Royal, Aberdeen. His first appearance at the Royal Princess's was in September 1868, playing Richelieu. In 1869 he produced a play of his own entitled *The Gloamim' and the Mirk; or a Story of Modern Athens*. This topical satire about Edinburgh proved a great success and ran for fifteen months. When he died in 1884, his son W. A. McNeill continued to run it against powerful opposition from the Theatre Royal, Broughton Street, and the newly opened Royal Lyceum Theatre in Grindlay Street. The outcome of this competition was the closing of the Royal Princess's Theatre on 22 May 1886. It was occupied for a time by the Salvation Army, which later built its congress hall next door. In 1912 it was bought by a local syndicate and demolished to enable construction of La Scala cinema. That early picture house, designed by the grandly named Hippolyte Blanc, is now the heavily altered Empire Bingo hall.

THE SOUTHMINSTER

After Paterson moved out, the old Dunedin Hall was demolished. The following year a more substantial amphitheatre was erected on the site. It was leased to Charles Hengler. He called it the Southminster Music Hall and it opened as a circus on 7 March 1863. At this point, the Henglers (who were a large and respected travelling circus company) were abandoning tented circuses in favour of proper theatres with a circus ring where the stalls would normally be. Their circus company visited these in turn and other variety shows appeared during the rest of the year. The Southminster may have had a distinguished pilastered stone facade, but the iron-framed theatre behind was otherwise clad in plain brick. Inside, there was one large balcony with boxes below and much ornate plaster work.

Hengler's venture at the Southminster was, by all accounts, not particularly successful and came to an abrupt halt when the building was destroyed by fire in 1875. It was rebuilt later in the same year and re-opened with drama as the Queen's Theatre under the direction of J. B. Howard. The first performance was *La Sonnambula* on 13 December 1875. But only two years later it was badly damaged by fire. Within months the theatre was rebuilt as Weldon's

Circus. In the following year James Newsome took it over and it became known as Newsome's Hippodrome and Circus.

THE OPERETTA HOUSE

Meanwhile, at the foot of Chambers Street, where the Adam House office block stands, the Operetta House was built in 1875 for the impresario Carl Bernhardt. Its seasons of light opera were not a success and it soon became the Gaiety Music Hall, which opened on 5 July 1875. The building was rectangular with a large pit and a narrow balcony with long slips around three sides. The barrel-vaulted ceiling was supported by slim iron columns and the narrow proscenium was flanked by Corinthian pilasters. The Gaiety soon developed a reputation for risqué fare, hardly surprising given that the manager had previously worked in the disreputable New Star Music Hall in Leith.

In 1877 Edward Moss took it over and renamed it Moss's Theatre of Varieties, featuring the best talent available in the country. He even bought adjacent shops and the University Hotel above the theatre – the former to make additional foyers and a ladies' room, the latter to house his artistes. On his tours they had to work hard, most travelling from London, doing two shows a night, before being whisked to Moss's Princess's Theatre in Leith (see below). Moss (born in 1852) was later to found the Moss Empires chain – Britain's foremost variety circuit. He was determined to make variety theatres as respectable as drama houses – quite a challenge at the Gaiety! A season of bills at Moss's Varieties might consist of the following star turns, usually direct from their London bookings.

Jenny Hill – affectionately known as the Vital Spark
G. H. Chirgwin – the White-Eyed Kaffir
James Fawn – famed for 'If You Want To Know The Time, Ask A
    Policeman'
Vesta Tilley – the legendary male impersonater
Charles Coborn – 'The Man Who Broke The Bank at Monte Carlo'
Dan Leno – legendary clog dancer and character comedian

Although patronised mainly by students, the theatre was so successful that Moss's salary list for his artistes averaged some £250 a week. A big star like Vesta Tilley was paid £100 for six performances. The former Gaiety continued until 5 November 1892 when the much larger Empire Palace superseded it but it was quickly sold to local impresarios Lees and Sanders and retitled the Operetta House once again. In 1900 they presented Edison's Animated Pictures and six years later the hall became a full-time cinema. As such it had an uneventful career, but like so many primitive former theatres converted to picture houses, it was sidelined by the 1930s 'supers', with their 'talkie' equipment. It closed in December 1939, becoming a furniture store until the early 1950s. A small plaque on the wall of Adam House commemorates Sunday religious services given in the old Operetta House and is the only visible reminder of this early variety theatre.

Meanwhile, live entertainment was thriving in other parts of Edinburgh. The Albert Hall in Shandwick Place was built in 1876 by D. S. Mackay as the Albert Institute of Fine Arts, the basis of what Mackay hoped would eventually be a kind of Victoria and Albert Museum for Edinburgh. By 1880 it had failed and was being offered as premises suitable for wine merchants. In 1882 it opened as a music hall for a visit by the Christy Minstrels. However by 1886 it had become a Methodist Mission, before turning into a cinema in 1908, run by J. J. Bennell. Even that was intermittent and on 1 February 1910, the *Evening News* heralded a grand re-opening – Tindle's Picture Concerts. Tindle was brother-in-law of Richard Thornton, then partner in the Moss Empires theatre chain. By 1915 it was a cinema once more, and although closed in 1932, the ornate entrance portico can still be seen today.

THE EDINBURGH THEATRE

The **Edinburgh Theatre** was one of the grandest, yet tragically least successful theatre ventures in Scotland. It was conceived by a private syndicate of Edinburgh businessmen and civic dignitaries who wanted Edinburgh to have a drama and opera house to match the finest in Europe. The owners engaged Sir Robert Gowans, one of the top architects of the period who was also responsible for the fine Castle Terrace tenements nearby and the Rockville mansion. Originally, a baroque opera house complete with winter garden and aquarium was mooted by the developers, but their architect thought that such an indulgent design would be in bad taste, and furthermore, prohibitively expensive. The theatre as built was actually less elaborate than originally proposed, yet it cost a staggering £65,000. Architecturally, it was magnificent with an austere and monumental frontage, punctuated by five soaring arches and executed in grey sandstone. Within, it was handsomely appointed in neo-classical style with three tiers, a solidly pilastered anti-proscenium and what was described as 'the most elaborate machinery for working everything on stage yet seen in a British theatre'.

It should have been a recipe for success, but architectural grandeur and technical innovation did not come cheaply and the owners were heavily in debt when the theatre opened under Letters Patent on 20 December 1875, although it was not called 'Theatre Royal'. To make matters worse, Wybert Reeve, the manager had neither the experience nor the charisma to attract consistently

Figure 2.4 Frontage of the Synod Hall (ex Edinburgh Theatre) prior to demolition (Tony Moss).

large audiences. The Edinburgh Theatre opened on 20 December 1875, and while the press raved about its gilded and plush auditorium, the stock actors employed by Reeve came in for criticism. The first performances were of *Used Up* (in which Reeve took the lead) and *His Last Legs*, the latter with

R. H. Wyndham highly praised for his lead role as Felix O'Callaghan. A season of Shakespeare followed but admission prices were much higher than at the well-established Theatre Royal and this too must have had an adverse effect on audiences. After a summer break, the theatre re-opened on 14 August with *Princess Toto*. On 17 August, it had a unique moment of glory when Queen Victoria unveiled the Albert Memorial in Charlotte Square. That evening, members of the royal entourage visited the theatre. This event must have alerted Edinburgh society to patronise it, for the autumn season was markedly more successful than hitherto. There was a 'magnificently staged' performance of *The Lady of the Lake*, adapted from Sir Walter Scott's poem. Mapleson's Italian Opera Company took up residence that November, proving that the Edinburgh Theatre also had outstanding acoustics. Carl Rosa's Opera Company visited the next spring, producing *Pauline, Fidelio, Zampa, The Flying Dutchman* and *Siege of Rochelle* on successive nights. The travelling opera companies were an outstanding feature of the Victorian theatrical scene. Their ability to present wide and fairly polished repertoires during short residences in cities throughout Britain was quite remarkable when one considers the nightmarish logistics of moving musicians, costumes, lighting and scenery at that time. A 'spectacular' production of *Henry V* was followed by a twelve-night run of plays starring Mrs Stirling. All the while, the Edinburgh Theatre had been losing money and the owners were forced to declare bankruptcy. Mrs Stirling's run ended on 2 April 1877 with *Masks and Faces* and after only two years, the career of what was probably Scotland's most architecturally significant mid-Victorian theatre came to an abrupt end.

The building was shortly sold by auction to a break-away group of Presbyterians for a quarter of its original cost. The entire fittings and furniture were sold off. Obviously the lush, gilded exhibitionism of the theatre was disliked by the stern churchmen; the heavy, neo-classical facade must have found favour as it was retained when the radically reconstructed building re-opened as the Synod Hall and offices of the United Presbyterian Church. In 1900 it was acquired by Edinburgh Corporation and subdivided. The offices were let to small businesses and the halls were used for bowling, rifle ranges and by the Royal Scottish Geographical Society.

In 1906 the Poole family brought their diorama show from their native Gloucester to a hall in this building. Indeed, Poole's Synod Hall Cinema eventually occupied it and became one of the most popular in Edinburgh. Ironically, by the 1960s, Edinburgh's civic leaders felt that their city should have a grand opera house and so the Poole's lease was terminated and the Synod Hall closed in 1965 to be demolished. The project was stillborn and tragically the magnificent neo-classical edifice of the former Edinburgh Theatre was destroyed in the name of culture.

THE ROYAL LYCEUM

The failure of the Edinburgh Theatre would have discouraged most dispassionate businessmen from investing in drama theatres in Edinburgh, yet almost within sight of what was by then the Synod Hall, the redoubtable Howard and Wyndham set about developing a new high-quality playhouse on a large, regular site on Grindlay Street. (This had previously been home to the Cook brothers original tented circus, but they had moved on to a permanent amphitheatre in East Fountainbridge; see below). Howard and Wyndham were successful not only because of their business acumen, but, moreover, their enthusiasm. They simply lived for the theatre; Howard's management of the old Theatre Royal had been exemplary, being particularly noted for spectacular and entertaining pantomimes and by the time the **Royal Lyceum** opened in 1883, he was probably the best-known figure in Edinburgh theatrical life. At twenty-nine years old, F. W. P. Wyndham was very much the junior partner. Edinburgh born and bred, he was, like Howard and the elder Wyndham, an actor who had played all over Britain. Whereas Howard was a fine actor who knew how to manage, Wyndham was a sound administrator who could be

Figure 2.5   Frontage of Royal Lyceum (author).

Figure 2.6   Auditorium of Royal Lyceum (author).

relied upon to give a competent performance when required. The launching of the Royal Lyceum was planned in meticulous detail by Charles J. Phipps. It was, for example, the first in Britain to be fitted with an iron safety curtain. Externally, it was a competent essay in French classical style with a fine order of Corinthian columns supporting a centrally placed pediment and a steeply pitched mansard roof. The foyers were slightly cramped to cope with an audience of over 2,000, but congestion was an accepted part of Victorian theatre-going. A large open fire provided a warm welcome. The auditorium was, and still is, a feast for the eyes. It is delightfully intimate with three horseshoe balconies supported by slender iron columns and three proscenium boxes set into either side of the first balcony, divided by more slim columns. The tall, rectangular proscenium is inlaid with exquisite filigree plaster work in the Italian Renaissance style. The balcony fronts and richly decorated circular ceiling are finished in the intricate, swirling low-relief plaster for which Phipps's theatres are renowned. The original colours were crimson plush with cream, lavender and tones of gold leaf. It was completed within a tight budget of £17,000, or a quarter of the cost of the Edinburgh Theatre. In addition the Royal Lyceum did not employ any permanent cast, instead relying on travelling companies and actors on short contracts, which also saved money. Interestingly, the Royal Lyceum was the first Scottish theatre to use electricity for house lighting.

Howard and Wyndham achieved a considerable coup in booking Henry Irving and the London Lyceum company for the first two weeks, performing *Much Ado About Nothing, The Belle's Stratagem, Hamlet, Louis XI* and *The Merchant of Venice*. The critics raved about the shows and Irving was presented with his portrait by the Edinburgh Pen and Pencil Club, a prestigious body which included in its membership many of the leading figures in Edinburgh society. *The Scotsman* said of *Much Ado About Nothing* 'Never before did Shakespeare's comedy receive an interpretation so adequate in essentials and in every detail so artistically complete.'

Subsequently the Royal Lyceum presented a wide variety of fare from straight drama to opera and even occasional lectures, but the great annual money-spinner, then as now, was pantomime. Howard and Wyndham had become legendary for their lavish pantomimes and the tradition began at the Royal Lyceum in December 1883 with a production of *Little Red Riding Hood*. It ran for a record three months, with an adverse effect on the competition. When the rival Theatre Royal countered by advertising their own *Bluebeard* as 'The Young People's Pantomime', the Royal Lyceum management struck back immediately with:

> Little Red Riding Hood!
> The Young People's Pantomime!
> The Parent's Pantomime!
> The Middle-Aged Pantomime!
> The Old People's Pantomime!
> *Everybody's* Pantomime!

J. B. Howard died in 1895 and Wyndham continued alone to expand the company. In 1912 Howard and Wyndham absorbed the Robert Arthur group of six theatres and by the 1914 war, it controlled one of the largest groups in Britain. The dynamic Stewart Cruikshank took control of Howard and Wyndham in 1928. He was a builder's son who chaired the rival King's Theatre, which was a splendid addition to their portfolio. There was no point in running two theatres in direct competition, so the King's developed a considerable reputation with musicals and pantomime, while the Royal Lyceum presented straight drama, opera and more sophisticated light entertainment. Each theatre was given firm policy objectives – the role of the Royal Lyceum being to showcase 'the best works of modern writers, together with the classics of the past'. As the same time, all shows, pantomimes and touring productions were transferred to the King's. Responsibility for carrying out this policy went to John L. Masterson, one of the most capable and popular of all Lyceum theatre managers. During the 1930s, theatres all over Britain began to feel the effects of competition from luxurious new 'super' cinemas, whose cheaper prices and air-conditioned luxury left the cramped Victorian theatres feeling sadly outclassed. This threat could only be countered by investing the theatre with a degree of glamour and spectacle which black and white cinema films could not match. The Lyceum was given a very necessary refurbishment before the first of three glittering gala nights which did just that. The first was on 11 July 1931, when King George V and Queen Mary attended a performance of Barrie's *The Admirable Crichton*, presented by the Masque Theatre with Esme Percy in the title role. This was a historic occasion, the first Royal Command Performance in Scotland since 1822, when George IV had seen *Rob Roy* in the old Theatre Royal.

During the 1930s the Lyceum continued as Edinburgh's top drama theatre with a mixture of new work and some 'old favourites', such as *Marigold*, a simple love story set in Victorian Edinburgh, which seems to have captivated audiences. Such escapist offerings were entirely in keeping with the public mood during a time of recession. Yet the diversity of Lyceum programmes can be gauged from the fact that in 1935, no fewer than 35 plays were presented, including 12 new works.

During the Second World War many popular plays, such as Noël Coward's *Private Lives* made their Scottish debuts at the Lyceum, but once victory seemed assured, a more adventurous policy began with David Belasco's *The Return of Peter Grimm*. In 1946 King George VI and Queen Elizabeth visited the Lyceum again as part of the Victory celebrations. The year 1947 was, of course, that of the first Edinburgh Festival, and the Lyceum became one of the key sites for Festival drama. Many international companies brought their repertoires to the Lyceum during successive festivals, as they do today.

By the 1960s the Lyceum had passed from Howard and Wyndham to the Meyer Oppenheim property group and it became increasingly obvious that the new owner was acquiring all the adjacent properties as he intended to demolish the entire block for a commercial development. Oppenheim's plans caused much alarm in the City Chambers. The loss of the Lyceum would seriously affect the stability of the Festival, which had become vital to the city's economy. The Festival apart, it would be unthinkable to allow a private developer to wreak havoc on a much-loved part of Edinburgh's city centre. Oppenheim's scheme would alter the entire character of the area, if not the city itself and with so much at stake, the 'city fathers' decided that they could not afford to play a passive role in this affair. They had no intention of saving the Lyceum, however. In November 1963 Provost Duncan Weatherstone had described it as 'a lousy theatre . . . the sooner it goes over to bingo the better'. Although he later apologised for his ignorant remark, it was still obvious that the Corporation wanted the redevelopment of the nearby Synod Hall to proceed so that a new theatre could be erected. None the less on the eve of its closure on 26 February 1964, the Corporation stepped in and bought the theatre from Oppenheim for £100,000. Clearly, they became involved with the Lyceum only reluctantly and would have much preferred to see the theatre in the hands of another more suitable owner. The Corporation's commitment to the Lyceum at the time was an extremely unusual and by no means popular move. Had it not been taken, however, the cultural life of Edinburgh and Scotland would have been deprived of a building now treasured as a theatrical jewel. The Corporation immediately formed the Edinburgh Civic Theatre Trust to administer their new acquisition, the aims of the latter being to encourage the performance of drama, music and dance by establishing a resident group of performers not only to tour but also to assist in the training of drama students. From being reluctant saviours in the 1960s, the Corporation set about transforming the Royal Lyceum into one of the most vibrant venues in Britain today. Clive Perry, a young and unknown Englishman, was appointed as artistic director. He had the balcony closed, reducing the theatre to an intimate 1,647 seater. Like F. W. P. Wyndham in the early days, Perry ran the Lyceum with a great deal of enthusiasm, firmly re-establishing it on the theatrical map. By reducing some ticket prices and using his flair for publicity and canny management, Perry was able to cut the Lyceum's deficit in half during his first year.

The building was physically transformed in 1977 in what was only the second rebuild in its entire history. This controversial makeover was carried out on the instructions of its new owners, the Edinburgh District Council, who had superseded the Corporation at the 1975 local government reorganisation. At the same time the Edinburgh Civic Theatre Trust was wound up and the Royal Lyceum Theatre and its occupier, the Royal Lyceum Theatre Company, became separate entities (the latter paying the council rent). The refurbishment work carried out by the City Architects Department repaired the fabric of the building, upgraded the front of house areas, the stage and dressing rooms while the auditorium was refurbished from top to bottom and the entire building rewired and fitted with air conditioning. This was necessary work to make the old theatre more comfortable and flexible than hitherto, but the gaudy redecoration of the auditorium in powder blue, gold and pink was less than appropriate.

The Royal Lyceum re-opened on 28 September 1977 with a Royal Gala performance of Otrovsky's *Diary of a Scoundrel* in the presence of Princess Margaret. Ludovic Kennedy, chairman of the board of directors, made a speech suggesting that the Royal Lyceum Company might grow into the National Theatre of Scotland. Although this was the expression of an ideal rather than a declaration of policy, it demonstrated the optimism of the company at the time. The Royal Lyceum Company had grown and developed in many directions over the previous decade and had reached a point where it was practically the only theatre company in the country which could pitch its ambitions at such a height of excellence.

In 1986 further renovation work saw the creation of a large glass-fronted entrance hall and box office facing Grindlay Street with the addition of a rehearsal rooms complex in buildings opposite. The Royal Lyceum Theatre continues to play a pivotal role in the annual Festival programme and presents innovative and quality music and drama all year round. Moreover, it is a charming and beautiful building, rich in history which is loved by theatre-goers from Edinburgh and beyond.

THE EMPIRE PALACE

Following the success of his Theatre of Varieties in Chambers Street and Princess's, Leith, Edward Moss now believed that Edinburgh would be an ideal location to develop the first of his lavish **Empire Palaces**. He already owned the site of Newsome's Hippodrome on Nicolson Street. With the deaths of the principal circus proprietors, and the fast increasing land values in central Edinburgh, circuses tended to decline towards the end of the 1880s. Music-hall artistes' salaries, on the other hand, were escalating. It must have been in Moss's mind that many circus acts were available cheaply. The Victorians were obsessed with horse racing and the British Empire now embraced all sorts of countries with many species of exotic animals. A new style of 'Empire' enter-tainment was in the making. Moss would ensure that it would appeal to young and old alike. Morally, it would be above suspicion. It would place the very best of the old with the new and it would be highly profitable.

Vesta Tilley, a male impersonator and star performer at the Moss theatres, recalled a meeting with Moss in her memoirs:

> I remember him telling my husband and myself at dinner at his house in Edinburgh, that he had bought a site in that city and intended to build a magnificent theatre on most up-to-date lines for the exploitation of variety... Of course, we listened to his schemes with interest, and as he proposed to float a company in Edinburgh to finance the scheme, my husband agreed to take two £1 shares, but as he afterwards told me, he was very doubtful as to the success of the scheme, and I too could not see how a theatre costing some £50,000 to build and equip could succeed in Edinburgh.

Although Moss may have had doubts about the scheme, he was careful to keep them hidden. His philosophy for success required the Empire Palace to be a family theatre. 'They want something that is bright and cheerful without

Figure 2.7   Facade of the Empire Palace (author collection).

being vulgar, something that is amusing without being coarse.' If Moss was able to provide suitable entertainment, he left it up to Frank Matcham, acknowledged as Britain's greatest Victorian theatre architect, to express these ideals through 'a building which is at once charming to the eye, and comfortable to the body, a building majestic in its proportions, refined and classical as becomes Modern Athens in its architectural feeling, and at the same time a building equipped with all the luxuries which modern developments in matters theatrical can supply.'

Matcham's brief was to provide the largest, best-looking, best-equipped theatre in the country. Apart from its massive 3,000 capacity, his design incorporated many innovations. To save money, the building was set back from Nicholson Street, allowing commercial property to front the main road. The main theatre frontage may have been narrow, but Frank Matcham devised a flamboyant gilded oriental tower with a copper onion dome surmounted by a

Figure 2.8   Interior of the Empire Palace (courtesy Edinburgh Festival Theatre).

life-size female figure – it was neither 'refined' nor 'classical', but it was conspicuous. This was but a foretaste of the wonders housed within. At the Empire Palace, Matcham showed for the first time the real inventiveness and imagination that were to be the hallmarks of his long career. His highly idiosyncratic style was ideal for the fantasy world of variety.

The stalls and circle foyers had multi-coloured marble floors, mahogany dados and balustrades carved with Moorish designs, swirling patterned carpets, deeply modelled gilded rococo plaster work, coffered ceilings and frescoes of Indian scenes. The whole ensemble he swamped with the lush crimson drapes and replica Louis XVI-style furniture, producing an astonishing, breathtaking theatricality which suited the brave new world of light entertainment. But the auditorium, itself was surely the *pièce de résistance*!

It was huge with three well-spaced galleries, all supported by cantilevers and smothered in sensuous mock-Indian fibrous plaster work. These were a Matcham innovation and ended the need for supporting columns and so an uninterrupted view could be enjoyed from all seats. There were long slips and four stage boxes, swathed in velvet and capped by domes studded with gold stars. The walls were covered in maroon and gold flock wallpaper. The height of the auditorium was designed to take into account sight lines for aerial trapeze acts. There were gangways spaced at four-seat intervals to allow the audience to come and go whenever they pleased. There was a sliding roof for ventilation (essential if up to three performances a day were to take place). The stage was claimed to be the most flexible in the country; the entire proscenium arch could be folded away to accommodate circus acts and the stage divided into modules which quickly retracted to reveal a circus ring underneath. So successful was the arrangement that it was possible to stage a complete circus in the afternoon and variety that evening (the stables from Newsome's Hippodrome were retained behind the Empire Palace). There were plush tip-up seats in the stalls and circle, but pit and gallery customers had a very different experience. They had to enter round the back, where they paid at the door and climbed stone stairs. There were upholstered benches mounted on the gallery steppings, tough linoleum floors and ceramic tiled walls. A sign on the ceiling warned 'DO NOT SPIT – OFFENDERS WILL BE EXPELLED BY THE MANAGEMENT.'[5]

The new Empire Palace staged its first show on 7 November 1892. It consisted of music (massed military bands and an orchestra of thirty players), singing (a soprano, contralto and baritone), comedians (a mimic, 'musical eccentricities' and a knockabout), animals (an equestrian sketch, performing cockatoos and performing dogs) and finally acrobats.

On 13 April 1896 the Empire Palace made history when it was the venue of the first cinema show in Scotland, using Lumière equipment. The newspaper critics were dismissive, but the audiences were impressed and the Lumière cinematograph returned for a fortnight from 1 June. Films shown were *Dinner Hour at the Factory*, *Children Playing*, *A London Stage*, *A Small Life-boat*, *The Arrival of the Paris Express* (a Lumière classic), *A Practical Joke on the Gardener* and *Trewey's Hat* (Mr Trewey managed the Empire Palace).

The theatre was a revolutionary success. Frank Matcham's achievement brought him many more commissions from Moss. The business confidence of the time was summed up in Moss's remarks when asked by *The Scotsman* if he thought the Empire Palace concept would pay:

'Pay!' he repeated the word with a satisfied smile, and said, 'Do you think I would be in it if it was not going to pay? My dear boy, the London Empire is already paying 50 per cent and the Alhambra [Leicester Square] 26 per cent. My firm belief is that there is no risk, so to speak, in conducting a place of entertainment. If such a place does not pay, it is the fault of the management.'

There may have been few financial risks in the variety business, but fire was still a very real threat. On 9 May 1911 the Great Lafayette (an American illusionist whose real name was Sigmund Neuberger) was performing an act where he appeared to enter a lion's cage but he was really using an ingenious system of hidden double bars to separate him from the beast. In addition, the floor was metal and periodically charged with electricity – a cruel device to make the poor lion roar and plunge about. That night, there must have been a flaw in the cable as some hanging scenery caught light. Hot ashes fluttered down and soon the whole stage was ablaze. The iron curtain stuck half way and the resulting draught fanned the flames. The Great Lafayette stood in a trance and even the pleadings of his black servant could not budge him. Suddenly, the blazing fly tower collapsed and he was engulfed by the inferno.

The fire tragedy happened just a few weeks before the first Royal Command Variety Performance was to have taken place at the theatre. There had been years of negotiations to achieve this royal patronage, and the respectability it would bring. It proved a double blow for Sir Edward Moss (he was knighted in 1905), for he had worked hard on the project. His health broke down and, eighteen months later, he died.

The Empire Palace was rebuilt later the same year. Only the stage and dressing rooms had been destroyed and in his design for their replacement, Matcham used fireproof materials wherever possible; wood was almost totally dispensed with. The Empire Palace re-opened on 7 August 1911 and the policy of 'Variety twice nightly at 6.40 and 8.50 pm' was resumed.

By the 1920s variety theatres were experiencing tough competition from the new generation of luxurious cinemas – the Picture House, the Caley and the Rutland to name but three. The Indian decor, benches in the pit and warnings not to spit found in the old Empire Palace theatre all looked dated. The theatre was closed for demolition in November 1927, and during the following ten months an entirely new Empire was built, to the design of the Newcastle-based architects, Milburn and Milburn. They had replaced Matcham as designers of theatres for Moss Empires. Their approach lacked his flamboyance, being safely classical and much more angular. To achieve a capacity of around 2,000 with wide aisles and luxury seating for all, the new Empire also had to be much bigger, which diminished the intimacy and rapport between artiste and audience. While the new Empire was some 88 feet wider than its predecessor, it still had a narrow frontage, this time with two fluted pilasters framing a window containing a hoarding. The new auditorium, however, was a monster. It had three levels with what looked like an acre of maroon plush, tip-up seats. There was no place for lavish plaster work this time – the cream walls were divided by simple frames of silver filigree moulding and the ceiling was coffered with a dome in the centre. It was imposing in scale, but rather too formal for a variety house.

The new Empire opened on 10 September 1928. During this period lavish variety shows with long chorus lines and high-kicking dancers became popular (anything less would have been lost in such an enormous proscenium). The big bands of the 1920s and 1930s became Empire regulars, as did the debonair Scottish singer and dancer Jack Buchanan, who invited his admirers to 'Stand Up And Sing!'

During the 1950s, big American stars like Laurel and Hardy, whose fans blocked Nicolson Street when they appeared in 1954, and the crooner Johnny Ray, who had tearful teenagers screaming in the aisles, kept the Empire at the forefront of the Edinburgh entertainment scene. By the early 1960s, it was no longer possible to fill such a big theatre and the Empire closed on 27 November 1962. It was sold to Mecca for £165,000 in March 1963 and spent the next thirty years as a bingo hall. All the while, the Edinburgh Festival organisers and City Council had been looking for a first-rate venue as the centrepiece for Festival productions. By 1992 Mecca were experiencing financial problems, so they sold the theatre to the council who leased it to the **Edinburgh Festival Theatre** Company, chaired by Lord Younger. The building was found to be in good condition and was pressed into use during the 1991 Festival,

Figure 2.9   Interior of the Edinburgh Festival Theatre (author collection).

complete with bingo apparatus while a radical rebuild was planned at a cost of £21 million. The existing foyers were dull and cramped, and the building had very little architectural presence. The architect, Colin Ross of Law and Dunbar-Naismith, proposed radical changes; the existing facade and foyers would be demolished and replaced by a dramatic, glazed structure with a gently curving concave frontage. The auditorium would be restored to its original splendour and the stage, fly tower and long-abandoned dressing rooms would be thoroughly modernised.

The results are most impressive. The new front of house spaces are bright and inviting; the all-glass exterior looks wonderfully animated, especially at night with the audience milling around its three levels. The ground floor is stone with a stylish back-lit opaque glass bar (the Café Lucia) and a boldly curved ticket counter. Surprisingly, this high-tech design actually complements the beautifully restored auditorium. Here, great care has been taken to restore even such tiny details as the marquetry inlays on the seat backs. The silver, cream and pink colours are shaded with darker tones to enrich what remains a fairly stern design and the expanses of new carpeting and maroon velvet upholstery look very inviting.

Yet, this splendidly resurrected theatre was to prove controversial. It opened on 18 May 1994, under the enthusiastic management of Paul Iles. He believed that the theatre should start where the old Empire left off – with a variety show. This included in its bill the Krankies, a puppet show, the Lothian and Borders' Police Pipe Band and Rikki Fulton. The packed audience loved it, but inevitably there was one Edinburgh councillor, Nolan by name, who was unimpressed by such populist offerings! The second gala, at which Scottish Opera gave its new production of Wagner's *Tristan and Isolde*, was attended by a glittering gathering of people prominent in the arts, business and politics, from Scottish Secretary Ian Lang to culture guru Bernard Levin.

Paul Iles was adamant that the theatre had to and would be self-sufficient from day one. The first Festival season was certainly a tremendous success with no less than eighteen different productions, ranging from modern dance to Val Doonican. During the rest of the year, the building's size became as much a disadvantage as during its final years under Moss control – it simply could not be filled on a nightly basis. With so much money and effort invested, the theatre could not be allowed to fail, so the management set about reducing overheads and applied for a grant to the cash-strapped City Council. Overheads were reduced and a funding package was finally agreed in March 1997 when the managements of the King's and Edinburgh Festival Theatre were merged to save money. The theatre has many influential advocates, so hopefully, given time, its financial position will stabilise. Its resurrection is a magnificent achievement which deserves many decades of success.

Figure 2.10   Facade of Edinburgh Festival Theatre at night
(courtesy Edinburgh Festival Theatre).

THE PALLADIUM

To complete the story of variety in Edinburgh we must go round to East Fountainbridge and to the Palladium, a popular, if smaller music hall. The building dated from 8 November 1886 when it opened as the permanent home of Cooke's Circus. The site of their tented circus on Grindlay Street had been sold three years previously to enable the Royal Lyceum Theatre to be built. By then, under the control of John Henry Cooke, the third generation of the circus family, it had become an Edinburgh institution. Cooke was born in New York in 1836 and by the time he was five he was an expert tight-rope walker. Brought up among horses and ponies, he became a respected trainer, and even prepared horses for Queen Victoria.

Cooke's clowns, acrobats and jugglers were highly popular, but his circus was best known for its equestrian spectaculars. From 1908 Cooke used the Palladium as a cinema, films being projected on to a screen hung across the middle of the ring, with those members of the audience behind seeing the action the wrong way round. Interest in circus was waning and with his own health declining, Cooke sold the building to R. C. Buchanan, who controlled a syndicate of variety halls and cinemas throughout central Scotland, It was rebuilt as a proper cinema, re-opening on 11 February 1911. The Palladium did not survive the difficult transition to sound, being less glamorous than purpose-built rivals. It closed on 13 August 1932 but by December had become a circus once again with the stalls converted to a ring for a Pinder's Royal Circus season. Spring 1933 saw the arrival of Millicent Ward's Repertory Players, who had their Edinburgh base at the Gateway, a studio theatre on Elm Row. They fitted it with a proper stage and dressing rooms and remained for three years. From 11 April 1935, the Palladium was run by George Young with a variety policy. Although it always retained the look of a converted cinema with a single balcony and little decoration, the intimate 966 seater was filled with the atmosphere of infectious bonhomie of a music hall. In 1941 Mr Young's widow sold out to the Glasgow firm Stagecraft Ltd.

Many of the best-known Scottish comedians appeared at the Palladium, and in later years London names like David Frost (starring in an Oxbridge revue at the Festival), Tommy Cooper and Morecambe and Wise graced its boards. The list of Scottish comics was long – Dave Bruce, Bert Denver, Clark and Murray, Alec Finlay, Dave Willis, Andy Stewart, Duncan Macrae, Jimmy Logan, Denny Willis, Chic Murray and Maidie, Johnny Victory and especially Lex McLean. The gruff Glasgow comic's suggestive patter was clearly popular as he held the longest period of top box-office returns with a 25-week run in 1958. He would tell the story of a woman in Morningside who asked for a plumber to call, to repair a pipe. Invited to have coffee, he begins to chat to her 'This is a nice house, Mrs McTavish . . . It must be four or five apartments . . . aren't you worried about the rates?' 'Young man,' she replies, 'we do not have rates here . . . only mice!' or 'What is sex in Morningside? . . . the things coal's delivered in!' Jokes about 'posh' districts of Edinburgh were popular with Palladium audiences, who mainly came from the Tollcross area; Morningsiders might have preferred drama at the Royal Lyceum or an operetta at the King's.

A Glaswegian, Dan Campbell, was manager for twenty years. As a young soldier, he had entertained his comrades in France and Belgium. After the First World War, he toured London theatres, then returned to Scotland with his own concert party, the Sparkles, formed in 1928. He later claimed the only places they avoided playing had less than 1,000 inhabitants. Dan used to call the Palladium the 'University of Music Halls', the place where many future stars graduated. On the night of the fire which destroyed the Theatre Royal, Broughton Street, in 1946, Dan Campbell went down to see it after being informed by phone before leaving the Palladium. On his way home to the West End of the city he had a strange urge to go back to his own theatre and unlock the door; he could never explain why he did this, but he searched the Palladium and in the stalls found a seat smouldering. It was red hot! Someone had left a lighted cigarette on the cushion, so a double disaster was averted by Dan's sixth sense that night.

The Palladium, the last of Edinburgh's variety halls, clung on until October 1968, when Jim Johnstone and his band gave the last show. Patronage fell when many of the Tollcross citizens were moved to better housing in the outskirts. It became a discotheque for a while, then lay derelict until the demolition workers wreaked havoc on East Fountainbridge during the summer of 1984.

The Tivoli at 99 St. Stephens Street, Stockbridge, opened as a theatre in November 1901. It had previously been a roller-skating rink and was a large hall with a single stadium-type floor plan. This made good use of the sloping site, but the auditorium did not look anything like a conventional theatre. If you sat at the back, you were too far away to hear or see the stage properly. The different price zones were only kept apart by low dividing walls. There was bench seating at the front and upholstered tip-ups to the rear.[6]

The Tivoli was promoted by Thomas Barrasford, a variety impresario of Newcastle origin. He ran a large chain of variety theatres, mainly in working-class areas of industrial cities. His prices undercut the 'posh' Moss and Stoll circuits, so he saved money with shorter shows, squeezing as many as three performances into an evening. The acts he booked were often obscure, but the cinematograph shows proved popular. Barrasford only began his quick expansion after the turn of the century, ironically when the variety era was about to be usurped by the cinema. As most of his theatres already had projection booths, they were easily adapted.

The venture became the Grand Theatre in the winter of 1904, opening with the pantomime *Cinderella*. During this phase, cine-variety was tried, but because of its awkward shape, it was never a serious competitor to proper theatres like the Empire Palace. In 1909 the building became home to the Edinburgh Horse Repository and Riding Academy which had moved from Northumberland Street before re-opening as a full-time cinema at Hogmanay 1920. It was later absorbed by the George Taylor circuit of Glasgow, and from 1956 by Green's. The last performance was in May 1960. Since then the building has had many uses; part was a garage and a furniture warehouse; the remainder has been used first as a Mecca ballroom and subsequently as a nightclub. It has now burned down.

Few now recall that behind the unassuming red sandstone facade of what is now Marco's Leisure Centre in Grove Street, there was once a small theatre. The three arches accessed the pit, stalls and circle (there was no balcony) of the New Pavilion, opened on 15 February 1897. The proprietors were Edinburgh Pavilion Ltd, whose managing director was one P. Sturrock-Campbell. The first attraction was John L. Lundie's Great Anglo-Australian Combination Company in the antipodean drama *The Great Bank Robbery*. Attractions were many and varied – in December 1902 we find 'Hillcoat's Famous Cinematograph and Grand Variety Show' appearing. In 1906 it became the Prince of Wales and a melodrama house, the Alhambra, in November. Two years later from 9 November 1908 it opened as Pringle's Picture Palace – a full-time cinema. Within a decade it was being operated by the former lessees of the Broughton Street Theatre Royal, Edinburgh Varieties Ltd, controlled by Horace Collins as the Garrick commencing with the revue 'Hullo Baby' on Hogmanay 1917. Prices ranged from 8d (3p) for the pit to 1/10d (9p) for the 'orchestra stalls'. Later shows included 'real natives' – the Hawaiians and Mlle Leilan doing the hula-hula dance; music from J. M. Hamilton's Concert Party and comedy burlesque from the Atlas Vulcana Girls, displaying feats of strength. The singer Mary Connolly, from Dublin, topped the Garrick's last programme when fire engulfed it after the evening performance on 4 June 1921. Her vaudeville company stood watching their belongings burn; many lost everything they had and none was insured. Too badly damaged to be worth repairing, the auditorium was dismantled, but the facade was kept and a bakery developed on the site; the building has been a leisure centre for the last fifteen years.

THE KING'S

Although famous as one of the Howard and Wyndham chain, the building of the **King's Theatre** in Leven Street was actually commissioned by the Edinburgh Building Company, a syndicate of businessmen, led by Councillor Robert C. Buchanan, as a rival to the successful Royal Lyceum. Buchanan already controlled a large number of provincial variety theatres, but this was to be his most ambitious project to date. On 18 August 1906 Dr Andrew Carnegie laid the memorial stone and copies of current newspapers and coins were buried underneath. During construction, the owners experienced financial difficulties, so before the project was complete, the syndicate transferred its rights to the King's Theatre Company. It was formed by Stewart Cruikshank, the builder, whose firm had constructed the theatre and he became the major shareholder. Buchanan was managing director and he took charge of the day-to-day running of the King's. Despite his guidance and expertise, he was soon ousted by Cruikshank's son, A. Stewart Cruikshank, who was a dynamic businessman with a soft spot for theatre.

The King's was designed by James Davidson and J. D. Swanston. Davidson was a distinguished Coatbridge architect. He designed many banks, schools, offices and churches in Lanarkshire and was probably responsible for the facade of the King's. Its appearance was typical of his 'Lanarkshire municipal' style; a dour and solid, red-sandstone mass which resembles the offices of an insurance company rather than a theatre. While undeniably handsome, it looks misplaced among Edinburgh's refined grey-sandstone classicism. Inside, the

Figure 2.11   Facade of the King's Theatre when new (author collection).

spacious foyers mellow slightly into the good taste of a gentleman's club, with solid mahogany dados and heavily carved door frames, amoebic patterns of stained glass, solid pilasters, marble stairs and fine parquet floors. But once inside the auditorium! The senses are assailed by an Aladdin's cave of fruity Viennese baroque, all swathed in plush and gilt. This can definitely be attributed to Swanston, a Kirkcaldy architect with several similarly flamboyant theatres to his credit. The towering ranges of boxes, nine each side, are exuberantly decorated with lush plaster and separated by voluptuous nudes holding masks. Richly opulent and very seductive the theatre's design may have been, but its architects did not quite have the expertise of Matcham or Phipps. Sight lines from the upper boxes were very poor and the three balconies slammed into the statues and ornaments of the boxes in a completely arbitrary fashion. As a result, the original balcony patrons looked out on the deep decorative panels above the proscenium, rather than into the stage. None of this mattered to the proud owners; the new King's Theatre was incredibly luxurious and very glamorous!

There was seating for 2,500; tip-up seats in the stalls, grand and dress circles and upholstered benches with backs and metal armrests in the balcony. The King's opened on 8 December 1906, appropriately with a festive production of

Figure 2.12   Side boxes in the King's auditorium (Graham Carnie).

Cinderella. The King's was initially advertised as 'The House of Variety' and was run to a high standard; the management must have wanted to emulate Moss's Empire Palace, or Oswald Stoll's magnificent London Coliseum of 1905, which had captured the imagination of the variety business. The King's also had regular visits from the travelling Carl Rosa Opera and Richard D'Oyly Carte's company. The latter had exclusive rights to perform Gilbert and Sullivan's operettas, which were popular with Edinburgh audiences and their performances helped to establish the King's as a number one touring venue. Stewart Cruikshank became an enthusiastic owner and he took special pride in producing lavish pantomimes each winter. Cruikshank must also have realised that his theatre was at a disadvantage by not being part of one of the large circuits. In 1928 he merged his theatre with the Howard and Wyndham empire, and became chairman of the company.

During the summer season, the King's traditionally closed down. In 1934 Stewart Cruikshank decided it would be worthwhile to experiment with a summer season in Edinburgh along the lines of seaside entertainment. The show, known as *Half Past Eight*, had already been a hit in Glasgow, where comic Jack Edge filled the house for fourteen weeks. Edge was brought to open *Half Past Eight* at the King's, but it was a flop. With meagre audiences, it lasted just six weeks. In the meantime, Howard and Wyndham brought Charles and Ilona Ross to produce and choreograph their pantomimes. Charles Ross thought that closing the King's for the summer was a wasted opportunity and wanted to revive the summer revue. Not surprisingly, at first Stewart Cruikshank was sceptical, but in 1937 he eventually succumbed to Ross's pestering. He gave the show only four weeks to succeed or be closed down. Everything seemed to be against its success; Ross could not even find a big star to front the show. Eventually he tracked down a young and relatively unknown comic, Dave Willis, at the Paisley Theatre. Willis was warm, outgoing and sharp – just

Figure 2.13 King's Theatre, Edinburgh (author collection).

what Ross was looking for. The *Half Past Eight* show began on 31 May 1937, billed as 'An after dinner light revue of song, dance and laughter – also starring Cliff Harley, Florence Hunter and the Charles Ross Girls'.

At first only a few hundred came to see the show and by the end of the third week Stewart Cruikshank was about to close the theatre, but what seemed like a miracle happened. News of the show was spread by word of mouth and by the following Friday, the King's was experiencing full houses; on Saturday, there was standing room only. As the leader articles of newspapers commented on the grim political situation in Europe and gossip continued about the Duke of Windsor's abdication, people turned to the *Half Past Eight* show for light relief and glorious entertainment! The show was varied every week. There were big opening and final numbers with the dancers in sequinned dresses, gliding across lavish sets; Dave Willis was a hard-working anchorman who appeared throughout most of the show, sometimes dressed as a dame; Cliff Harley was his straight man. The outcome was that *Half Past Eight* became a summer tradition at the King's, initially running for three months from the end of May; Edinburgh audiences loved Willis, and he starred in the show for the next five seasons. By 1941 it had stretched to twenty-eight weeks. When, Dave Willis moved to open a Glasgow version of the show, Harry Gordon took over for three years, and subsequent comedians were Stanley Baxter, Rikki Fulton and Jimmy Logan. After initial doubts, Stewart Cruikshank took to promoting the shows with vigour. It was a terrible blow for Howard and Wyndham when he was killed in a road accident in 1949, aged 72. Nevertheless, their success continued – at least for a while.

With capacity audiences spilling sweets and fizzy drinks at pantomimes, and equally busy summer seasons, after the war, the King's was in need of major refurbishment. In 1950 the magnificent old canopy, with its metal pillars at the pavement's edge and stained-glass panels, was replaced by a modern cantilevered design. Next, attention was turned to improving the interiors and Howard and Wyndham sensibly used the opportunity to improve the atrocious sight lines. The King's was closed for radical structural alterations and redecoration which lasted ten months. The balcony was demolished while the rake of the upper circle was increased and it was extended back. The new rear portion was separated from the front by a broad gangway and seating was reduced to 1,530. Although everyone could now at least see the whole stage, seats from the rear were now too far away for shows to make an impact. Furthermore, with no balcony, the dress circle had an empty space above and big bare side walls.

With the dress circle sealed off, the theatre was temporarily re-opened in May to host many touring productions during the 1951 Edinburgh Festival. After this, it was closed so that the refurbishing could be completed. It re-opened with the pantomime *Puss in Boots* on 14 December 1951.

During the 1950s and early 1960s, spectacular revues featuring leading comics, singers and dancers, as well as international cabaret acts were the order of the day. By the late 1960s, inflation, the lure of television and the greed of a few agents had pushed the fees for some top stars out of the reach of theatres. Without subsidy, large touring theatres like the King's were doomed.

Happily, the King's was sold to Edinburgh City Council in 1969 and continued to operate much as before. It was particularly useful during the Festival; with the Empire on bingo and the Playhouse still used as a cinema, the King's Theatre had the biggest stage and most dressing rooms of any in the city. The only problem was the fabric had again become badly worn, although the gilded decorations, mellowed with age, looked better than ever but the seating had begun to seem very cramped. After much procrastination, a £1.25 million refurbishment scheme was approved in 1985. The woodwork, marble and stained glass in the foyers were restored. In the auditorium, the aisles were widened and new, pullman seats, such as one finds in multiplex cinemas, were installed. The capacity was reduced to 1,330 (or just over half the original total). The orchestra pit was enlarged to a depth of ten feet and a hydraulic lift installed to raise it, thereby forming a stage apron when required. The plaster statues and ranges of boxes, now accurately restored to their original delicate tints, still delight the eye and the King's is undoubtedly one of the most luxurious theatres in Scotland.

Edinburgh has now the best theatre provision of any British city outside London. In the winter of 1989–90, the Playhouse, a 3,000-seat former cinema designed by John Fairweather, was opened by Apollo Leisure as a venue for the touring productions of blockbuster London West End musicals.[7] Within two years a further 1,900 seats were added to Edinburgh's total when the Festival Theatre opened in the old Empire. There is also a clutch of smaller theatres and performance spaces, of which the handsome new Traverse Theatre, opened in 1992, is the most prominent. During the Festival, these are an asset, but so many large auditoria can be difficult to fill the rest of the year. London has become an international tourist magnate partly because of the reputation of its theatres. Surely Scotland's beautiful capital could do the same.

LEITH

In the 1860s Leith was a bustling port to which ships traded from the Baltic, Scandinavia, Western Europe and the rest of the world. It was also notorious for its drinking dens, brothels, illegal betting shops and tatooists, hidden up narrow streets amid teeming slums. The mixture of bawdy entertainment known as 'music hall' probably began in Leith in November 1865. The fish market section of the Market Hall in Riddle's Close was converted to a cavernous pub fitted with long tables at right angles to a narrow stage. It belonged to a local merchant, John Davidson and the lessee was John Scotland. As the male audience smoked and drank, they would be entertained by 'turns'.

The Leith Royal Music Hall, as it was known, stood in a square bounded by the Kirkgate and Market Street running north and south and by Tolbooth Wynd and St. Andrew Street running east and west. The bills included Negro minstrels and burlesque acts. The manager, Alfred Macarte, left the Leith Royal Music Hall to open his own rival 'temple of varieties' – the Theatre Royal – which opened in 1867 on the corner of Bonnington Road and Great Junction Street, featuring touring acts from all parts of Britain. The name may have had aspirations to the grandeur of the famous Edinburgh drama houses, but the Leith Theatre Royal, while superior to the Leith Royal Music Hall, was still little more than a pub. The bill on opening night included various burlesque dancers acquired from music halls as far apart as Leeds, Liverpool, Dublin, Newcastle and Manchester. Performers included Master George Calvert, champion comic singer, and the bill was topped by Alfred Macarte himself, a 'Pantomimist and Step Dancer'. These acts would have had to battle against the raucous, smoke-filled atmosphere of such early music halls. The female dancers had to endure shouts and wolf whistles. Empty bottles and other missiles were thrown about; every so often a fight would break out while drunks peed or vomited on the floor; music halls were dirty, smelly and disreputable places!

At the same time, the Assembly Rooms in Constitution Street were advertising 'Better Class Varieties'. Drink was not served and audiences faced the stage, not each other. In an atmosphere more akin to a proper theatre, folk were entertained by 'Hypnotists, Mesmerists and Phrenologists who give Amusing (and Amazing) demonstrations'. By 1874 the New Star Music Hall, a pub at the corner of Leith Walk, was running shows under the direction of the proprieter, Mr Albert Cruvelli.

The old United Presbyterian church in Kirkgate burned down in April 1888 and in the following year, the site was leased to Edward Moss, who used the salvable remains as the basis for the Princess's, an entirely new theatre to present lightweight plays and melodrama. The grand opening was on 30 December 1889 under the management of Frederick Wright (lessee and manager of the Southminster Theatre in Nicolson Street, where Moss later built his Empire Palace). It opened with a play called *False Nights*. It had a small two-floor red-sandstone entrance with columns and a pediment which was built into an existing tenement. The large brick auditorium and stage all but filled the back court and fire escapes were knocked through ground floor flats at intervals around the block. Foyer space was minimal and seating was cramped (the pit and balcony alone could hold over 1,000 on wooden benches). There were two stage boxes at circle height and the whole ensemble was ornately plastered in French baroque style with elaborate gilding and crimson drapes.

Moss's expertise lay in running variety shows, and when the rickety Empire Music Hall in nearby Henderson Street was demolished to make way for housing, the Princess's became a variety theatre (the Empire was a small wooden building opened in 1881 – city magistrates must have thought it a fire risk). His lease was terminated in 1899 and he decided to devote his energies to developing his famous nationwide chain of Empire Palace theatres. Moreover, the cramped stage and dressing rooms were inadequate for housing the spectacular London productions for which the Moss circuit was by now famous. Briefly closed, the Leith theatre opened again on 30 October 1899 as the Gaiety, leased to Julian Malvern. He installed electric light so that cinematograph shows could be added to the theatre's variety bills. Indeed, from the turn of the century onwards, most new theatres would have projection rooms and the novelty became a part of most variety bills.

Within a few months, the Edinburgh councillor and city treasurer R. C. Buchanan had taken over control of the Gaiety, adding it to his expanding theatre chain. Like Moss, Buchanan's interests in the variety business were widespread and circuit strength allowed him to afford the best international acts.

The theatre was enlarged in 1914 when shops on either side of the main entrance were transformed into waiting rooms and a café. This coincided with programmes alternating between moving pictures and stage shows. The closely knit community of shipyard workers, dockers, whisky warehousemen and their families in the port identified with the Gaiety, especially after Leith's enforced amalgamation with Edinburgh in 1920. Affectionately known as the 'Gaff', the theatre's occasional Friday-night talent shows drew big crowds to support their neighbours trying their luck on stage. Shop owners who advertised the theatre were allowed in for a penny by showing a red pass.

During the 1930s and 1940s, the Gaiety became a cinema – a role for which it was quite unsuitable. It was probably cheaper than hiring expensive live acts during times of depression and war. The Gaiety reverted to full-time variety on 3 July 1944 under the management of Leith Entertainers Ltd. They installed Claude Worth, an experienced manager with a background in the R. C. Buchanan circuit. Worth lost no time in booking shows led by local comic Aly Wilson, Tommy Hood, Denny Willis or the Logan family. Latterly, the Gaiety also provided an outlet for young talent – in March 1953 an unknown Andy Stewart, who became a legendary singer and dancer on television, and Don Arrol, later host of television's *Sunday Night at the London Palladium* made their debuts. The Lex McLean and Johnny Victory shows were big draws before the Gaiety closed in September 1956 with the revue show *Laugh of a*

Lifetime starring Tommy Loman, Johnny Beattie and the Four Kordites. It was demolished in 1963 as part of the Kirkgate slum clearance scheme.

The **Alhambra**, fronted by a severe grey-sandstone loggia of Doric columns, was one of the most distinctive buildings on Leith Walk, the work of local architect J. M. Johnston. The owners were a syndicate, headed by the businessmen Henry Lees, Robert Saunders and James Baird, who had billiard and dance halls in the area.

It opened as a Theatre of Varieties on 26 December 1914 during the First World War with a concert in aid of the Prince of Wales National Fund and the Belgian Relief fund, presented by Leith Town Council.

The Alhambra's interior followed the Edwardian fashion for purer classical architecture. There was a spacious entrance hall with a fine barrel ceiling and white marble staircases. The pit, circle and gallery had upholstered seats for all

Figure 2.14   The Alhambra, Leith Walk, prior to demolition
(Tony Moss).

1,550 patrons and handsome teak dados. The balcony fronts were adorned with low-relief plaster work in Adam style and the auditorium ceiling had a flattened dome over the stalls. The proscenium was framed by enriched plaster work and the tympanum arch above was filled by a decorative panel symbolising the spirit of harmony; it was a complete contrast to the gilded baroque of the older Gaiety in Kirkgate. While undeniably well appointed, many found the Alhambra's decor rather humourless for a variety house. Naturally, the theatre had a well-equipped stage, twenty dressing rooms and a cinema projection box. It was also fitted with the only two privately owned street lamps in Edinburgh (the first mercury vapour lamps installed in the area) and there were electrical sockets in all parts of the auditorium to allow the use of 'electric vacuum cleaning apparatus'.

The Alhambra's management proudly advertised the 'Grand Orchestra of Fifteen' and its proximity to Pilrig and Leith Central Stations. The economic climate of the Great War worked against the Alhambra. Its 'High Class Varieties in Comfortable Surroundings' inevitably demanded higher ticket prices. Only a few months after opening, a cine-variety policy was introduced. A mix of variety, revue and drama was staged until 1930, when the Alhambra became a full-time cinema. It closed on 8 March 1958, a victim of falling attendance and Entertainment Tax. Permission was granted to demolish it in 1960 but the demolition did not actually take place until January 1974.

PORTOBELLO

Portobello, on the Forth estuary, was Edinburgh's seaside resort, renowned for its fine beach. It was also the town where Sir Harry Lauder was born. With aspirations to become a major resort town, and facing the cold North Sea, some indoor attractions were needed.

The first recorded amusement in Portobello was that of Ord's Circus in the late 1790s. This annual event took place on what was then the Links. Its site is now known as Elcho Terrace. By the summer of 1808, Portobello did not even have a church, but it had a theatre; seemingly a wooden building erected by a company of strolling players in Tower Street. This was only two years after the first stagecoach service to Edinburgh was established.[8]

Portobello pier, one-third of a mile in length, extending in a line with Regent Street, between Bath and Wellington Streets, was built in 1871, one year after Harry Lauder's birth, by the Galloway Saloon Steam Packet Company. At the end of that great structure, there was a variety pavilion featuring two shows daily, said to be offering 'first class refined entertainment'.

Portobello became a district of Edinburgh in November 1896. In 1905 Harry Marvello and his concert party, the Geisha Entertainers, arrived. They erected a stage and dressing rooms on the Harbour Green at the foot of Pipe

Figure 2.15   Portobello pier (author collection).

Street (their previous season had been at Ayr). It was the first time that Portobello had seen such a large open-air show. Success was immediate and within a few weeks, seating had to be doubled. Encouraged, Harry Marvello purchased the Tower Hotel on the promenade in 1906. In the large front garden, he erected the Tower Pavilion, just a marquee, which was Portobello's first big variety venue. As Archie Foley recalls:

> Outside, it was a big canvas circus tent with a wooden facade covered in hundreds of flashing bulbs . . . but when you went in, it looked like a proper theatre with wooden fittings and a proscenium. Both hotel and theatre may be long gone, but the tower itself is still a feature of Portobello. It is covered in relics from historical sites all over Edinburgh and built to satisfy the Victorian's taste for antiquities.

In May 1910 Portobello's pride and joy, the **Marine Gardens**, Seafield Road East, was officially opened. This amazing development spanned an area of 27 acres of ornamental gardens stretching west from King's Road. There was a concert pavilion, skating rink, Bostock's Jungle and American Animal Arena, a host of 'sensational devices and laughter compellors', a scenic railway, theatre, cinema, bandstand, ballroom (the Empress had space for 1,000 dancers and was the centrepiece of the complex), dog racing and a speedway dirt track.

Such an enterprise back in the early years of the twentieth century puts modern leisure complexes quite to shame.

Sadly, Portobello's giant pier was prone to storm damage and shortages of material during the First World War meant that it could not be adequately maintained and thus it was demolished in 1917. The fabulous Marine Gardens were commandeered by the government in 1914, becoming a barracks for troops in the First World War and a factory for the construction of amphibious landing craft in the Second World War. Eventually it was demolished – to make way for an SMT bus garage.

Andre Letta's Pavilion in Bath Street opened in 1921. Letta had long been famous in Portobello for his summer Pierrot shows. His Pavilion was a large tented structure with one level of seating. There was a flamboyant stucco facade, lit by hundreds of bulbs, and a similarly decorated wooden proscenium inside. Letta had a remarkable knack at spotting young talent and many variety greats, like the comedians Dave Willis and Tommy Morgan and the singer Donald Peers made their debuts there. The Pavilion was removed in 1937 to enable the construction of the County Cinema, later the George and now a bingo hall.

Visitors were also entertained by Tower Amusements on the promenade and with live shows in the Concert Hall at the foot of Wellington Street and the Town Hall. All this made up a richness of entertainment for those fortunate

Figure 2.16 The Marine Gardens, Portobello (author collection).

enough to know the area in those days. It earned Portobello the title of 'The Brighton of the North', which, alas, no longer applies.

NOTES

1. Edinburgh was at the epicentre of the Scottish Enlightenment in the mid-eighteenth century. Fired by a new interest in neo-classicism, particularly the art and culture of ancient Greece, this was manifest in all the arts. Ramsay was one of the movement's leading thinkers, along with artist Gavin Hamilton (who painted epic illustrations of Homer's *Illiad*), and the philosopher David Hume. Edinburgh became known as the 'Athens of the North' and a copy of the Parthenon was even attempted on Calton Hill.

2. During the 1740s, Edinburgh newspapers were seemingly more interested in reporting on the escapades of Bonnie Prince Charlie. Despite pages being devoted to the Pretender and his followers, there were regular notices advertising theatrical performances and the drama seems to have flourished.

3. Popular in the court of King George III, she had recently performed as Alicia in *Jane Shore* in the Theatre Royal Covent Garden before George III and the King of Denmark. After a large banquet, the Danish king fell asleep in the royal box during what Mrs Bellany considered to be her finest scene. Doubtless realising the opportunity of international patronage which the proximity of the Danish monarch in a stage box presented, she shouted her line 'OH THOU FALSE LOVE!' close to his ear. Waking with a start, he turned to George III and said audibly 'By God! I vould not marry dat voman vere dere none oder on earth!' From J. C. Dibdin, *The Annals of the Edinburgh Stage*.

4. Alexander Naismyth was the best-known society portrait artist working in Edinburgh at that time. Also much in demand as a designer of scenery, some of his sketches for stage sets are kept in the National Gallery of Scotland.

5. See also Brian Walker (ed.), *Frank Matcham: Theatre Architect*.

6. Stockbridge pubs made the most of their proximity to the new music hall in advertisements which highlighted the fact that they were equipped with electric bells timed to ring two minutes before the curtain rose for the next act, thus allowing patrons to dash across the road for a drink between turns. See Brendan Thomas, *The Last Picture Shows: Edinburgh*.

7. The history of this remarkable building as a cine-variety venue and cinema is covered in detail in Thomas, *The Last Picture Shows: Edinburgh*.

8. Much information on the history of Portobello as a place of entertainment was provided by local music hall historian, Archie Foley.

3   GLASGOW

The first evidence of a venue for regular performances of drama in Glasgow was a hall up an alleyway, known as 'Burrell's Close', located off Duke Street. Performances took place surreptitiously in a small room at the end, accessible from a narrow staircase. The proprietor was Daniel Burrell, a dancing master who had been invited from London by the Duchess of Gordon to teach 'the poetry of motion' to Glasgow's aristocracy. Inevitably, at the behest of the Church, the magistrates imposed tough restrictions. Men and women could only be taught separately, the former being dismissed before the latter were allowed in. Few came to these rigid and gloomy dances, so 'variety' performances were tried, beginning in September 1751. These proved to be more successful.

The first purpose-built theatre in Glasgow was a wooden lean-to booth which opened in 1752 against a retaining wall of the Bishop's Palace in an area called Castle Yard, just by the Cathedral. This precarious wall overhung Kirk Street to such an extent that a superstition spread that if the wisest man in the city touched it, it would collapse on him. Rudimentary though it was, the Castle Yard Theatre was fashionable. The richest customers were carried there on sedan chairs, with servants to protect them from the religious zealots who shouted abuse outside. In 1753 the Reverend George Whitefield, a loud-mouthed and inflammatory preacher, came to Glasgow. Whitefield, who once acted himself, was feared among the acting community as wherever he preached, he goaded his audiences into destroying theatre booths and assaulting the performers. In Glasgow, he preached outside the Cathedral and incited his mob of supporters to riot, telling them that the Castle Yard Theatre was a house of Satan. The place was destroyed and it was not until April 1764 that a new theatre was erected, this time well away from the Cathedral precinct.

When Mrs Bellamy had made her Edinburgh debut at the Canongate Theatre, five Glaswegian businessmen were in the audience. They persuaded John Jackson, the manager of the theatre, to allow Mrs Bellamy to come to

Glasgow, where they promised to build a theatre for her. Jackson rode to Glasgow with two Edinburgh managers, Messrs Beatt and Love, to help to persuade the city magistrates to allow the theatre to be built. They grudgingly permitted the Alston Theatre to be erected outside the city boundary at Grahamston; the site is now at the junction of Hope Street and Argyle Street. The land was sold by a Mr Miller from Westerton at the then enormous price of 5s per square yard. When the developers complained, Miller told them that as this was to be a temple for Belial, they could well afford the price. The Alston was a solid hall, built of stone, with a small portico of four Doric columns in front and was initially managed by Mr Beatt. Two nights after the theatre opened, a Methodist preacher, after claiming he had a dream in which the devil drank Mr Miller's health, incited a crowd to destroy it. As the building was soundly constructed, only the wooden seats and roof were burned and it was soon repaired. Mrs Bellamy, who opened the theatre, became a regular performer. Successive managers, including Mr Digges whose term in Edinburgh had been so successful, were faced with constant intimidation from the clergy and left after short seasons. In 1780 John Jackson, the ambitious manager of the Edinburgh Theatre Royal, formed a consortium with two actors, Mr Bland and Mr Mills to lease the Alston Theatre. On 3 May Jackson arrived from Dumfries, where one of his companies had performed in the Assembly Room Theatre, to see a crowd gathered around the Alston Theatre and smoke rising in the clear morning air. His hopes sank; he had invested heavily in the building and had a company of actors expecting their salaries. In the fire Mrs Bellamy lost all her fine costumes and jewellery, valued at £800.

The fire had evidently been started deliberately by religious fanatics in the middle of the night. The spring of 1780 was a period of public unrest and violent bigotry; a few weeks before, a mob had destroyed a nearby Catholic church during a Sunday service and rioting, looting and arson were common-place. Nobody was arrested for burning the Alston Theatre. The drama was still loathed as devil worship by the poorer classes and this feeling was shared by the civic authorities. Dr Cleland later wrote in his *Annals of Glasgow* 'I was at the fire and I heard the Magistrate direct the firemen to play on the adjoining houses and not mind the Playhouse.'

Public opinion had already started to change, and among the educated, the theatre had been attracting increasing numbers of influential supporters. In destroying the Alston Theatre, many now thought that the zealots had gone too far. A group of local businessmen made good the loss of the building, while ladies gave Mrs Bellamy forty silk dresses as part compensation for her loss. The anti-theatre lobby was silenced for a time and the Glasgow magistrates eventually gave permission for a theatre building to be erected within the city boundary.

THE THEATRE ROYAL, DUNLOP STREET

As the Alston Theatre's owners did not want to risk more trouble, it was Jackson himself who developed the next theatre. He thought that Grahamston was too far from the city centre, so he found a site on what is now Dunlop Street, then an elegant area of mansions looking across a green to the Clyde. Jackson purchased land from Robert Barclay, a writer who had no qualms about a theatre being built there, but Jackson had not reckoned on his other neighbours, Dr Gillies (Minister of the South Parish Church) and the Reverend Mr Porteous, who lived opposite. When Jackson (himself the son of a vicar) came to lay the foundation stone on 17 February 1781, he was handed a note from the clergymen stating they were lodging an interdict against him, on the ground that a theatre would spoil their area. Jackson ignored the note and instructed the builders to proceed as quickly as possible. Once back in Edinburgh, he consulted his lawyers, and with legal opinion in his favour, he wrote to the ministers:

> Let me persuade you, Gentlemen, to take the advice of one who has seen enough of the world to point out your imprudent conduct on this occasion. Would you live in neighbourly comfort with one who has pitched his tent so near you? Molest him not in the pursuit of *his* profession, for believe him, he means to deport himself with the greatest deference to *yours*. The son of a clergyman, and brought up for holy orders, he will ever pay honour to the sacred characters of that order. Let it be your study to preach sanctity without austerity . . . let us show to each individual of the world, that brotherly love and charity are the characteristics of good Christians. That it may be so with me shall be the constant care of,
>
> Gentlemen, your humble servant,
>
> J. JACKSON.

The letter had the desired effect. The theatre was completed on time and without further interruption from the clerics, in fact property in its vicinity actually rose in value.

The Theatre Royal opened on 11 January 1782 having cost almost £5,000 to build. It was Glasgow's 'major' theatre, meaning that it alone had the right to perform plays in the city. Jackson ran it in conjunction with other Theatres Royal in Edinburgh and Aberdeen alternating the companies on a monthly basis.

Glasgow's first Theatre Royal was a handsome one with a yellow-sand-stone facade of four bays, rusticated to first-floor height and with columns flanking the entranceway. Inside, the accommodation was rudimentary. There were two shallow galleries round three sides of the auditorium with three rows of benches in each. These were supported by iron columns. The audience was packed on to the wooden forms, giving a capacity of over 2,000. People were smaller in stature then. There was a commodious stage with a small apron and doors in front of the proscenium to allow the performers to make dramatic entrances and exits close to the audience. On 12 August 1785 the legendary Sarah Siddons performed at the Glasgow Theatre Royal. Her visit captured the public's imagination and she played to capacity audiences for a week. The acclaim surrounding her visit helped to make the theatre respectable for the first time. Over a space of five years, Jackson brought many of the greatest actors of the period to the Theatre Royal – Henderson, Lewis, Pope, Henry Siddons and John Kemble. His stock company for the 1790 season was highly acclaimed, but the next year many of the brightest stars moved on and business was suddenly bad. In the autumn of 1791, he went bankrupt, probably as a result of trying to perform in five theatres as far apart as Glasgow, Dundee and Dumfries all at once. His estate was put in the hands of trustees and the Theatre Royal was sold to Stephen Kemble by public auction. Kemble was previously a subordinate in Jackson's company and was reputedly fat enough to play Falstaff without padding. After a dispute over the terms of sale, he banned Jackson from the theatre. Jackson then spent the next eight years plotting to oust Kemble and in 1799 a syndicate of Jackson's well-to-do acquaintances bought the theatre and he became manager once again.

THE THEATRE ROYAL, QUEEN STREET

By 1802 business was sufficient for Jackson to extend the auditorium, but ironically the theatre's new-found reputation led to the construction of a new Theatre Royal, paid for by public subscription. A committee of Glasgow merchants each bought £25 shares. The Dunlop Street theatre lost its Letters Patent and was forced out of business but Jackson's expertise was still in demand and he became manager of the new theatre until his death in 1806.

The new **Theatre Royal** was located in Queen Street among the grand mansions and banking houses of the prosperous Merchant City. It cost £18,500 to complete and was described as 'the most magnificent provincial theatre in the Empire' when it opened on 24 April 1805. It was designed by David Hamilton (1768–1843), Glasgow's most prolific and sought-after architect of the Georgian era. The Adam-style exterior was rather severe for a place of entertainment. It was three storeys high and of grey sandstone. There were five arched doorways: the three in the centre leading to the boxes while the north and south entrances were for the galleries and pit. Above, a loggia fronted by six Ionic columns soared 30 feet. If the exterior was grand and aloof, within the theatre was elegant and intimate. The auditorium accommodated 1,500

Figure 3.1   Queen Street showing the Royal Bank of Scotland and the Theatre Royal (author collection).

with two complete tiers of boxes, a large pit and two galleries. The balcony fronts were ornately plastered with delicate-looking latticework. The proscenium had a gilded surround, resembling a picture frame, with neither side doors nor stage apron. Performances took place behind the proscenium only and to heighten the sense of illusion an elaborate set of lush scenery was painted by Alexander Nasmyth, a fashionable Edinburgh portrait artist. The Theatre Royal was open four nights a week and the winter season lasted from early November to late January with summer performances from April to July.

The new theatre was initially popular with the rich and fashion-conscious merchant families, netting £250 a night during its first week, but later it was not a commercial success. Its posh location and luxurious appointments perhaps deterred the audiences who had filled the benches of the Dunlop Street theatre. Moreover, the long journey from London and the salaries demanded by the biggest stars compelled the management to make do with lesser attractions. Few if any London stars visited Glasgow until June 1807, when it was announced that 'an engagement has been made, for a few nights only, with the greatest living actor – Mr George Frederick Cooke'. He was to open as *King Richard the Third*, followed by Peregrine in *John Bull* and, on his last evening, Petruchio in Macklin's *Man of the World*. This event caused great excitement and tickets were sold at a premium for the opening night as Cooke's portrayal

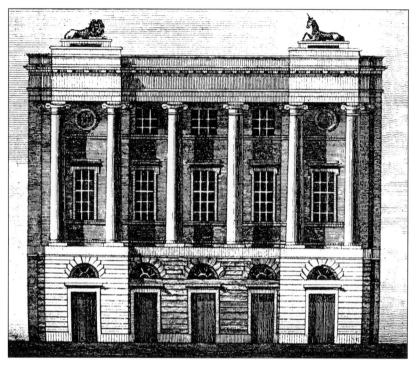

Figure 3.2   Facade of the Theatre Royal, Queen Street (author collection).

of Richard III at Covent Garden had become legendary; even the great John Kemble, once thought the definitive Richard of the day, subsequently refused to play the role.

These occasional visits of such distinguished actors did not, however, always go well, as is shown by an account in the *London Courier* of Edmund Kean's last appearance in Glasgow in April 1817. The play was *Bertram, or the Castle of St. Aldobrand*. A tremendous crush took place when the doors opened and 'many had their clothes torn and others their pockets picked'. All went well until 'the audience conceived that the fourth act had been shortened, and immediately groans, hisses and catcalls re-echoed from every quarter of the house. The fifth act proceeded, but it was no better than pantomime – complete dumb show, nothing could be heard for the hisses, groans and marks of disapprobation of every kind. During this uproar, Kean came forward and motioned to be heard, and with a look of ineffable disdain, turned up his countenance to the galleries, and addressed the Gods with, "What is your pleasure, Gentlemen?"' This laconic remark only made the circle and stalls patrons join in the now even louder abuse. A local critic wrote 'The audience retired in great disgust . . . as they were surprised by a careless, inanimate, and uninteresting representation. The general opinion . . . was that Mr Kean was labouring under the effects of intoxication – an opinion which, I am sorry to say, there was finally too good reason to believe.'[1]

The remaining career of the Theatre Royal in Queen Street was marred by uncertainty as successive managers struggled to make it pay. In August 1809 the entire stock of scenery, wardrobe and furniture had to be auctioned to pay off creditors, and when William Charles Macready leased it, redecorated it and put on lavish production of *Aladdin* (a huge success at Covent Garden), he still did not make enough profit. The Theatre Royal continued to decline as a description of it in a book of contemporary etchings by Joseph Swan, published in 1828, emphasises:

> The drop-scene is as fine a landscape painting as the eye need wish to rest on. Many of these fine paintings have, however, been much injured by carelessness and want of attention. The machinery was at first very complete, but has also, we learn, been considerably deteriorated.
>
> Notwithstanding, however, the inhabitants of Glasgow have provided and still possess this splendid theatre, it has become proverbial that they do not support the drama; and unfortunately this is but too true. Indeed, the building of this theatre and its decoration is the only exertion they have ever made for the support of the drama; but having done so, they have left it to sustain itself, – to go to ruin and decay. Ruin has indeed followed most managers who have had anything to do with it; and strangers are astonished on entering this place of public amusement, to find unhappy actors performing to empty benches.

In 1818 the newly formed Glasgow Gas Light Company had chosen the theatre to demonstrate the possibilities of their new innovation. The lighting of its new crystal chandelier was a novelty at first, but due to a lack of funds, it was not properly serviced and was blamed for a devastating fire in January 1829, which destroyed the theatre, leaving only the facade. The management was not insured, so the ruins were demolished.

After the fire, the old Theatre Royal in Dunlop Street made a come-back. John Jackson had sold it by auction in 1807 and the new owner, Andrew Thomson, had it partially converted to a warehouse for West Indian goods. The remains of the auditorium were let out for occasional public meetings. In 1825 it became a full-time theatre once again, renamed the Caledonian. The basement was converted into a secondary hall, known as the Dominion of Fancy and run by one John Henry Alexander. It opened with *The Battle of Inch or, For My Ain Hand*. Because of their close proximity, the noise from each theatre's production permeated both houses and great rivalry ensued. The matter had to be settled in court and alternate nights for performing were allocated. J. H. Alexander later became the proprietor of the entire building. When the rival Queen Street theatre burned down, the Dunlop Street theatre management saw their opportunity and rebuilt the latter to take the place of both. The architect was William Spence. At the same time, Alexander paid £1,050 for new Letters Patent and restored the name 'Theatre Royal'. Its productions were scarcely of high quality, most of them being melodramas performed by his stock company, but Alexander knew his market as the area stretching from the theatre towards Glasgow Cross was now the city's main entertainment area. Pubs and shebeens abounded and it attracted both the new working class and sailors on leave.

With immigration, Glasgow quickly doubled in size, reaching a half million by mid-century. There was now a huge market for entertainment, so Alexander enlarged his theatre in 1839–40, again to a Spence design. This later rebuild was radical; the existing theatre was almost entirely demolished and after nearly two years' work, a new Theatre Royal emerged. This was a splendid neo-classical edifice of eight bays with columns, pilasters, arches and niches, which contained statues of Shakespeare, David Garrick and J. H. Alexander himself. The interior was ornately decorated with painted panels depicting scenes from Shakespeare on the boxes and 'the most striking scenes of the dramatised works of Sir Walter Scott', interspersed by gilded medallions, on

The old Theatre Royal in Dunlop Street, as it was about a century ago.

Figure 3.3 Facade of the Theatre Royal, Dunlop Street (author collection).

the front of the upper circle. The decoration of the Theatre Royal with scenes from the National Drama reflected its prominence and popularity.

The Theatre Royal witnessed a terrible tragedy on 17 February 1849 when sixty-five people, mainly youths, were trampled underfoot (the usual cause of death in theatre fires) on a staircase after an irresponsible cry of fire. There was none on that occasion, but there was after the last night of the pantomime, *Blue Beard*, on 31 January 1863, when the whole place went up in flames. Alexander's health broke down and he died shortly after. He is buried in the Necropolis at Glasgow Cathedral, where his tomb is modelled on the proscenium of a theatre, a fitting tribute to a hard-working manager.

With the extraordinary optimism of the time the Theatre Royal was yet again rebuilt behind the existing frontage. It re-opened on 17 December 1863, under the management of Mr and Mrs Edmund Glover, but was only to last another five years and was sold to the City Union Railway Company for £27,500 to enable the construction of St. Enoch Station to commence. After the sale, the Glover family transferred the Letters Patent to their new Theatre Royal in Cowcaddens. The Dunlop Street theatre closed for good on 28 May 1869.

THE PENNY GEGGIES

In the *Glasgow Journal* of 4 August 1763, we find the earliest known advertisement for a 'music hall' performance in Glasgow – although this was decades before the genre had been invented:

THIS IS TO ACQUAINT THE CURIOUS, that there is to be exhibited by the inventor and maker, S. Boverick, from nine in the morning till eight in the evening, at the sign of the Mason's Arms, opposite the main guard, Trongate, at one shilling each person, the so much admired collection of miniature curiosities consisting of the following pieces:
1. An ivory chaise with four wheels, equal to the size of a grain and drawn by a single performing flea.
2. A flea chained to a chain of 200 links, with padlock and key, all weighing less than one third of a grain.
3. A miniature landau, with four persons therein, two footmen behind, a coachman, a dog and six horses, all drawn by a single flea.

According to *Glasgow Past and Present*, a country wife from Pollokshaws was in Glasgow selling her fowls and eggs at the time of the demonstration. She did very well at the market, and on her way home she saw a queue at the Mason's Arms. Not knowing what she was going to see, she paid her shilling, and entered just as the flea was about to pull the ivory coach. All she saw was the flea, so she quickly put her nail on it and cracked it, exclaiming 'filthy beast, wha could have brought you in here?' 'Professor' Boverick went mad and seized the woman by her throat, demanding how she dared kill his flea. Freeing herself, the wifie said 'Losh me, man, 'makin' sic a wark about a flea. Gif you come with me back to the Shaws, we'll gi'e ye a peck o' them and be muckle obliged to ye for takin' them!'

Despite such minor setbacks, these primitive entertainments became popular, and during the following century, the area was overrun with rudimentary theatres, show booths and pubs, which put on turns to attract drinkers. The booths, known as 'Penny Geggies' (derived from an old Scots word 'gegg', meaning show), were wooden stages fronted by ornately carved proscenium frames, which frequently burned down. The audience stood in the street outside and were entertained by numerous competing booths along the western edge of Glasgow Green.[2]

The most notorious of the 'Penny Geggies' was William **Mumford's**, opened in 1834. Mumford first came to Glasgow from his native Bedfordshire with a puppet show. At his booth, he presented dramas, such as Scott's *Rob Roy* with small casts but at bargain prices. He spent most of the profits on cheap whisky and was a notorious drunk. He recited the prologues himself, leaning against the proscenium for support. 'You're drunk', a voice might shout from the audience. 'Me drunk?', was his indignant reply, 'Wait till you see Baillie Nicol Jarvie' (a reference to a character in *Rob Roy* whom he was about to play). Frequently, Mumford's prologues became emotional temperance lectures; he used himself as a bad example. Soon other 'Geggies', such as Calvert's Booth and Dupain's, opened and competition was tough. Later fully enclosed 'music halls', like Whitebait's, the Jupiter and David Brown's, were opened as an adjunct to public houses. Brown was a spirit dealer who ran a music hall on the west side of Dunlop Street from 1852, then took over the Royal Olympic, a pretentiously titled rival which had opened in 1855. Both were drinking dens with a small stage at one end. At the same time more substantial theatres, in which the audiences faced the stage, were developed around Jail Square. The Adelphi was a wooden hall which opened on 21 December 1842 with Shakespeare's *King Richard the Third*.[3] Its owner was David Prince Miller, who had a small company of players with a three-piece band. The Adelphi was a short-lived venture, for it burned down overnight on 15 Novenber 1848. Charles Calvert bought the site and on it he built a brick hall which had its facade to Greendyke Street. It was opened on 20 October 1849 as the Queen's Theatre, to commemorate the recent royal visit to Glasgow. Notwithstanding its regal name, the Queen's had a reputation for lewd performances which attracted drunken and disorderly predominantly young male audiences. It was run with three shows a day – often burlesque

Figure 3.4   Musicians at Mumford's Geggie (copyright source unknown).

acts or foul-mouthed comics – and an extra late performance on Saturday
night. The congregation of the Episcopal Chapel next door were furious and
repeatedly asked the city magistrates to close it down. What went on in there
was, after all, totally illegal as all theatrical performances had to be vetted by a
censor. This law was difficult for the authorities to enforce, for at the first sight
of officialdom, the management saw to it that the audience was calmed down
and that no swear words or rude jokes were uttered on stage until they left.
The problem was eventually solved when the Revered John Henderson bought
the hall to be a centre for Sunday mission work and evening classes in 1859.

The City Theatre was built on a narrow site between the Adelphi and
Cooke's Circus Amphitheatre in Jail Square. It was opened in July 1845 by
Professor Anderson – the Wizard of the North, actor, manager and illusionist.
Despite the imposing entrance portico of four Doric columns, this theatre was
poorly constructed – the walls were single brick and the wooden beams that
supported the gallery and boxes were reportedly very thin. Early in the morning
of 19 November, only four months after opening, the City burned to the
ground. The *Illustrated London News* reported:

At five minutes past twelve on Wednesday morning, flames were seen leaping from the roof . . . and in an inconceivably short space of time they had spread over all parts of the building. Engines were on the scene with the utmost possible dispatch but by then the roof had given way. The firemen directed their force and skill to protecting the Adelphi Theatre, in the immediate vicinity, from a similar fate. The wind was blowing rather strongly from the south, and the consequence was, that a constant shower of sparks and pieces of burning wood was thrown on the roof of the Adelphi, rendering its safety a matter of great uncertainty, especially as it is composed entirely of wood. A plentiful supply of water was, however, poured on it . . . and no part of the Adelphi was permitted to catch fire. Meanwhile, the flames raged in the City Theatre with uncontrollable fury, illuminating the whole city and surrounding country. The spectacle, though in itself a melancholy one, was full of sublimity and grandeur. Thousands of spectators were attracted to the spot. After raging for fully an hour and a half, the flames subsided, having consumed every article the theatre contained; and the brick walls and portico alone remained, presenting a most desolate picture. The action of the fire upon the walls was so intense that they cracked in various places and have since fallen. On Wednesday evening, the opposite wall fell down with a tremendous crash at the time Mr Sheridan Knowles was performing in the Adelphi. The house was crowded and the alarm was intense. The audience rushed towards the doors, but happily without serious accident. Nothing now remains but the ruins of two staircases, a portion of the wall nearest the Clyde and four columns of the portico.

We may observe, in conclusion, that however much we regret the loss which Mr Anderson has sustained, it was a mercy the theatre *was* destroyed by fire without any loss of life; for that calamity, in all probability averted a much greater one. The City Theatre was calculated to hold 5,000 persons, and very far short of that number have, it would seem, been within its unstable walls, with no symptoms of danger occurring. Yet in the case of a tumult, or in the lapse of a short time, when decay began to operate, the worst was to be dreaded from an overcrowd in this extremely insecure structure.

The destruction of the City Theatre had shaken public confidence so the city magistrates worked to toughen up building regulations to ensure that all future theatres were solidly built, had an iron safety curtain and adequate exits for their entire audience to escape within minutes of a fire breaking out.

THE BRITANNIA

Every day, hundreds of Glaswegians walk down Trongate towards the famous steeple in front of the modern Tron Theatre, passing on their way a fading Italianate building with an amusement arcade on the ground floor. This once-grand edifice, designed by Gildard and MacFarlane, is now unique, for on its second and third floors, hidden from the public eye, there still exists the **Britannia** Music Hall – the only remaining example of its type in Scotland.

The Britannia started life in 1857 as Campbell's Music Saloon, an unlicensed music hall, owned by a Mr Brand and run by an actor called Willie Campbell. The entrance was a few doors wide, and was sandwiched between the shop fronts. Looking along the street, it was marked only by two gas lanterns. There was a small hallway with ticket booths on either side and the auditorium had a single wooden balcony on iron columns with bench seating throughout.

Figure 3.5 *Trongate showing the Britannia* (Glasgow City Archives).

Arthur Hubner moved his cinema shows from the Ice Skating Palace, taking over the lease of Campbell's and renaming it the Britannia to show silent films but music-hall acts still appeared there as well. Marie Lloyd, Little Titch, Dr Bodie and Harry Lauder all played this basic little hall. Prices ranged from 3d in the pit to 6d in the cushioned forms of the circle. The *Glasgow Weekly Programme* informed readers that 'To those who like music-hall business, the BEST and CHEAPEST is undoubtedly the BRITANNIA in Trongate.' However, competition was intense and many better equipped rivals were opening nearby. **Crouch's Wonderland** was a small music hall further west in Argyle Street,

Figure 3.6   Crouch's Wonderland (author collection).

developed by Herbert Crouch in 1882. When its popularity began to fade, Hubner left to run the Alexandra Music Hall in Cowcaddens and the Britannia closed in 1903.

It might have been the end, but for Albert Ernest Pickard, extrovert Yorkshire-born showman who had come up to Glasgow to make his fortune. He was already running a waxworks and museum of grotesques a few doors away from the abandoned Britannia. There, alongside the wax grotesques, Pickard advertised such live performers as 'LEO WHITTON, The Colossal Canadian, The Heaviest Man Ever Exhibited, The Bearded Lady Triplets, A Leprechaun from Ireland and an African Snake Charmer'. Pickard bought the vacant Britannia in 1906 and re-opened it as a low-cost music hall, at first employing some of the strange performers from his waxworks, with four shows daily. Pickard later had its early history recorded in verse:

> He bought it for a million,
> Or as near as that he could,
> And ca'ed it the Panopticon,
> which naebody understood.
>
> The dossers frae the models,
> An' a' the big fat fleas,
> Found it a 'Home from Home',
> Where they could rest at ease.
>
> An' great was the night wi' scratchin'
> While groans and growels grew louder,
> But greater still the oncost,
> On tons o' Keating's Powder.
>
> An' once a week the amateurs
> Danced round wi' active legs,
> But 'lang ere a' the play was played',
> They were drooned in Lipton's eggs.

The Panopticon's Friday-night amateur talent contests became an institution. If you had no money, you could add your name on the list beside the door to do a turn. The Panopticon's audience threw coins at the stage, so before an act was yanked off from the side with a shepherd's crook, they could pick up the coins. Even school children tried their luck; a wee boy, billed as 'Funny Clive', later became the renowned comedian Dave Willis as a result of his debut in Pickard's talent show. The education authorities got wise to what was happening as boys with comic talent such as Stan Jefferson, the son of the manager of the rival Scotia in Stockwell Street, repeatedly played truant from school to appear there. Stan's father had tried hard to keep his boy off the stage, but in 1906, he secretly applied to perform at the Panopticon with a mixture of songs, jokes and dancing. By chance, his father was talent-spotting in the Panopticon that night and was horrified to see his son doing so well on stage. With his father's encouragement he joined Fred Karno's troupe and eventually found fame and fortune in Hollywood as half of Laurel and Hardy.

The Panopticon was a big success and Pickard soon acquired the floors around his theatre in Trongate House, filling them with all kinds of odd side shows. The *Daily Record and Mail* reported:

> Apart from the variety entertainment, people will find plenty of cheap attractions in this building. There are various tableaux in wax, these including a representation of a torture chamber in the Middle Ages, the story of a Paris crime, and human sacrifices in Dahomoy. In addition, there are various mechanical and automatic machines, an electric rifle shooting machine and many paintings and statues.

In 1908, in an attempt to emulate the success of the Scottish Zoo and Circus in New City Road, Pickard installed a menagerie in the Panopticon's basement, and with his customary bravura announced the opening of 'Pickard's Noah's Ark', an action which prompted a furious publicity war with the zoo's owner, the formidable E. H. Bostock – much to the hilarity of the Glasgow public.

The novelty eventually wore off and by the 1920s, the Panopticon had become the Tron Cinema. In 1931 Pickard gave the place to his son, Peter. By then, Glasgow's entertainment district had shifted away from the Trongate to the Sauchiehall Street–Renfield Street axis as a result of the tramway system. The Panopticon was dirty, uncomfortable and hopelessly outmoded by the new 'super' cinemas, so it closed in 1938 and has lain abandoned but virtually intact ever since. There have been several attempts to find a new use for this unique space.

THE PRINCE OF WALES

James Bayliss came from England with his wife in 1842, attracted to Glasgow by its sudden prosperity as a major port and industrial centre. He was to become an important figure in the development of Glasgow's variety theatres. He began with a rough apprenticeship as a waiter at the Jupiter, a particularly sordid music hall in Saltmarket. There, he lost an eye when a soda bottle was thrown at him. In the early 1850s Bayliss became chairman at the rival Sloan's

Oddfellows Music Hall, a couple of doors away. Bayliss was ambitious and soon did well enough to buy the Milton Rooms at the junction of Stewart and Cowcaddens Streets in 1860. These were old meeting halls which he re-opened as the Magnet Music Hall and put on a standard of performance much higher than in some of its coarse rivals. Alas, the Magnet went the way of most early Glasgow theatres – it burned down. Perhaps this was a blessing in disguise, for James Bayliss built a new theatre – the Scotia across the city in Stockwell Street in the Merchant City.

The site of the Magnet was cleared and a very large new theatre was developed by Alfred Davis and Edward L. Knapp for melodrama, comedy and opera. As with Bayliss, Davis started in the business as a music-hall chairman, while Knapp came from a theatre background. The Prince of Wales was part of an audacious development which included a new and suitably ornate block of tenements facing Cowcaddens Street. The 2,800-seat two-tiered auditorium stood in the space behind and the 'orchestra stalls' and 'grand circle' were reached along a long, low marble-clad entrance foyer below the tenement. It was designed by David Hamilton,[4] the distinguished Glasgow architect of numerous grand buildings, and opened on 4 August 1867. The first season ended in a blaze of glory, but the second finished in a blaze of a different kind, the theatre burning to the ground overnight during a run of the pantomime *Valentine and Orson*. It was rebuilt, again by Hamilton, as a vast three-tier house of operatic splendour. Emerging from the long, dark foyer to the frescoed heights of the new theatre must have been a thrilling sight with its three wide serpentine galleries encrusted with delicate plaster lattices and arches soaring majestically to a fine circular domed ceiling. It opened again on 30 September 1869 with the Exeter-born impresario Fred Belton in charge, but misfortune still clung to it. It proved difficult to fill and only a decade later, in February 1879, there was another less serious backstage fire.

In March 1881 the Prince of Wales closed for an extensive rebuild, re-opening in August as the luxurious 2,030-seat **Grand Theatre**. Run by Thomas Charles, who was also chairman and managing director of the Theatre Royal in Nottingham, it kept very exacting standards and many of the finest performers of the period visited the Grand. When touring productions of pantomimes were given, smoking was allowed in the auditorium (as in the variety houses), but for drama and opera it was banned, just as in other so-called 'legitimate' theatres. In the 1890s the touring opera companies, like Carl Rosa's Royal Opera, were at their peak of popularity. These amazing outfits toured Britain's provincial theatres with a week's engagement at each and a different opera was presented every night. At the Grand, for example, they performed *Don Giovanni* on Monday, followed on consecutive nights by *Othello, Bohemian Girl, Faust* and *Carmen*, with *Tannhauser* and *Il Trovatore* on the Saturday. In densely populated working-class areas like Cowcaddens,

Figure 3.7   Cowcaddens Street showing the Grand Theatre (author collection).

such programmes were then highly popular and the theatre would have been as full as for a pantomime or comedy.

In 1903 the Grand was sold to the fast expanding circuit controlled by R. C. Buchanan. He gave it a further refurbishment, costing £8,000. The stage was rebuilt with fireproof materials and the auditorium was again modernised to a design by James Davidson.[5] The *Glasgow Herald* acclaimed it as 'The most spacious and luxuriously furnished theatre in the city' and it re-opened on 25 September. The theatre was sold to Moss Empires in 1909, and from May 1915 was operated as a cine-variety house. With local cinemas now attracting the bulk of Cowcaddens audiences, and people from outside the area preferring the Theatre Royal nearby in more salubrious Hope Street, the Grand was inevitably doomed as a theatre. It was finally destroyed by a fire after the last show on 5 September 1918, demolished and replaced by a modest picture house.

THE SCOTIA

James Bayliss next developed the **Scotia Theatre** across the city in Stockwell Street. It was to be Glasgow's first modern variety theatre. On the relatively cramped site of a joiner's yard behind the famous Scotia pub, his architect, James Sellars,[6] designed an elegant, intimate theatre with seating for over

2,000 patrons. Incredibly, Sellars was only nineteen years old at the time and he later went on to design such magnificent buildings as St. Andrew's Halls, Kelvinside Academy and a clutch of fine parish churches, including Kelvingrove, Belmont and Hillhead. He entered into the spirit of the variety theatre with vigour; the Scotia had a narrow frontage in red sandstone with pilasters flanking an advertising hoarding and a small pediment. The front-of-house spaces were small and dingy with stone floors, but the auditorium had very rich neo-baroque plaster work on the two balcony fronts and the boxes were handsomely framed with gilded Corinthian columns. The gilding, flock

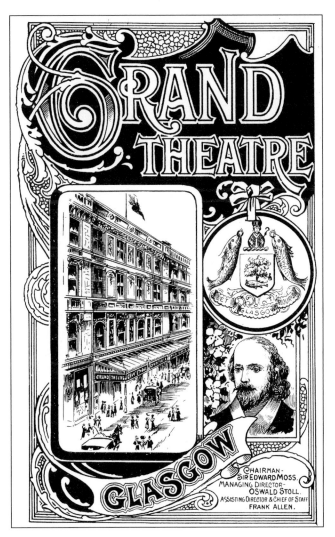

Figure 3.8 The Grand Theatre, Glasgow (author collection).

Figure 3.9   The auditorium of the Grand Theatre (author collection).

wallpaper and frescoes must have looked particularly seductive when softly lit by gas mantles. The Scotia opened on 29 December 1862 with 'high class varieties' twice nightly.[7] There was a serious backstage fire in May 1874, but fortunately this happened at night when the safety curtain was down and the building was easily repaired.

In 1893 H. E. Moss (proprietor of the Moss Empires theatre chain) formed a syndicate with the local impresarios Richard Thornton and James Kirk to buy the Scotia. With a large circuit, Moss had access to the best acts and the queues which stretched along Stockwell Street in both directions were longer than ever. Ironically, it was the Scotia's popularity which persuaded Moss to develop his Empire Palace in Sauchiehall Street and when that opened in 1897, the Scotia was closed down. It was subsequently renovated, renamed the Metropole, and leased to Messrs H. H. Morell and Frederick Mouillot. They attempted a melodrama policy, but being located in a dishevelled area and surrounded by drinking dens where the music-hall tradition was strong, it was unable to attract sufficient audiences. Arthur Jefferson[8] took over in 1901 and restored variety with three shows daily. He advertised it as 'The Most Centrally Situated of All the Glasgow Theatres – St. Enoch, Queen Street and Central Stations within easy access'. The proximity of the railway made it easy for Jefferson to book acts from all over the country, even animal acts were tried and the sight of camels and even elephants being lead down Stockwell Street was not uncommon. A pantomime was given every spring and Harry Lauder made his professional debut in Glasgow at the Metropole – a result of Jefferson's famed talent-spotting.

In 1914 the Metropole was sold to Bernard Frutin. Frutin was a make-up artist, who had left Russia in 1902 because of the unrest prior to the 1905 rising. Once in Glasgow, out of necessity he opened a barber's shop in the

Figure 3.10   Interior of the Scotia Theatre, Stockwell Street
(author collection).

Gorbals, but his first love was the theatre. His management of the Metropole became legendary. The small proportions of the theatre helped to create personal artiste–audience relationships and there was great camaraderie backstage in the cramped dressing rooms. The Metropole never had pretences to elitism, but provided down-to-earth fun and excitement for working-class families packed into tenements around Gorbals and Glasgow Cross. Mothers with weans wrapped in shawls were a familiar sight in the gallery and pokes of sweets were passed freely across the cramped rows of benches. Bernard Frutin died in 1940 and his son, Alec, took over.[9]

The Logan family was closely associated with the Metropole. Jack and May Short (alias Pa' and Ma' Logan) were its heads and their son, Jimmy, was soon acclaimed as one of Britain's finest comic actors. Under Alec Frutin's guidance, the Logans sang, did comic sketches and danced, becoming a Scottish show-business institution.

Tragically, just fourteen months short of its centenary, and by then Scotland's oldest operating music hall, the Metropole was destroyed by fire during the night of 28 October 1961. The roof, circle and gallery were destroyed and only smouldering rubble was left. Deemed to be beyond repair, its site was cleared and an integral part of life for countless Glasgow families and entertainers quickly vanished.

THE THEATRE ROYAL, HOPE STREET

Bayliss made a great success of his Stockwell Street variety house and went on to higher things. He opened his Royal Colosseum and Opera House on 28 November 1867 on a site at the junction of Hope Street and Cowcaddens Street opposite the burned Magnet. The Royal Colosseum was a solid building, designed by George Bell and made of sandstone quarried on site. The architect was known for his imposing neo-classical facades – the Justiciary Courthouses in Saltmarket and the magnificent Merchant's House and Courthouses in the Merchant City, for example. The new theatre looked prosperous with a fine Corinthian portico topped with an Italianate tower facing Cowcaddens Street. Inside, it had three horseshoe tiers with space for 4,000. It was reportedly rather sombre and classical with little of the fine plaster and drapes found in its contemporaries, although it cost the high price of £30,000. Bayliss intended the Royal Colosseum to be Glasgow's number one venue for straight drama and opera – this was Glasgow's answer to Covent Garden and a vast improvement over the ageing Theatre Royal, Dunlop Street. Unfortunately it appears that Bayliss did not have as sure a hand with the 'legitimate' theatre business as he had with music halls. Apart from the hugely popular pantomime *Let Glasgow Flourish*, which played to capacity houses for three months, the Colosseum was a financial disaster. Bayliss sold out to Messrs William Glover, son of Edmond, and George Francis in 1869. With the Dunlop Street theatre site sold for redevelopment as part of St. Enoch railway station, they were able to transfer the coveted Letters Patent to the Royal Colosseum. First, the theatre was closed for two months from the end of May for radical alterations to redecorate the interior and enlarge the stage and fly tower, before a grand re-opening on 12 June as Glasgow's third **Theatre Royal** when the Grand English Opera Company staged *Il Trovatore*. This time it was to be a success; Francis retired in 1878 and his place was taken by Edward L. Knapp.

On the night of 2 February 1879, disaster struck when the Theatre Royal suffered the first of its periodic fires; it was burned to the bare walls. Knapp left at once to manage the brand-new Royalty theatre in Sauchiehall Street and left the ageing Glover to carry on alone. A new auditorium was designed by Charles J. Phipps. Although the original walls were retained, a new main entrance with a domed tower was knocked through existing buildings on Hope Street. This made commercial sense as the theatre now faced the city centre, but the design was necessarily cramped. In shape, the auditorium was similar to the original, but this time the tiers were encrusted with low-relief plaster latticework and the capacity reduced to 3,000. The theatre was back in business on 26 October 1880 with Marie Litton in *As You Like It*. In 1882 Glover finally retired, not only exhausted by the rebuilding but also his subsequent effort to re-establish the Theatre Royal's prominence. It was sold to the Glasgow Theatre and Opera House Company, a firm set up by the ambitious Charles Barnard, lately manager of the Gaiety in West Nile Street. Like Bayliss long before him, Barnard had started his career as a manager trying to improve the reputation of music halls. A trained tenor, he also had a passion for opera and drama – hardly appreciated at his previous postings. In 1884 he had electric light installed throughout the Theatre Royal – any advance which might cut the risk of another fire was more than welcome. Barnard's tenure was short; he had attempted to run the theatre at premium London prices – a mistake as competition in Glasgow was intense. Having spent most of the profits on improvements and new scenery, Barnard left and the Theatre Royal was boarded up.

The next few years were difficult; a variety of inept managers spoiled its reputation and there were intermittent periods of closure. In 1891 J. B. Howard and F. W. Wyndham got a bargain when they bought the vacant theatre for just £7,500 (it had cost £30,000 to build). They were the shrewd operators responsible for the recent success of the Royalty, Sauchiehall Street. Its money-spinning policy of touring opera companies, plays, musicals and pantomime was successfully copied at the Theatre Royal, which re-opened on 10 September 1888 with Henry Irving and Ellen Terry in *Faust*. Sadly, it was just four years until the place was devastated again by a fire on 1 March 1895. The insurance assessors estimated £30,000 worth of damage – but only then did the owners discover that their policy had run out two days before!

THEATRE 'ROYAL,' GLASGOW.
Destroyed MARCH 1, 1895.

Figure 3.11   Theatre Royal, Glasgow (copyright source unknown).

Others might have despaired at such bad luck, but Howard and Wyndham had a good reputation as managers and easily secured a bank loan to begin all over again. Phipps was called back to revise his existing design for a third auditorium within the same old blackened walls. The budget was tight and to get the theatre back in business, the construction took place at break-neck speed. In the event it was ready in a little over six months and opened on 9 September 1895. The theatre was now in a form similar to that seen today. There was a tiny foyer for stalls and circle customers, but the rest had to use entrances around the block. Despite hasty and shoddy building work, the spacious auditorium design (seating 1,966) was one of Phipps's finest. The balconies were unusually deep at eleven rows and originally were fully supported by iron columns. The grand and dress circles were serpentine with delicate low-relief rococo decoration. The top balcony was a horseshoe frieze, the design of which was continued above the proscenium. The boxes were framed by giant Corinthian columns with richly decorated shafts, and high above there was a beautiful, circular panelled ceiling. It was chastely decorated in cream, grey, lilac and light gilt with crimson drapes and blue upholstery.

By then, the theatre had become very popular. There were some memorable pantomimes, starring comedy greats Harry Lauder, Will Fyffe, Tommy Lorne and Dave Willis. The finest actors brought their companies; Sarah Bernhardt, Sir Henry Irving, Ellen Terry and Donald Wolfit all trod its boards. In the 1930s and 1940s, in conjunction with Howard and Wyndham's similar Royal Lyceum in Edinburgh, it nurtured the developing Scottish repertory theatre companies.

In 1949 Stewart Cruikshank (Jnr) took control of Howard and Wyndham. He was more interested in expanding the mass-market variety and pantomime side of their business. In 1954 the modern Alhambra was added to their portfolio, and the Theatre Royal was now the most old fashioned of their three Glasgow venues. When Scottish Television (STV) was established in the mid-1950s, it considered two buildings as possible homes – the Theatre Royal and the Haymarket Ice Rink. Howard and Wyndham were among the original investors in STV, so they forcefully offered the Theatre Royal. The theatre closed on 16 February 1957 with the pantomime, *Robinson Crusoe*.

STV removed the stalls and built a flat thick concrete floor in what was now known as Studio A. Happily, the Scottish variety tradition was kept alive in the daily television broadcasts of *The One O'Clock Gang*. The audiences queued down Hope Street for tickets for the television show, though they had not supported the place latterly when it was still the Theatre Royal. Other programmes, like John Grierson's networked documentary series *This Wonderful World*, were made in the smaller Studio C, converted from an ice store at the back of the theatre.

By the end of the 1960s, it was nearly seventy-five years since the Theatre Royal had had a fire, so it was perhaps inevitable that one was due. At four in the afternoon on 2 November 1969, the fire brigade was dealing with a small electrical blaze in the sub-basement. An hour later, the whole building was evacuated and foam pumped in. A fireman was killed when he fell through a trap door into the basement and drowned and it was feared that the old theatre would blow but by late evening the foam had contained the blaze.

Repairs were effected and the television broadcasts went on for a time until STV's extensive new headquarters were completed on a site adjacent. In the meantime, prominent figures in Scotland's musical community, led by the conductor Sir Alexander Gibson, were agitating for the creation of a first-class opera house for Scottish Opera. What followed seems miraculous. The 1970s were a bad period for the arts. The government was too occupied in dealing with recession and industrial strife. New arts developments tended to be 'showpiece' examples of modern architecture – concrete boxes like the National Theatre, while everywhere old Victorian buildings were ruthlessly torn down. In Scotland there was the inevitable Glasgow–Edinburgh debate. Many thought the capital was the only serious contender for an opera house. The Theatre Royal was an unlikely choice. Beautiful as its curving tiers and fine plaster decorations undoubtedly still were, its structure was described by the surveyors as 'a particular form of nineteenth century Glaswegian rubbish'. There was not even a decent foyer, far less the elegant bars required of a modern opera house.

Undaunted, Scottish Opera bought the building from STV for £300,000. A budget of £1.5 million was secured with the help of the Scottish Arts Council, and Arup Associates were contracted to carry out a massive rebuild. Their team was lead by Derek Sugden, a veteran of several auditorium restorations, who remarked that the Theatre Royal would be by far the most challenging.

> My first view of the Hope Street elevation and entrance to the Theatre Royal in 1972 was depressing, but penetrating inside, under the accumulated debris of sixteen years of Scottish Television's occupation, the achromatic remains of a once superb interior... A few weeks after work had started, any problems with the medieval Scottish building regulations, paled into insignificance compared with keeping the structure in position and tolerably stable. When the inner skin of stonework was drilled or cut away, the internal rubble ran out as if the life blood of the building was running away. Our client was enthusiastic and kept wanting more and more alterations, which ate into the budget. To improve sight lines, we had to remove two columns (supporting the first tier). This revealed a system of timber cantilevers, which particularly in the slips, could only be described as 'having been left to the carpenter to work something out'. These were stiffened with new structural steel beams and new steel cantilevers were inserted with long bolts and connectors through the full thickness of the masonry walls. We altered the boxes on each side and achieved an elegant solution of which my firm was very proud.[10]

This was expensive work, some of it then at the cutting edge of technology, but it was only the start. The fly tower had to be strengthened, the orchestra pit enlarged to take a full 100-piece symphony orchestra and the stage re-equipped to the highest standard for opera and ballet productions. Somehow, enough space was found by annexing neighbouring buildings to create a stylish new foyer two floors high with stone floors and elegant mouldings in a successful pastiche of the Phipps's manner. The entire building was then redecorated from top to bottom in a predominantly brown and gold scheme (architects seemed to be addicted to brown in the 1970s). Finally costing over £2.2 million, the project went away over budget, but nevertheless was a wonderful job completed in the same year as the splendid former Palace Theatre in the Gorbals was pulled down. Its successful outcome probably helped to tip the city planners attitudes towards conserving Glasgow's past, rather than destroying everything as had been the case until then.

Scottish Television brought their cameras back to record the opening ceremony on 14 October 1975 when Scottish Opera performed *Die Fledermaus*, and popular extracts from other operas, for a glittering audience of civic dignitaries, politicians and personalities. The *Herald* reported 'The Lord Provost of Edinburgh looked a bit amazed – the Lord Provost of Glasgow elated.' What an achievement for his city when the capital was still dithering over a vacant sight in Castle Terrace! For the doyen of Glasgow journalists, Jack House, it seemed 'one of the greatest events in Scotland this century'. He continued 'Since you can now get from Edinburgh to Glasgow in 43 minutes, why

Figure 3.12   The auditorium of the Theatre Royal, Hope Street, when restored for Scottish Opera (Arup Associates).

shouldn't the Festival Opera be presented in the Theatre Royal ... Some chauvinistic Edinburghers might not like the idea, but it makes sense to me.'

Original administrator Peter Hemmings saw the Theatre Royal as a venue on the touring circuit of Sadlers Wells, Glyndebourne Touring Opera, the Royal Shakespeare Company, and the National Theatre companies which had then not visited the city for many years. At first, this vision was thwarted by Scottish Opera, who had an agreement to veto the appearance of rival companies on its patch. Since occupying the Theatre Royal, Scottish Opera has gone through numerous cash crises, which this policy cannot have helped – an empty theatre is a heavy liability. More recently, a wider variety of plays, musicals and even jazz concerts has been sanctioned. The Theatre Royal played an important role in Mayfest and the highly popular Glasgow Jazz Festival.

In 1995 as the Theatre Royal celebrated the centenary of Phipps's last rebuild, and twenty years as the grand home to Scottish Opera, the company went through another financial crisis. The future of its orchestra, its status as a full-time national company and even its home were under threat. How such a state of affairs could be allowed to develop defies comprehension. The Scottish Office, its hands tied by a tight spending round from the Treasury in London, could not fully assist. A cost-saving deal was eventually achieved by which the opera and ballet companies would merge and share one orchestra. The Theatre Royal was saved for the time being.

After twenty-two years of intensive use, in 1997 the Theatre Royal was in need of redecoration. The team of cleaners had taken a great deal of pride in their good housekeeping, but the seats and carpets were getting worn and the once fashionable brown colour scheme had not improved with age. Happily, the newly established National Lottery came to its aid, allowing Scottish Opera to employ the Edinburgh architects, Law and Dunbar-Naismith to design a refurbishment. This time, the theatre has been beautifully restored to something similar to its original colour scheme, so that once again, for the first time in more than a century, theatre-goers can enjoy the subtle tints and radiant gilding chosen by Phipps in a theatre that is surely one of his masterpieces.

THE GAIETY

Few realise that there was a theatre on the corner of West Nile and Sauchiehall Streets for many years before the advent of Moss Empires. The **Gaiety** opened on 30 March 1874 in the old Choral Hall, an imposing church-like building which fronted West Nile Street. When the hall was built around 1810, the street was but a country lane and the land behind was a farm run by a William Harley, who later built the first public baths in Glasgow, thus Bath Street was named.

Once converted to a variety house, the Gaiety could seat 1,369 with 22

Figure 3.13   Auditorium of the newly-restored Theatre Royal, Hope Street
(courtesy the Theatre Royal, photographer Kevin Low).

standing. The hall had one tier with long slips, supported by iron pillars and a vaulted roof, again like a church. A new flat ceiling was installed well below the original, the proscenium and balcony front and boxes were all smothered in florid rococo-gilded plaster and the walls had flock wallpaper. It would have looked very cosy and intimate. It was run by D. S. Mackay, who also ran primitive music halls in his native Dundee.

It must have been hard for Mackay to run the theatre from his Dundee

Figure 3.14 Interior of the Gaiety Theatre (author collection).

base, so a few months after opening, it was sold to a Glaswegian, Charles Barnard. He was an accomplished tenor and an ambitious owner. According to *The Bailie*, the Gaiety was 'certain to be a success'. Perhaps the journalist was influenced by an accompanying advert, placed by Barnard, announcing that it was 'one of the most elegant and commodious places in the United Kingdom, replete with every comfort and convenience, superbly decorated, elegantly furnished, perfectly ventilated, well lighted, unsurpassed in acoustics, and unique in construction!'

Mr Barnard had big plans for his small theatre, and programmed it with Shakespeare and opera to keep up with the rival Theatre Royal. The pantomime was followed by Shakespeare's *As You Like It*, Officers' Amateur Dramatics production of *Hamlet* and *La Fille de Madame Angot*. When the Theatre Royal advertised Scott's *Rob Roy*, the Gaiety management went for head-to-head competition with the same play. It was a Scottish favourite, and both versions were a success. The Gaiety even revived it again for the Glasgow Fair. With new drama theatres proliferating, Barnard was soon forced to lower his sights and although populist offerings made more money, he was not really interested in producing them. He sold out in 1880 to T. T. Brindley, an entrepreneur who made the Gaiety into a music hall after closing it for improvements to its lighting and ventilation, designed by Frank Matcham. In 1894 Moss Empires became lessees and flushed with the success of his magnificent Empire Palace in Edinburgh, Moss quickly decided that the Gaiety was too small to cope with demand. After a final night on 25 January, Burns Night, when the company was augmented by highland dancers and the audience linked arms to sing 'Auld Lang Syne', the demolition gang moved in. In the seventy-five years it had stood, the Gaiety's surroundings had been transformed from an almost rural scene to the busy heart of Britain's 'second city'.

THE QUEEN'S THEATRE

The Queen's Theatre was one of Glasgow's most extraordinary variety halls. It was formed out of the upper floors of a gaunt, four-floor warehouse building with a dull pilastered frontage of dressed sandstone, hidden up Watson Street, just east of Glasgow Cross. All one saw in passing was a small pedimented doorway with two gas lanterns. The interior, reached up tortuous flights of stairs, was actually remarkably ornate with two serpentine balconies encrusted with fruity plaster garlands and a proscenium framed by fluted Corinthian columns. Seating, for 1,800, mainly consisted of hard-backed benches.

Its early career is still something of a mystery, but it opened in 1878 as the Star Music Hall, a speculative venture by Dan S. Mackay. Colourful posters advertised programmes 'specially organised for the working classes . . . this is the only place of amusement in Glasgow that studies the welfare, comfort and pocket of the working classes by giving them only the very best talent, an extra strong band, gorgeous scenery at reasonable prices which are never changed'. These were from 2d in the gallery to 6d in the two rows of cushioned orchestra stalls.

On 10 October 1881 it re-opened as the Shakespeare Music Hall, managed by Arthur Lloyd, and by October 1884 it had become the New Star Theatre of Varieties and then, on the evening of 1 November, disaster struck. Some foolish person shouted 'Fire!', and in the ensuing panic, fourteen patrons were trampled to death on the stairs as the audience panicked to escape. A further eighteen were injured in what proved to be a false alarm. The theatre remained closed until 28 November 1892, when it became the People's Palace, billed as 'The Most Popular Hall in the City... No Vexatious Extra Charges... Pre-Eminently THE WORKING MAN'S HOUSE.' Apparently, other music halls had started to charge extra to let patrons leave early, or put a penny on the advertised price for those who wanted to move to another part of the house. Some halls even refused refunds if the auditorium was full and the ticket holder failed to find a seat.

The theatre was run by Thomas Colquhoun (grandson of James Bayliss and his wife, who ran the Scotia) and Barney Armstrong, with Joe Lanty doubling as assistant manager and resident comedian. With extra fire escapes added, it now seated 2,300, with standing room for a further 320. A report in the *Daily Record*, evidently written by the theatre's management, stated:

> The People's Palace has the finest Dressing Rooms, Lavatories &c., of any theatre in the city... The new proprietor has spent about £1,000 in putting this place in order, and mark you, has abolished almost every known grievance, and they are not a few, of those who frequent music halls and theatres. It is worthy of note that this hall is not run merely for profit and that an excellent, not to say brilliant, programme can be given at nominal prices of admission. The Empire in London has just declared a dividend of Seventy per cent, which may be taken as the ordinary music hall profit. Twenty per cent is quite enough for the People's Palace – the other fifty will be given to the people in reduced prices and special quality of entertainment.

A typical bill included such wonders as 'Paula The Reptile Queen, With Her Crocodiles, Alligators and BOA CONSTRICTORS', followed by 'Captain Alf Diey's Gathering of the Clans'.

In 1902 the enveloping warehouse, and consequently the theatre, was bought by Glasgow Corporation for £15,000 and renamed the Queen's Theatre of Varieties. Bills were presented twice nightly and consisted mainly of local comedians, singers, dancers, magicians and novelty acts. From 1907 it was leased to the cinema pioneer Ralph Pringle and temporarily restyled Pringle's Picture Palace, and in 1914 Bernard Frutin (of the Metropole) took it over for cine-variety. The Queen's was hopeless as a cinema as many of the seats were at right-angles to the screen, so by the end of the First World War, only variety bills were given.

In 1930 Harry Hall became lessee and manager, and the Queen's reputation for earthy performances continued. Hall's special interest was the annual pantomime, the book of which was reputedly written on an F2 school jotter by

Hall and Sammy Murray, the Queen's resident comic, in a neighbouring pub called the Crystal Bells. John Fairley, who worked in the City Collectors department of Glasgow Corporation, recalls that the results of this collaboration were frequently

> very, very vulgar, in fact that is putting it mildly. One year it was discovered that the script had not been licensed by the Lord Chamberlain, so the police came to arrest and fine the cast on the opening night, which was great publicity. At that time all scripts had to be passed by the censor, so the F2 jotter was produced, and sent down to St. James's Palace . . . What the censors made of lines like 'Gonny no' keep us waitin' fur wur grub? Ah'm that gaspin' fur ma chuck ah cid git beasted intae a scabby dug, so ah cid!' Probably they couldn't understand a word of it, so they gave it permission and it went on.[11]

The shows invariably starred Frank and Doris Droy with Sammy Murray in the lead. A loud-mouthed and hilarious performer, he referred to everyone as China and thought nothing of swearing on stage, something unheard of in the 1930s. Somehow, the Queen's management always evaded the censors and people came from all over Glasgow to revel in the theatre's good-natured jollity. Harry Hall was manager for twenty-two years until 1951. John Fairley recalls an office trip to the Queen's after the Second World War:

> It happened that someone had tipped off Sam Murray that the audience was to include a fair-sized group from the City Collector department that evening. Most of us have seen leading members of theatre casts come forward to congratulate folk in the audience for birthdays and such-like. Down at the Queen's they did things differently for, on this night, Sam suddenly broke off from his script, to exclaim in a stentorian bellow, 'Aw here! Ah've jist went an' remembered somethin'. There's a loat a' fullas in here the night frae the City Collector's oaffice – ye didny know that, did yis, eh? But ah'm tellin' ye – don't pey yer gas bill, an' big Tommy Douglas ower therr, he'll get yis cut aff. Aye, an' whit aboot Reggie Scott, eh? He's here an' a' the night. Whaur ur ye, Reggie? Gonnie pit yer haun up? Naw? Ah well, never mind, he's here tae, so yis better get inty John Street an' pey up or the baith o' them's gonny get yis.' Reggie Scott, our boss was not amused at being singled out like this, but the rest of the party enjoyed the whole thing immensely.[12]

Sadly, the Queen's was hit by a night-time fire on 24 January 1952, when the dressing rooms, stage and ceiling were destroyed.

HER MAJESTY'S, THE ROYAL PRINCESS'S AND THE CITIZENS'

In 1846 municipal Glasgow more than doubled in size by a single Act of Parliament and for the first time the city crossed the Clyde to take in the ancient Barony of Gorbals. During the industrial revolution, the Gorbals, a rural village with farmed land, was overrun by industry and densely packed cheap slum housing. The well-to-do left, their houses were split and filled with many immigrant families. The spaces between were filled with tenements and workshops, the notorious 'backlands'. Without proper sanitation, these airless slums were a risk to public health. There were many other such ghettos around Glasgow but through the City Improvement Act 1866, the old Gorbals was swept away by the City Improvement Trust, and a wide new main street substituted for the old, narrow, crooked one. The ground to the east side was feued by John Morrison, the builder, who in 1876–7 built a range of tenements along the street. Although not every flat had sanitary facilities, the scheme was a vast improvement over what had gone before, and the architect, James Sellars, was given exacting specifications of what was to be built – churches, public houses, schools and a theatre.

At the same time the premises of the Union Bank in Ingram Street were being extended. These had originally been a mansion rebuilt by David Hamilton as a bank with a tall classical portico in 1841. Because the site was limited, the portico had to go. Morrison was also responsible for this building work and he rescued it because it seemed ideal for the facade of his theatre, then under construction back in the Gorbals. The facade was modified by Sellars and rebuilt; the giant order of Tuscan columns that had once stood on the ground was now at first-floor height and separated by tall windows. John Mossman made six imposing statues – four muses, flanked by Shakespeare and Robert Burns – which were mounted on the parapet. An elaborate glazed cast-iron arcade was built over the street to shelter patrons outside the somewhat pretentiously titled Her Majesty's Theatre and Royal Opera House.

The auditorium, the work of a different architect, Campbell Douglas, seated 1,479, but was very intimate with two deeply curved serpentine balconies, supported by slim iron columns. The dress circle had just six rows of upholstered seats, so most folk were to be crammed on to the wooden benches which filled the balcony and pit. Furthermore, 162 had to stand against railings at the back. There was no room for a proscenium frame, the arch being defined by the pilasters flanking the stage boxes. Yet, despite its spartan facilities, Her Majesty's had fine gilded plaster decorations, draperies and a large stage.

The opening performance was on 28 December 1878, under the management of James McFayden. The theatre started in the colourful manner that has distinguished it to the present day – with a riot. The pantomime *Ali Baba and the Forty Thieves* was going badly as the ambitiously designed scenery was

Figure 3.15   Frontage of the Royal Princess's Theatre
(author collection).

too heavy for the flying system. The *Glasgow Herald* found it hard to be encouraging:

As regards the scenery, all of which is fresh from the hand of the painter, and much of it highly artistic in character, it was in a state of mechanical rebellion, and the hard working staff, whose duty it was to reduce it to subjection, found their efforts more than once unavailing on Saturday evening . . . the audience manifested a good deal of impatience, although Mrs McFayden craved their indulgence in a sensible, business-like speech which might have had a kindlier response.

Folk in the pit began to pelt the performers with missiles, and when the safety curtain was lowered, they threw the seat cushions! It is hard to shake off the bad image such an inauspicious start creates, so within a few weeks, the McFaydens had quit and Her Majesty's closed down. Shortly after, it was leased to Harcourt Beryl and made a fresh start as the **Royal Princess's Theatre**. Beryl promoted a mixed diet of melodrama, variety and pantomime, a successful policy continued by his assistant, Richard (known as Rich) Waldon. Waldon, an Englishman, took control in 1886 when Beryl was lured away to manage the Grand in Cowcaddens. His interests in the business were widespread, for he had shares in many suburban variety theatres, in Glasgow and across the north of England. As managing director, he worked hard to build the reputation of the Royal Princess's as a family theatre open twice nightly all year round until his death in 1922. Waldon had already identified a young Harry McKelvie as a suitable successor, so the Royal Princess's was gifted to him in his will. McKelvie, also involved with the thriving Pavilion in Renfield Street, was a brilliant writer and producer of hugely popular pantomimes at both theatres. He probably thought he could avoid disasters of *Ali Baba* proportions with shows called *Tammie Toddles*, *Gaggiegalorum* or *Bletherskeite*; he always used thirteen-letter titles – a superstitious pantomime tradition. With the exception of the villain (who, naturally, had to be English) his pantomimes used casts who were predominantly Scottish. Lanky Tommy Lorne was a favourite from 1920 until his untimely death in 1935. Then George West, with his outlandish outfits and absurd farcical expressions, took over and reigned supreme in Royal Princess's pantomimes for twenty-one consecutive seasons – a world stage record. Such was demand that the panto seasons kept getting longer. By the 1930s, they lasted from October until June the following year with a short season of variety in between. McKelvie soldiered on, while all around one by one the local theatres were going over to cinema.

In 1945, now dogged by ill health, he retired. He had become a rich man as a result of his writing and managerial skills. He leased the Royal Princess's to Dr O. H. Mavor, the playwright better known by his pen name, James Bridie. Although he was the son of a well-to-do West End family, Mavor had first come to prominence when he organised a student riot in the Coliseum in 1909. He had founded Glasgow's Citizens' Theatre Company in 1943 to promote Scots-dialect plays using Scottish actors and so create a national theatre. Such an achievement would have required serious financial backing and Mavor was well connected. First he secured a grant from the CEMA (the forerunners of the Scottish Arts Council), then Sir Frederick Stewart generously gifted £10,000 to help with setting up costs. The Citizens' was supported by prominent businessmen and art lovers: T. J. Honeyman, George Blake, Guy McCrone, Norman Duthie, Paul Vincent Carroll, R. W. Greig and the cinema magnate George Singleton.[13]

Mavor died in 1951, but during the 1950s his vision became reality; the Citizens' Theatre was bought by Glasgow Corporation in 1955 for £17,000 and continued to present a mixed repertoire of innovative Scottish plays and standard classics. The 1960s were to prove difficult. The Gorbals had reached rock bottom. The streets of tenements around the theatre had once been held up as prime examples of urban renewal, but decades of neglect had reduced them to slums. The local inhabitants were not remotely interested in plays at the cutting edge of new writing, and the soot-blackened surroundings, with urchins playing in the gutters, were not inviting for those coming from outside. A succession of managers kept the Citizens' ticking over, but even with capacity reduced to a comfortable 880 seats, the theatre could not be filled.

In 1969, amid uproar in the local theatrical community and nationalist outrage, Giles Havergal came up from Watford and changed the Citizens' course entirely, starting with an all-male production of *Hamlet*. He had been appointed at a time of acute crisis, and quickly installed the most radical, chic and arousing young company in Britain, with a majority of English actors. His immediate predecessors had failed because, however nationalistic its pretensions, the Citizens' had become just another ordinary repertory theatre. Havergal realised he could use the Citizens' dishevelled auditorium and insalubrious surroundings to its advantage; a flat-rate admission charge of 50p was introduced to attract cosmopolitan student audiences; his overtly camp set designs had added significance in the context of the theatre's devastated neighbourhood. When London critics came up for the premiere of Noël Coward's *Semi-Monde* in 1977, the local vandals helpfully torched some cars in the Citizens' car park. Such clashes of style and culture were now the ethos of the Citizens' operation.

If Havergal revived the Citizens' Company, the theatre building was still in mortal danger. Plans for a new cultural centre in Glasgow first surfaced in 1965, and the Corporation had since allowed the venerable theatre to fall into a state of disrepair. William Taylor, a lawyer, Citizens' board member and Labour councillor until retiring undefeated in 1969 to become the theatre's chairman, had been heavily involved in planning Glasgow's inner ring road. The eastern flank would plough straight across the Citizens' Theatre. Taylor was saved from embarrassment by the lack of capacity in the Corporation budget to execute this wanton scheme. Even so, all around the theatre, property was blighted by compulsory purchase orders.

Much of the time in the early 1970s was consumed with discussing and approving plans for a new Citizens' complex within the proposed cultural civic centre at the top of Buchanan Street. Models were displayed in 1973, and very hideous they looked too. In addition to the theatres, there were to be two concert halls – one for the Royal Scottish Academy of Music and Drama and the other for the Scottish National Orchestra – and a banqueting chamber. It would be a veritable little Barbican of the north. By the late 1970s the recession put paid to these plans, and only the 2,500-seat Scottish National Orchestra hall and banqueting suite were eventually built to modified plans as the architecturally controversial Glasgow Royal Concert Hall.

To their considerable relief, the Citizens' was given an official reprieve in December 1976 and Havergal started agitating for substantial renovations. Although when built nearly a century previously, the theatre had been intended for variety, its intimate auditorium had proved ideal as a repertory venue. It would have been a great loss to the performing arts. As it was, what happened next horrified the company. In July 1977 the demolition men moved in and within a few weeks, the once handsome Gorbals Street tenements had been razed to the ground. They didn't stop there. Before action could be taken, the facade – regarded as a masterpiece and listed – was bulldozed until only four stumps remained. For the first time, the gaunt outside walls of the old theatre were in full view. The remaining broken sandstone pieces of the original frontage had gouged claw marks from the excavators and the Citizens' now looked like an assault victim. The city planners had made a botch up of the first order. The Scottish Development Agency landscaped the devastated surroundings as best they could, and it was even suggested that as the statues had been rescued from the parapet, the old frontage might one day be replaced. In the meantime, the auditorium and backstage areas were given a thorough renovation and redecorated in red, gold, green and black.

Eventually, a new entrance foyer was proposed, and although this was part of a dull office development, rather than a re-creation of the magnificent original, it was, none the less, an improvement. Designed by BDB Architects, it has a high-tech, fully glazed pediment with the rescued statuary on prominent display inside. At night, light floods out and its highly original red and gold decor with blood-like paint gushing down the walls looks intriguing, yet ever so slightly dangerous. Its glass roof high above makes this an airy, elemental space. The auditorium, however, retains its dark allure. It too was redesigned with new pullman seats in strawberry plush, a line of closely packed naked lightbulbs around the circle and sponge-stippled gold and red paint painstakingly applied over everything. It was ready for the Mayfest season in 1989, when *A Tale of Two Cities* was presented. The 1990 season, when Glasgow was 'European City of Culture', saw full houses night after night. After 120 years of performances, the Citizens' Theatre is still alive and kicking.

THE ROYALTY

During the summer of 1879, people passing along bustling Sauchiehall Street had watched as a palatial new block took shape on the corner of Renfield Street. The front building had shops, offices and a hotel and was in the elaborate French Renaissance style favoured by its architect, James Thomson. The Royalty Theatre was developed on the space behind and was approached through ornate arches at the corner. It was a delightful little-known work by Frank Matcham. The foyers were small and cramped, but intricately decorated with plaster latticework on the ceilings, polished woodwork and multi-coloured marble. The auditorium was an intimate theatrical jewel. Here, Matcham was more refined than in his later Empire variety theatres. The plaster decoration was crisp and delicate looking in French Renaissance style. There were two tiers; the balcony was flat-fronted and decorated with low- relief swirls in a Phipps-like style. The circle had only seven rows and a bulbous front with plaster latticework and cupids holding lights. This was continued through the stage boxes, which were framed by Corinthian pilasters and topped by broken pediments containing statues. The proscenium had simple egg and dart mouldings and an outer frame of Corinthian columns. Unbelievably, the seating capacity was given as nearly 2,000. Pit and balcony patrons must almost have had to sit on each other's knees.

The Royalty opened on 24 December 1879, under the ownership and management of Mr E. L. Knapp. The first performance was of Offenbach's *Madam Favart*, but during the next thirty years as a leading professional theatre, the Royalty offered its audiences everything – Grand Opera to Moore and Burgess Minstrels, Shakespeare to Shaw, the Divine Sarah to Little Tich. In 1884 it passed to the Edinburgh-based actor-owners Howard and Wyndham, who regularly appeared there. They sensibly reduced the capacity to a more bearable 1,432 seats. Later, having established the larger King's as their principal Glasgow outlet, Howard and Wyndham sold the Royalty to the Scottish Playgoers Company for use as a repertory theatre. It was renamed the Lyric – more appropriate to its new use.

During the First World War, the entire block, including the Lyric, was sold to the YMCA. The hotel became a soldiers' and sailors' home and the Lyric was used as a cinema to entertain the troops. When the war ended in 1918, the amateur dramatics returned. YMCA members had frequently suggested to officials that a drama club should become part of the association's recreational programme, but it was not until 1935 that the deficiency was remedied. In October that year, the first enthusiastic group of thirty met to appoint officials and choose plays; soon rehearsals were in full swing.

Their first show took place in the **Lyric Theatre** on 18 February 1936. This mixed bill of four one-act plays was given in front of a packed audience and although the highest priced seat was only 2/-, a profit of £17 was made. In October the club was renamed the Lyric Players and until May 1940 they gave two seasons a year at the theatre. The rest of the time, it was used for professional productions and occasional conferences and lectures. In common with other dramatic groups, the Lyric Players were shut down during the war years as, once again, the YMCA dedicated its resources to the war effort. Shortly after hostilities ended, they re-formed and were back performing on the Lyric's stage in the spring of 1946. In post-war years the Lyric Players' activities expanded to taking their shows on tour between their seasons at the Lyric. The theatre now also became the Glasgow venue for Royal Scottish Geographical Society lectures until after a performance of Chekhov's *The Seagull*, early in the morning on 21 March 1953, disaster struck. The fire began in the stage, but the safety curtain had been left open, so by the time the fire engines arrived, the entire theatre was engulfed in flames. The main worry was that it might spread to the adjacent YMCA hostel, or to Green's Playhouse, a gigantic cinema complex across the narrow lane behind. It was a close shave as flames leapt

Figure 3.16   The grand edifice of the Lyric Theatre, Sauchiehall Street
(author collection).

Figure 3.17   The Lyric Theatre, Sauchiehall Street,
after a fire (author collection).

high from the Lyric's roof. Green's escaped with a few broken windows and a
blackened wall, but the poor old Lyric was burned to the rafters.

The owners were determined that the theatre tradition should continue, so
a careful survey was made of the charred remains, then a new theatre was
planned by Glasgow architects Frank Burnet and Boston. In order to make use
of existing undamaged structure, the new Lyric would be a much simplified
version of Matcham's original. The backstage arrangements were brought right
up to date and seating was reduced to only 847. The grand re-opening was

attended by the Lord Provost, Andrew Hood, and Robert Maclellan's *The Road to the Isles* was performed by a cast including the Lyric Players and members drawn from other Glasgow amateur drama clubs. Everyone connected with the theatre rejoiced at its phoenix-like return; but the rebuild had cost the YMCA £112,000 and there was still a £25,600 shortfall. This debt severely stretched the charity's finances and as the decade progressed, money was urgently needed to tackle Glasgow's mounting social problems. In 1959 all the YMCA property in central Glasgow was sold to property speculators. The Sauchiehall Street buildings went to an outfit called Gula Kalumpong Rubber Estates Ltd. The Lyric Theatre was closed and everything was demolished. Sauchiehall Street lost one of its most elegant frontages to an ugly grey concrete office block called St. Andrew's House. With an equally brutal development replacing the Empire opposite, that stretch of Sauchiehall Street became cold and uninteresting, a state which has not improved since.

THE ATHENAEUM

In 1886 the Athenaeum, a further-education college specialising in music and drama, moved to new premises in St. George's Place (now Nelson Mandela Square). The new college was a particularly handsome building by the eminent Glasgow architect Sir J. J. Burnet. In 1893 the college extended its site with a new building facing Buchanan Street, also by Burnet, which contained a small theatre. It was a remarkably tall and narrow building, crammed on to the site of a Georgian house (one of the first of many such plots to be redeveloped during the late Victorian period). Following the new fashion for art nouveau, the facade was an eclectic, but very successful, mixture of arches, decorative railings and sinuous windows, topped by minarets.

The theatre was small and unadorned with a single balcony, supported by iron columns and upholstered benches for 796. It was to be used by the college to train drama students, with regular productions open to the public. Soon local amateur dramatic groups performed and the Citizens' Theatre Company found its first venue there. The Athenaeum, now part of the highly acclaimed Royal Scottish Academy of Music and Drama, suffered during the 1995–6 winter when frozen pipes thawed and the auditorium plaster work was soaked. It took nearly a year to restore and the grade A-listed Athenaeum is one of Scotland's hidden theatrical gems. Used latterly by amateur and youth companies for whom its small size was ideal, the Athenaeum was sold in 1997 to a London-based property developer and is presently threatened with conversion to a shop. Given that Glasgow has a surfeit of retail space, this historically important building should remain intact and used as a theatre.

THE EMPIRE

On the demolished site of the old Gaiety, and almost directly opposite the Royalty in Sauchiehall Street, H. E. Moss set about developing the second of his mighty Empire Palaces. Once again Moss put the design of the new theatre in the capable hands of Frank Matcham. It took more than a year to build and the completed building even outdid the splendours of its Edinburgh namesake. Whereas at Edinburgh, Matcham had to make the most of a cramped site, here he had two long frontages at one of Glasgow's busiest street junctions. As ever, he rose to the occasion with vigour. The four-storey edifice was finished in red sandstone, boldly carved in mock Italian Renaissance style, but topped by soaring Indian minarets. The main entrance, on Sauchiehall Street, was below an Italianate high arch with flanking turrets rising from the first floor. A pediment was inscribed '**Empire Palace Theatre**' and the whole tour de force was capped by a large dome with a flagstaff. The stage was at the Renfield Street end, so bars and waiting rooms were built facing West Nile Street, where

Figure 3.18   Frontage of the Empire Theatre, Sauchiehall Street
(author collection).

dress circle and balcony customers used separate entrances. There were shop units between these to make more money and offices above. The foyer (for stalls and circle patrons only) had a richly plastered ceiling, this time in a free mix of French baroque and Indian styles, with voluptuous female torch-bearers peering down from the corners. Floors and walls were clad in pink, brown and white polished marble. The auditorium showed Matcham at his magnificent, most playful best. Previously, at Edinburgh, his balconies flowed in the same plane through boxes to a simple proscenium, and were merely enriched with applied decoration. At the Glasgow theatre he fully realised the possibilities of using his patented cantilevers to develop a vibrant three-dimensional arrangement. Boxes and balconies occurred at every possible plane, sweeping round, bending and bulging in and out. The decoration was no longer just superficial, but seemed to flow organically as part of the whole design. The central boxes were lowered and twisted towards the stage; those above were swept back and tied into the balcony. Seemingly useless spaces higher up were moulded into mysterious niches, painted with murals and filled with statuary. The 30-foot-wide proscenium arch was rounded, but even this was hung with an open latticework of gilded plaster trimmings. There was seating for 2,500 and, curiously, the air was somehow 'flavoured with the fragrance of choice vanilla'.[14] It was one of the most sensuous theatre interiors in Britain.[14]

The Empire Palace was finally ready for opening on 5 April 1897. There was a serious traffic jam that night around the theatre as crowds struggled through double-parked horse-cabs to get inside. When the curtain rose, the whole company was on stage for the National Anthem. There were eleven turns on the bill, and they were all warmly applauded, but when it came to Vesta Tilley, a Moss favourite, the audience went wild. They stood up and cheered and shouted 'Speech! Speech!' After Tilley had spoken, they stood up again and sang 'For she's a jolly good fellow!' Only then did they settle down and allow her to begin her act. Next to Tilley, the Russian Ivanoff Singers and Dancers received the greatest cheer. Not surprisingly, the *Evening Times* reported 'Unbounded enthusiasm attended the opening of the new Empire Palace last night, and it was admitted on all hands that this success was richly deserved.'

Exactly when the theatre became known as the Empire is not clear, but in 1901, a new 'Empire' name sign, lit by countless bulbs was put up. The Glasgow theatre always took acts the week after their Edinburgh Empire performances. Was this how the Glasgow theatre first got its reputation for difficult-to-please audiences? Glaswegians could have read Edinburgh reviews, and they would go to the theatre bar instead of sitting through a poor act. The vast majority were true professionals, though. They had to give polished performances week after week at different Moss theatres and it was punishing work. All the best-known variety turns in Britain, the leading American vaudeville stars, revues, pantomimes, so-called 'nigger minstrels', ballet companies,

Figure 3.19   Glasgow Empire, circular (copyright source unknown).

circuses, musicals, operas, dance bands and a symphony orchestra – the Empire staged everything!

Following the 1928 rebuild of the Edinburgh Empire, the Moss company next engaged Milburn and Milburn to expand their Glasgow theatre. Hemmed in by other buildings, the only option was to enlarge on the existing site. In 1931 the wonderful Matcham interiors were swept away, along with the foyers, shops and offices. Most windows in the old facade were bricked up; the dome, turrets and minarets were chopped off and an extra storey added. Because the rebuilt auditorium filled the entire space, the adjoining warehouse was bought and converted to a new entrance. It now looked dreadful outside – architectural botch-ups are not a recent phenomenon!

The opening night of the second Empire was on 28 September 1931. This time there was no fanfare, or even the National Anthem. The new Empire began with an ordinary variety bill, starting where its predecessor had left off. Topping the bill was Jack Payne and the BBC Dance Band, then by far the most popular throughout Britain; Billy Bennett, 'The Working Man'; and A. C. Astor, the ventriloquist. Since Scottish acts consistently brought the best audiences, it is interesting to note that there was not a single Scot in the line-up that night, but next week Tommy Lorne, the hilarious lanky comedian, starred in his own revue, *Happiness For Sale*.

Figure 3.20   Etchings of Glasgow Empire
(copyright source unknown).

Inside, the new Empire was very large, seating 2,100 in comfort similar to the latest super cinemas. When Moss Empires directors, R. H. and Colonel Gillespie, came up from London, they were faced with reporters who asked 'Is it true that the Empire is going over to talkies?' They denied any plan to make the Empire into a cinema. In fact, the Empire was wired for talkies and could have become a cinema at a moment's notice, but it stayed true to variety. The auditorium, in ivory and plum, could hardly have been more different from its predecessor. It was largely unadorned, save for some trivial classical details in silver and large decorative grilles in the then-fashionable angular 'jazz moderne' style on either side of the stage, concealing the ventilation system.

More attention was paid to comfort and technical innovations than in Matcham's era. There was painted cork panelling 'for perfect acoustics' on the walls and extractors to remove 24,000 cubic feet of stale air every minute. The old Victorian dressing rooms had been cramped, but the new Empire's all had washbasins and there were four suites of rooms with baths for the star acts to relax in – still a luxury in most theatres.

The new manager was Captain Bernard A. Leslie, an extrovert who retired to run a hotel in St. Andrews. In the mid-1930s the Gillespie brothers were replaced at Moss Empires by George Black, late of the London Palladium. One Christmas he came up unannounced to supervise the final rehearsals of a pantomime. He sat in the stalls, shouting instructions to change the lighting, scenery and even the running order. Eventually, he needed advice from the manager, so he leaned back and bellowed 'Leslie! Leslie!!' Being a military man, the manager had his staff well trained, so a stage hand said firmly 'I'm sorry, sir. Captain Leslie is not in the auditorium.' Black responded 'Well go to his office and tell Captain Leslie that Corporal Black wants to see him at once!'[15]

Figure 3.21   Exterior of the Empire after the 1931 rebuild
(Tony Moss Collection).

The Empire had long been considered a tough house to play, but in the post-war years, it struck fear into a new generation of English performers. Audiences for the second show on a Friday night were thought the most fearsome. Many had spent their early evening in nearby pubs, and well plied with drink, they were ready to exact revenge on any act not up to standard. Johnny Beattie explains why:

> You'd get some coming and giving their old act for the umpteenth time, beginning with ''ello, 'ello, 'ello, 'ow are yer? Awright luv?' And they didn't attempt to make any rapport with the audience, or they'd start with ''Ere, I'm goin' to tell you something . . .' and the Glasgow audiences would sit there and think, 'Oh, are you? We'll see about that, pal, so we will.' Also, the Empire was a very big theatre and there were no radio mikes like you have today, just one on a stand at the front of the stage. You really had to project your voice sometimes. I know that younger stars found the size daunting and so they didn't speak up to be heard, which also annoys audiences, who've paid good money.[16]

Maybe that is what happened when Mike and Bernie Winters were given 'the treatment'. Mike, the dapper, brisk-talking brother, was on first, all alone on that big Glasgow stage, and was making heavy weather with a stony-faced audience. After two minutes, as per routine, Bernie, the goofy one, wandered on. Pause, ominous silence – then, from a seat in the circle came the disgusted tones of a typical Glasgow man: 'Oh ma Goad!' he called out. 'There's *two* of them!'

The journalist and playwright Donald McKenzie remembers similar incidents in the Empire:

> I was working for the *Daily Express* at the time and went to review a show on a Monday afternoon with the Latin heart throb Ramon Novarro, who was then quite a well-known film star, but at the Empire he sang and his sister played piano. I guess he was used to adoring female audiences, so it must have been a shock for him to play to a theatre mostly filled with Glasgow men, who always kept their caps and raincoats on during the show. As per routine, Novarro threw posies of flowers for the women in the audience and he paid a heavy price! Fellows stood up and flung them back, shouting 'Get aff ya fuckin' wee pansie!' Poor Novarro ran from the stage and I later saw him in his dressing room, crying his eyes out.[17]

Experiences of such harsh encounters filtered back to London, where the Empire's reputation outgrew the reality. Young stars like Des O'Connor and

Roy Castle were warned by older 'pros' who had been badly received. They were so scared from hearing these tall tales that by the time they got to Glasgow, the former fainted on stage and the latter reputedly went through an eighteen-minute routine in four minutes.

The reality was somewhat different; Glasgow had its own tradition of very funny men from the shipyards and the East End, but they were quick to spot a talented, warm and outgoing personality. Many English performers did extremely well at the Empire – the all-round entertainer Max Bygraves was one. The stylish crooner Frankie Vaughan was not only loved for his song and dance routines, but also for generous charity work. He gave much needed support to youth clubs to help to end gang violence in the city.

Because of its size, Moss Empires could afford the biggest American stars who did lengthy British tours. For Glaswegians, they brought unattainable glamour and could do no wrong. Crowds welcomed Frank Sinatra, Dorothy Lamour, Jack Benny, Abbott and Costello, Jerry Lewis and Dean Martin, and Bob Hope at Central Station. Their hotels were pestered by journalists and screaming lassies laid siege to the stage door at the Empire. There, the theatre's attentive stage staff had a warm welcome and protected the stars from the bustle outside (Bob Hope later said that they were the best in the world). Glaswegians could relate to them through their work in Hollywood films and there was the thrill of seeing screen idols in the flesh.

The Scottish singer Andy Stewart was always well received and had record-breaking summer seasons at the Empire from 1959 to 1961. Thousands came to see him in *The Andy Stewart Show*, a kilt and pipe entertainment, based on his popular *White Heather Club* on television. More and more Empire regulars were finding new audiences through the medium of television, without the travel, hotels and smoke-filled theatres to contend with. The new generation of pop stars – including Adam Faith and Cliff Richard – appeared at the Empire in its final years, but time was running short. Important Moss shareholders were also investing in television and property speculation. Countless variety palaces throughout Britain were now torn down to make way for office blocks. Moss's managing director, Leslie MacDonnell, was instructed that the Glasgow Empire had to go. The last performance was on Sunday, 31 March 1963. It was given a spectacular send-off. There were military pipes and drums, the fifteen-strong Empire orchestra, the May Moxon Dancers – the Empire's own troupe for over thirty years, the White Heather Girls – Highland dancers from the television show, George Penman and his Jazzmen and a cast including Johnny Beattie, Albert Finney, Rikki Fulton, Jack Milroy, Jack Radcliffe, Fay Lenore and Calum Kennedy. All had come to say goodbye for the last time to Scotland's most famous variety theatre. It was an emotional evening, for everybody knew that the Empire was not going because of lack of patronage, but rather to be demolished for a quick profit from a speculative office development.

There were letters of protest to newspapers and *The Stage*. But these were the 1960s, a time before the preservation of popular Victorian buildings, far less mutilated ones, was taken seriously. Sure enough, demolition took place shortly after and a rather brutal low-rise office development replaced the Empire and its neighbouring warehouse.

THE TIVOLI

A less famous music hall in a working-class district was the Argyle Street Theatre of Varieties near Anderston Cross. It began its career as a warehouse, then became a Salvation Army barracks, before a rudimentary conversion to the People's Palace music hall in 1893. It was set behind a row of tenements with its entrance through a shop unit. It had a large glazed canopy on iron pillars with a row of gas lights above. First-floor tenements were annexed to form offices and dressing rooms. The auditorium with space for 1,200 had two tiers with long slips and two boxes on either side. It was sold to Thomas Colquhoun and Bernard Armstrong in 1898. Many of their staff came from the Scotia in Stockwell Street, where Mrs Bayliss, Colquhoun's grandmother, had been manager. The theatre was renamed the Tivoli and re-opened on 2 January 1899 when attractions included the comic singers Charles Coburn, Tom Hughes and Morny Cash. Partly due to its success and partly to stricter licensing regulations, the Tivoli was closed in 1904 for an extensive rebuild by the original architect, James Thomson of Baird and Thomson, a firm best known for the remarkable cast-iron Gardner's Warehouse in Jamaica Street. The Tivoli was back in business on 28 December with a gala opening attended by Sir John Ure-Primrose, the Lord Provost, and the magistrates of the city. After the National Anthem, the distinguished audience was treated to Laura, the Gentleman Equilibrist, the Kronemanns acrobats, a comic equestrian sketch called Ginnett's Rejected Remounts and Mr W. F. Frame, a director of the theatre, in a burlesque of Sir Henry Irving. The reporter from *The Era* was impressed:

> Messers Colquhoun and Armstrong are to be congratulated on having constructed a building which holds its own in style with any other variety theatre in town. Constructed on thoroughly fireproof lines with concrete, stone and ironwork, the entrances are commodious in every respect with double swing doors in use throughout . . .

> Decorations are very fine; the scheme of colour being cream, blue, pink and gold with a handsome ceiling design of fresco work from which depends 12 handsome electroliers. Similar lights abut from the circle and gallery fronts giving great brilliancy to the entire interior. A magnificent tableau curtain and box hangings in flame coloured plush present a fine

proscenium effect and the scenery painted by Mr John Morris is most artistic . . . The new year holiday season at the Tivoli promises to be a busy one and the future success of the house seems assured.

The Tivoli was indeed at first a success, but soon audiences were being lured away by the cheaper spectacle of the cinema. Colquhoun and Armstrong's firm went bankrupt and in 1907 the Tivoli was renamed the Gaiety and leased to J. J. Bennell's BB Pictures Ltd as a cinema.[18] Some early films were of poor quality, so occasional, sometimes dire, variety turns were retained, and proved popular even in the 'talkie' era.

In 1935 the Gaiety was thoroughly rebuilt as a full-time cinema, losing all evidence of its music-hall beginnings. Even so, its final moment of glory still lay ahead. A smouldering cigarette end, left after a boxing match, started a fire which devastated St. Andrew's Halls, Glasgow's magnificent concert venue, so Glasgow Corporation commandeered the old Gaiety which re-opened as the Glasgow Concert Hall in January 1963. It began with a performance of children's classics by the Scottish National Orchestra, whose temporary home it became. Many famous international singers and musicians appeared in the shabby old cinema, but inevitably, it was only an interlude. Glasgow Corporation was then determinedly erasing Glasgow's poorer neighbourhoods from the cityscape in their massive comprehensive development programme. The old Gaiety lay in the path of the city's new motorway system, so closed for the last time on 31 July 1968 for demolition. Frankly, by this time it was a very dilapidated structure and hardly a great architectural loss, but the removal of the once vibrant Anderston community around it was a huge mistake. The section of Argyle Street in which the theatre once stood is no longer recognisable.

THE PAVILION

Unlike so many grand variety palaces, the **Pavilion** in Renfield Street is still gloriously alive and has now been entertaining Glaswegians for over ninety years. The theatre was the brainchild of Thomas Barrasford, a Newcastle-based variety impresario who financed many new theatres in the Edwardian period. His favourite architect, Bertie Crewe, was an expert at designing these temples of fun. His work often came close to Frank Matcham's exuberance. Crewe trained first in London, then in Paris at the Atelier Laloux – no wonder his theatres were frequently so Francophile.

The design of the Pavilion, opened on 29 February 1904, was most assuredly French. The curious French Renaissance exterior, clad in buff terracotta with touches of mosaic, ornate pediments and steeply pitched pavilions, has become a much-loved landmark. Though only three storeys high, its intricate small-scale detailing gives the illusion of far greater size.

As with so many variety theatres, the architect had to provide a big seating capacity on a relatively cramped site – so the foyers are small and the stairways bend and twist and double back on each other to reach the different tiers. The entrance hall was circular with a heavy cornice and, throughout, there were fine mahogany doors and colourful floors in swirling patterns of terrazzo. Upstairs, the circle foyer treatment was restrained in cream and gold with panels of green moire silk. The 1,800-seat auditorium was altogether more vibrant. Thick, cream, plaster decoration, gilded in different shades, encrusted

Figure 3.22   Renfield Street showing the Pavilion (author collection).

the boxes, circle and balcony fronts. The proscenium was painted with marbling and hung with layers of crimson drapery. Overhead, lively trompe l'œil panels in scrolled frames adorned the ceiling. A series of arches, supported by voluptuous women, soared above the balcony. All seats were tip-ups and there was Wilton carpet in the stalls and circle. Barrasford lured patrons by offering incredible luxury at low prices. To increase profits, he would run as many as three shows a day, so the Pavilion was fitted with a sliding roof 'to keep the atmosphere pure and fresh'. The latest backstage facilities meant sets could be replaced in seconds without long orchestral intervals between acts. That meant that a show which might previously have taken three and a half hours could now be over in two. After a quick clean and airing, the theatre would be ready for the next performance.

Matthew Ballantine, a theatre-loving Glasgow businessman, who had been a minor shareholder in the Pavilion company, replaced Thomas Barrasford as managing director in 1905 and started a long family link with the theatre. He guided it through its greatest years until 1922. From 1938 until his death in 1964 the Glasgow cinema magnate George Urie Scott was managing director. He presided during long decades of happy pantomimes starring Jack Anthony. In between, there were hilarious summer seasons with Tommy Morgan. The bluff, outgoing, Bridgeton-born comic enjoyed a cult status from fans who readily identified with his no-frills technique. His catchphrase was 'Clairty, Clairty' (I declare to goodness) and he became known for his impersonation of the GI bride 'Big Beanie McBride, the Pride of the Clyde'. Morgan hired buses to take theatre staff on Sunday trips and seemed inseparable from the success of the Pavilion. He lived and worked hard though, and died in 1958, aged only sixty years old. His ashes were scattered from the Pavilion's roof.

With Dumfries Ballantine, grandson of Matthew, at the helm, the Pavilion continued with full houses throughout the 1960s. Now, Lex McLean headlined the summer shows. As the 1960s drew to a close his summer seasons became ever more popular, and he literally colonised the place from May until the pantomime season started each November.

However, the future was to be fraught with problems. In the old days independent theatres did not have to worry about Equity minimum wages and musicians' unions. These overheads made original productions more expensive, so pantomime casts became handfuls and the orchestra a quartet. The old Green's Playhouse cinema, which faced the Pavilion across Renfield Street, became an unwelcome rival. It was restyled the Apollo theatre for live cabaret, comedy and rock concerts. When Lex McLean died in 1975, leaving no obvious successor, the Pavilion management seemed to lose their way. For the first time, the theatre was closed during the summer and it started to lose money. It seemed that McLean's pessimistic conviction that 'When I go, there'll be nobody to take my place' was true. Even so, it was a more intimate venue for

Figure 3.23   Interior of the Pavilion (David Trevor-Jones).

concerts than the Apollo. Lulu broke box-office records at her first appearance in 1975 and other Scottish pop stars, such as Sheena Easton and Barbara Dickson, also did well in a period of social upheaval for the Pavilion. New talents like Billy Connolly continued the tradition of top Glasgow comedy, but his generation preferred doing television to the long, gruelling summer seasons of Morgan and McLean.

With little money available, the theatre became scruffy. In 1979 it received an injection of nearly £100,000 from three London businessmen, Michael Abbott, Tom Malcolm and Stephen Komlosy (then deputy director of London's

Cambridge Theatre). In 1981 it made a loss of £26,000 and closure loomed. Some visitors, like Frankie Vaughan, cut their fees. The recession made matters worse, but having lost the Empire, Alhambra and Metropole, no one wanted to see another variety theatre go. The Pavilion started to reduce its losses by doing what it was best at – offering unpretentious, predominantly Scottish entertainment, to give folk a good night out at little expense. Regular performers like the comic Denny Willis (son of Dave Willis), Country and Western entertainer Sydney Devine and fitba'-mad Andy Cameron (dame in numerous Pavilion pantomimes sporting football-boobs) have never 'made it' outside the west of Scotland, but have a loyal following at the Pavilion. It could then claim to be the last completely unsubsidised commercial theatre in Scotland.[19]

Under the careful guidance of chairman Matthew Ballantine Jnr and manager Ian Gordon, the theatre enjoyed new financial stability in the 1980s. It still needed major refurbishment. When water tanks on the roof flooded the interior in 1989, the insurance pay-out partly enabled this to happen. The work was tightly budgeted though and, although the opening roof was reinstated, there was not enough to redo the gilding or draperies. As a result, the interior looks slightly coarse.

The summer show was revived in 1989. *Pride of The Clyde* brought established entertainers like Dorothy Paul to new audience. She later developed her own highly popular one-woman show at the Pavilion, which runs for weeks each year and has helped to revive her career. The future of the Pavilion theatre now looks brighter; the owners are proud of their financial independence, but it would be wonderful if money and willpower could be found so that this intimate, historic theatre could be properly restored to its original splendours.

THE PALACE

The history of the **Palace** actually went back long before the city improvements to the old rural Gorbals. When the area was developed in the 1870s, an old kirk was left standing in the back courts of the new tenements. John Morrison, the builder responsible for Her Majesty's next door, extended it to make a religious meeting-hall complex, the Grand National Halls of the Good Templars Harmonic Association. This was an organisation of temperance supporters who ran Saturday afternoon tea concerts, known as 'The Bursts'. At these concerts, a paper bag with an apple and an orange in it was given away to each patron (mostly to children), and at a given time during the show, all the empty bags were blown up, then, at the word of command, were burst!

Alcoholism had been a serious problem in the mid-Victorian era, but by the turn of the century there were stricter licensing laws and 'The Bursts' fell on hard times. In 1903 the hall was sold to Thomas Barrasford (later of the Pavilion) and Rich Waldon, who already ran the neighbouring Royal Princess's. Variety impresarios were shrewd businessmen, and they expected their architects to use as much of an existing structure as possible. When Bertie Crewe was engaged to make the halls into a very large variety house, part of the side wall was incorporated. Because Waldon was to run both theatres, the Palace also shared the Royal Princess's columned facade. That meant most of the budget could be spent on a fabulous interior.

In the late Victorian period, the Moorish–Indian style became very contagious – folk were fascinated by motifs from the far reaches of the British Empire. In variety theatres, Matcham started the trend by devising an Indian treatment for the Tivoli in London's Strand. Now Bertie Crewe temporarily abandoned his French principles for a ravishing mock-Indian scheme to outdo his old rival. It is no understatement to suggest that the Palace was one of the most audacious and spectacular theatres ever built in Britain. *The Era* enthused over its wonderful appointments:

> This luxurious and beautifully designed theatre was opened on Monday 14 March 1904 and crowded houses successfully inaugurated this latest addition to Glasgow's long list of amusements. The Palace is one of the largest variety theatres in Scotland with two balconies supported by the newest suspensory principals, so there is not a single column to obstruct the view of the stage. Even the pit seats are upholstered in velvet and the floor is of cork carpet. The grand circle has fifteen rows of exceptionally roomy chairs with spacious raised lounges and promenades, separated from the seats by marble balustrading.
>
> The decorations are on a sumptuous scale. The design is pure Indian, an outstanding feature being the ranges of boxes, supported by beautifully modelled Nautch girls and papier mâché elephant heads. Above them are gorgeous Hindu pagodas from which springs the elaborate domed and painted ceiling. The proscenium arch is executed in alabaster. Ivory, gold and red is the scheme of decoration with draperies, carpets and upholstery of peacock blue.

What a colourful, vigorous and lively sight must have greeted the audience at that first show, as they came in from the soot-blackened streets of the Gorbals. Alabaster! Peacock-blue carpets! Few then had carpets in their own homes; come to that, few even had their own toilets or baths. Yet, for the 'popular prices' of 2d to 2s, they could experience top-class variety in these surroundings. The Palace was well named indeed. *The Era* was characteristically impressed by the show:

> The programme submitted by Messers Waldon and Barrasford was received with much enthusiasm and between two of the turns, Mr Waldon stepped in front of the curtain and in a neat speech indicated

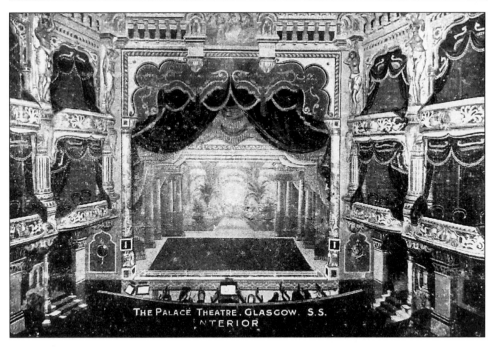

Figure 3.24   Interior of the Palace Theatre (author collection).

the scope for the new venture and promised a clean, healthy entertainment to which all the classes might bring their families without fear of hearing anything objectionable.

It is incredible to think that with 2,000 seats at the Palace and over 1,200 at the Royal Princess's next door, on a good night there would have been 500 more theatre-goers milling around Gorbals Street than could be packed into the three auditoria of today's Royal National Theatre in London. In 1905 Rich Waldon became the sole owner and because he had many theatres to look after, he installed Harry McKelvie, the Royal Princess's producer, as manager. Theatres were not allowed to open on Sundays, so to get round the regulations, seemingly high-brow 'Improving Lectures' were advertised. For example:

PLEASANT SUNDAY AFTERNOON
Lantern Slide Show On
Peace and War
Reverend James Barr, B.D.,
Will give his famous address on
SWEATING
Only Men Admitted

For all its splendour, and an ingenious management, the course of history was going against the continued success of theatres like the Palace. All over the Gorbals, cinemas were being opened. Most were rather downmarket compared with the theatre, but they cost as little as a penny (or failing that a returnable jam jar) to get in. Going to the theatre was still perceived as something one only did on a special occasion. When the Great War became a national effort, the Palace, already well equipped with a projection box when it opened, was leased by Rich Waldon to Walter Thompson's Picture House Syndicate. The new policy was for cine-variety, but whenever a popular film came, the 'live' section of the show was dropped to fit in more performances. In 1930 the projection box was moved to behind the balcony when 'talkie' equipment was installed and the increasingly sporadic variety was finally abandoned. Mrs Ann McCready remembers the Palace in cinema days:

It was advertised as 'The BEST in the DISTRICT', but the Palace still looked and smelled more like an old theatre. You went in a narrow door with a pay box, and up or down marble steps. There were fancy railings which the kids used to hide behind. I did it myself many times because you could spy through the wee holes. It was very dark inside, but quite posh still. As a wean you wouldn't get spat at in there. If you didn't have enough money for the stalls or circle, you'd walk up to the end of the block. There was another door there by a pub with its own pay box and stone steps to the top balcony. It got a noisier crowd and you sat on the floor – you had to tuck your dress in so that folk didn't put their cigarettes out on it.

The Palace survived largely unaltered until 1953 when it was sold to the Maitles family for only £9,000. It had never been redecorated since it opened and the once-vibrant colours were heavily smoke stained. The new owners were notorious for their shoe-string cinema operations, and they kept it going until 1962. Then, bingo was all the rage. The Palace was partly repainted in cream and gold (the owners could not afford scaffolding to do the ceiling) and fitted with tables in the stalls, becoming the Palace Bingo and Social Club. Now old wifies with headsquares queued at the Palace end of the columned facade while students and intellectuals waited at the other to see plays at the Citizens'. In May 1973 a fire destroyed the unused upper floors of the entrance foyer. They were boarded up and abandoned and in 1975 Glasgow District Council compulsorily purchased the fast-decaying old theatre for £160,000 to enable the completion of the ring road. This was controversial and provoked heated exchanges in the city chambers as Tory councillors demanded to know why a building worth only £9,000 when in good condition was now worth so much more in a state of disrepair. Surely the Palace could not be demolished as despite years of neglect, it was still regarded as the finest example of its type in the country. After many protests, it was grade B listed and the bingo sessions continued with a lease to the Maitles outfit. The ring road was cancelled, but still no repairs were made and the flashings became weak. Glasgow District Council had unnecessarily landed themselves with an expensive liability. The ceiling was waterlogged and parts of the fibrous plaster decoration started peeling off. After a rainstorm early in October 1977, the Palace suffered a serious ceiling collapse. The city authorities must have been relieved. As quickly as they could, a dangerous building warrant was served on the Palace and it was closed down. The authorities did, however, grant a short stay of execution to allow the retrieval of some of the unique plaster work.[20] Claire Blenkinsop, manageress of the Citizens' Theatre, adjoining the Palace, told the *Architects' Journal* 'It is a pity the Palace has to go, but there is no chance of raising the huge sums needed to restore it and there is no theatrical use for it anyway.' The Citizens' foyer provided a home for the statues and some of the elephants. A complete set of boxes went with other relics to adorn the newly formed Theatre Museum in London's Covent Garden. Before the demolition work started, Jimmy Logan made his first and last visit to the Palace, as he recounts:

> I well knew the financial problems of running theatres, after all I had been struggling for years to get rid of the Metropole, which was costing me a fortune. The Palace was clearly something special, though. It seemed just such a good quality of place. There were floors and floors of long-abandoned dressing rooms and each one had its own coal fire! If only it had survived a little longer, I'm sure it would have been renovated and used for the big London musicals.

It was not to be. The demolition started that November, and, within a week, one of Britain's most unusual theatres was no more.

KING'S THEATRE

In the first decades of the twentieth century, the theatre industry was well organised and booming. Pre-London trial runs of potential hit shows and post-London tours of acknowledged successes went out to the chains of splendid touring theatres. In Scotland Howard and Wyndham had become the acknowledged specialists, but their Glasgow Theatre Royal and Lyric could not alone cope with demand from an entertainment-hungry populace. Another theatre was needed, and fast, so once the site on Bath Street had been acquired, Frank Matcham was commissioned to design a new theatre which quite simply was to be the finest in the city. Even at this time, the local gentry and kirk-goers around Charing Cross were not amused at the prospect of a theatre appearing in their neighbourhood! Letters of protest were sent to the magistrates, and to the *Glasgow Herald*, but to no avail – the **King's** was given the go-ahead.

In designing what was an important touring theatre, costing over £50,000, Matcham was in a more subdued and dignified vein than usual. As with the earlier Empire Palace, he made the most of the prominent corner site, designing two show facades in Dumfriesshire red sandstone. The Elmbank Street elevation fronted the plush lounges to the rear of the auditorium. The fascinating symmetrical Bath Street elevation had overtones of art nouveau, but as with everything Matcham did, it was truly an enigmatic mixture of styles and influences. There were pavilions at either end; one contained the foyer while the other accessed the stage. When seen from a distance, the whole composition, topped by large ball finials, pediments and statuary, looked prosperous and inviting – everything one could want from a theatre.

The entrance hall still makes a wonderful impression on today's audiences, coming in off Glasgow's often cold, wet streets. The heavy, mahogany doors with their bevelled glass and lustrous brasswork, the warm pink marble of the walls, and that splendid barrel ceiling with statues gazing down from the corners prepare one to witness one of Matcham's most brilliant designs.

The King's 1,841-seat auditorium is unbelievably opulent in a free mix of baroque and rococo. There are three generously curved balconies, which engage with complex arrangements of boxes. The grand circle meets pairs of boxes with banded Ionic columns; the tier above slithers over the first box to larger

Figure 3.25 Frontage of the King's Theatre (author collection).

Figure 3.26 Interior of the King's Theatre (author collection).

stage boxes with elaborate half-domed canopies. Above, an arcade of conches rises to a magnificently decorated twelve-sided ceiling, the panels of which radiate from a single rose. The proscenium has several heavily modelled frames topped with a giant cartouche and angels. Everywhere one looks is a feast of gilding, flock wallpaper, marble, plum velvet plush and embroidery.

With such a theatre, small wonder the *Glasgow Herald* described the glittering opening, on 12 September 1904, as 'Brilliant!' and 'A notable addition to the recreative resources of the city'.[21] The audience, in their starched collars, tail coats and long evening dresses thoroughly enjoyed 'a fine performance' and one which set the tone for the following decades. The King's continued the policy of the smaller Royalty, which Howard and Wyndham then sold.

The big names from the West End came almost every week in the 1930s, but until 1933 it was the custom for city-centre theatres like the King's to have a long summer lay-off while city folk departed for the coast. Then A. Stewart Cruikshank decided that it would be worth experimenting with a summer show in Glasgow along the lines of the seaside entertainment. After all, a holiday

Figure 3.27   Foyer of the King's Theatre (author collection).

only took a week or two so what was there to do the rest of the time? It would start at half past eight and thus be a shorter show at a lower ticket price. The first performance was on 5 June 1933, described as 'an after-dinner liqueur of song, mirth and melody designed for summertime and at summertime prices'. The *Glasgow Herald* reported that 'it is simply an experiment in switching to music hall for a season. In its manner, it is quite an attractive and often amusing entertainment and the audience last night enjoyed it, and notwithstanding the fine weather outdoors, was one of considerable popularity.' *Half Past Eight* proved more than a simple change of direction for the King's. It was a response to changed circumstances. Glasgow was enduring the pain of the depression with mass unemployment and an uncertain future. Folk wanted light relief from these difficult circumstances and *Half Past Eight* shows in the palatial surroundings of the King's Theatre were the perfect tonic. They were enormously successful until 1954 when Howard and Wyndham added the Alhambra to their portfolio. This was altogether bigger than the King's, and the summer shows were transferred there. Another aspect of the King's year which remained unchanged was the pantomime each winter. Produced for Howard and Wyndham by Charles and Ilona Ross, these fantastic performances used ballet dancers, real horses pulling Cinderella's carriage, trap doors, smoke effects, elaborate costumes and scenery to delight generations of children.

By the mid-1960s Howard and Wyndham had all but abandoned serious drama and instead put their faith in the continued success of long seasons of pantomime and the summer show, now known as *Five Past Eight*, at the Alhambra. To finance these expensive productions, the King's was sold to Glasgow Corporation in September 1967. This purchase was a far-sighted act on the part of the city authorities. Few theatres were then in public ownership, and most municipal venues were recently-built multi-purpose halls of little merit or character. Maybe even then, at the height of the city's self-destruction, some in authority were beginning to worry about the demolition of so many theatres, and the burning of nearby St. Andrew's Halls. Whatever motivated them, Glasgow Corporation could not have found a finer theatre than the King's. It has become well known for staging touring productions of musicals, and the amateur dramatic clubs, displaced when the Lyric was demolished, have an even better venue. The pantomimes are subsidised by the city council, and during the 1970s and 1980s, Glaswegians' favourite stars from the Howard and Wyndham era, like Stanley Baxter, Jimmy Logan and Rikki Fulton, have played dame. Bus loads of children alight in front of the King's where a new generation sits enthralled, not only by the high standard of the show, but by the still sparkling gilt and plush of Matcham's architecture. In fact, when it was announced that Glasgow would be 'European City of Culture' in 1990, the King's was refurbished to a very high standard. Memories of *Half Past Eight* were rekindled when Rikki Fulton and Jack Milroy appeared as Francie and Josie in *King's High*, a new and hugely successful summer revue. Today, the King's hosts touring productions of hit musicals, amateur dramatics, occasional variety shows and, of course, the fine tradition for superbly produced pantomime continues.

More than ninety years after first opening, audiences still queue around the block to enjoy an evening at the King's. It is one of Scotland's most beautiful theatres and a great asset to the city of Glasgow.

THE COLISEUM

Today, emerging from Bridge Street Underground Station and looking at the acres of wasteland around Eglinton Street, it is hard to imagine that the city centre once extended over the Clyde and that this was a busy shopping street, surrounded by tenements as far as the eye could see. Here, Moss Empires bought a large plot of land to build a second big variety theatre – their existing Empire in Sauchiehall Street, though hugely popular, was thought to be too far away for Southsiders to reach conveniently. Once again Frank Matcham was asked to design this new theatre. The exteriors of Matcham theatres generally fall into two categories: the symmetrical facade with pavilions (such as the King's), or the big brick box with some architecture tacked on at the front. The **Coliseum** was definitely one of the latter; from most angles, it looked rather industrial – perhaps not entirely inappropriate in an area like Laurieston where workshops and housing existed in close proximity. The red-sandstone facade projected forward from the 120-feet-wide auditorium block. It had strong hints of the new fashion for art nouveau. The octagonal balcony stair tower had a carved stone frieze in the style and was topped by a spire with a minaret in which a rotating sign spelled its name in lightbulbs. The main entrance was through a high archway with a loggia above and a steeply pitched pavilion roof. The pit entrances were round the sides and the name was spelled out in giant raised art nouveau script on panels on the sides. It was hardly one of Matcham's best efforts at an exterior, but the 1904–5 period was exceptionally busy for his office. Around those years he designed nearly a dozen major theatres, including three important London venues: the Richmond Theatre, Hackney Empire and Stoll's London Coliseum. Motifs from all of these appeared in the interior of the Glasgow Coliseum.[22]

A novel feature of its design was that there were indoor waiting rooms for all customers. In variety houses, the audiences would come and go as they pleased during a show, so there were always queues waiting to get in. In the Coliseum, they could all buy a ticket at the door, go upstairs and sit in comfort until others came out. Even the pit waiting room was carpeted and had long buttoned velvet settees. The main entrance was 'boldly Italian' with white-marble columns, pilasters and staircases reaching an arched gallery at first-floor level and fresco panels in gilded surrounds on the ceiling. Patrons would walk along passages with Turkish rugs and settees in wall niches before emerging in the splendour of the 2,893-seat auditorium. The proscenium arch was of brown grained marble with a broken pediment topped by cupids and inscribed 'To Awake The Soul By Tender Strokes Of Art'. This was flanked by enriched columns, topped by statues of the muses – all obviously derived from Richmond Theatre. On either side, there were three boxes capped by domes and broken pediments with yet more statuary.

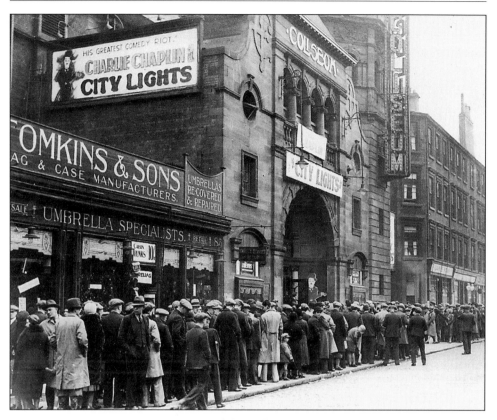

Figure 3.28   Frontage of the Coliseum (courtesy Allen Eyles).

There were two very deep cantilevered balconies and the ceiling was a flattened dome with painted panels and peacock fans in the corners. The interior was in shades of cream and gold and the rose-red embroidered velvet draperies and silk fringes alone cost nearly £1,000. The dressing rooms, in a separate block for fire protection, were fully carpeted with toilets and piped water heating. No expense was spared as Moss knew from personal experience the danger of theatre fires. The Coliseum was regarded as being one of the safest in the country; the steel safety curtain weighed 82 tons and there were three independent lighting systems. In the event of fire, the audience could be evacuated through thirty-six exits in three minutes.

The Coliseum opened on 18 December 1905. From then until 1919, variety was presented twice nightly at the Coliseum, which proudly advertised seats for 35,000 a week! The Great Carmo made a lion vanish, Harry Houdini escaped from handcuffs and torture instruments, but a favourite performer at Moss theatres was Dr Walford Bodie, MD. Bodie was not a real doctor – he claimed his title stood for 'Merry Devil'. He did a hypnotism act, tricks with

Figure 3.29   Interior of the Coliseum after conversion to a cinema
(author collection).

electricity and, more controversially, claimed he could cure people through these forms of 'bloodless surgery'. Of course, he was a fraud as he used to plant his subjects for cure in the audience, but his popular act was highly polished and well delivered. A typically baffling advertisement by Bodie read:

The Cock Crows Best That Crows Last
Ye Canna Sit Doon on the Thistle
THE ONE AND ONLY
DR WALFORD BODIE
THE FAMOUS BLOODLESS SURGEON
Supported by GIGANTIC STAR COMPANY
HUNDREDS TURNED AWAY NIGHTLY – SUCCESS GREATER
THAN EVER
3 – HOURS SOLID AMUSEMENT – 3
THIS WEEK AT THE COLISEUM FROM 7 PM
'Medicine is quackery with a University Stamp'

Not surprisingly, Bodie was loathed by doctors, who thought him dangerous as people with real illnesses might not go to hospital after seeing his act. Medical students were insulted by his advertisements as Glasgow University had one of the most respected medical schools. The students, led by the young O. H. Mavor (later known as the playwright James Bridie), decided to exact revenge. On 12 November 1909 a large group, well armed with eggs and rotten fruit, sat in the pit. When Bodie started castigating the medical profession, they heckled noisily. Thinking he was safe on the stage, Bodie unwisely replied, quoting Burns 'they come in stirks and gang oot asses'. This was too much for the students, who scrambled across the orchestra pit and pelted the hapless Bodie with eggs. The management must have been expecting trouble, but although there were police present, they were heavily outnumbered. Bodie and his assistants were chased out of the Coliseum, never to return. The event was enshrined in local folklore as the 'Bodie Riot'.

The theatre came to prominence again in May 1920 when the Carl Rosa Opera Company made a rare visit to perform Wagner's 'Ring' cycle. The *Glasgow Herald* reported that its acoustics were 'perhaps the finest in the city' – a tribute to Matcham's design principals. By then, the Coliseum had outlived its usefulness as a variety theatre. Its remoteness from the city centre and elephantine proportions hastened its demise, so it was sold in March 1925 to Scottish Cinema and Variety Theatres for use as a cinema. At first, there were few alterations, but once 'talkies' arrived in 1929, the Coliseum became hugely popular so the proscenium was demolished and seating extended into where the stage had been. Looking from the front, it was still recognisable as an Edwardian music hall. In 1963, interestingly at the same time as the London Coliseum was fortunately being less drastically adapted, the Glasgow Coliseum was radically rebuilt as a Cinerama theatre. The upper balcony was demolished, a new curtained auditorium built within the original and the facade was hidden behind a sheet-metal frontispiece – a classic example of how not to treat an old theatre. Cinerama was a flop, and in 1976 the Coliseum was compulsorily purchased by Glasgow District Council as it lay in the path of the proposed inner ring road. That was cancelled and cinema shows continued for a while. After a spell of dereliction, the theatre was rebuilt once again as a bingo club. No evidence of Matcham's interior is visible, but high above a suspended ceiling, the original is still extant.

THE ALHAMBRA

By the late Edwardian period, the great theatre-building boom was drawing to a close. However, as a final brave flourish before the 'picture palaces' conquered all, a generation of more technically advanced and very luxurious variety theatres was developed. To give more spacious aisles and seating without losing capacity, these had to be significantly larger than what had gone before.

The **Alhambra**, opened on 9 December 1910, was typical of this later style. It was designed by Sir John J. Burnet, one of the top architects of the period. Although contemporary fashion demanded a more serious classical look than in Victorian times, the Alhambra's designers tried hard to enter into the spirit of the theatre world. On a dingy site on Waterloo Street, among the canyons of offices in Glasgow's financial district, they produced a totally unexpected soaring, stripy bright-red brick pile with whimsical little towers, topped by domed lanterns. With its colourful Arabian terracotta details, it might have looked more at home in Manchester, or even Baghdad!

The foyer for stalls and circle patrons was an imposing double-height space with grand staircases on either side. There were recessed mirrors framed by hefty pilasters at first-floor height and a heavily panelled ceiling. The enormous 2,750-seat auditorium was less successful. The heavy, angular design attempted a French classical style, but lacked the finesse and sensuous flowing curves of most Victorian theatres. Its three vast unadorned tiers faced the stage squarely, as in a cinema. Most patrons enjoyed the superb acoustics, excellent sight lines, spacious aisles and sprung seats upholstered in plum velvet. Even so, the frighteningly steep balcony was still reached up stone stairs from a side entrance and only had upholstered benches with iron armrests.

Backstage, the Alhambra had a surfeit of technical gadgetry and could claim to be the best-equipped theatre north of London. There was the latest system for flying scenery and even a revolving stage. Glasgow Alhambra Ltd, its owner, was run by Alfred Butt and R. H. Gillespie – entrepreneurs who intended the Alhambra to be a very lavish music hall, with performances only once nightly. The opening was well attended by city dignitaries in evening dress, and early bills attracted such big stars as Harry Lauder, Vesta Tilley and Sarah Bernhardt. With competition from a host of cheap and well-established variety theatres, ordinary Glaswegians were not enthused about paying premium rates even if the show was three hours long and the Alhambra closed in the spring of 1910 while the management had a rethink. It was in business again that autumn with more successful twice nightly shows. The theatre's variety days were numbered as the big chains like Moss Empires were contracting all the best acts for months at a time and independently run venues were shut out. In 1926 the Alhambra's policy changed to musical comedies, operas and plays. The extravagant pantomimes continued. The late Jack House recalled a 1930s production:

> The big scene in *Queen of Hearts* was a trap door act which occupied the whole of the proscenium. It was like the front of a block of flats with doors on various levels. Lupino Lane (as the Knave of Hearts)

performed the most amazing acrobatics with a team of four French trap-door specialists. Its *raison d'être* was that the Knave was being pursued by secret police who were trying to catch him for all his misdeeds. The way the five of them hurled themselves in and out of the myriad doors defies description. Lane was always eluding his pursuers by a hair's-breadth, and you never knew on which level he would next appear. The timing was perfection and, of course, Lane escaped and the chase ended . . . I have never seen anything like it.[23]

The Wilson Barrett Repertory Company had regular long seasons of plays in the 1940s. In between the drama, opera and musicals, top comedians Harry Gordon and Will Fyffe starred in panto for six consecutive seasons from 1941. Aberdeen-born Gordon styled himself the laird of an imaginary north-east village called Inversnecky. He delighted Alhambra audiences with his pawky stories about it, told in his broad Aberdeen accent. He was a wonderful panto dame, taking meticulous trouble to appear in the year's latest ladies' fashions with a blue-rinse wig. Sadly, Fyffe died suddenly in 1947, but Harry Gordon eventually made a record sixteen panto appearances at the theatre.

In 1954 the Alhambra became a prestigious addition to the Howard and Wyndham chain. Although it already had a reputation for being smartly run, its best years lay ahead. At once, the new owners transferred their popular *Half Past Eight* summer revues from the King's. The Alhambra's cavernous auditorium was not sufficiently intimate for drama and it worked much better with these variety spectaculars. Since the Second World War, the shows had started earlier and eventually, in 1955, the name changed to *Five Past Eight*. Howard and Wyndham's producer, Dick Hurran, delighted in using the Alhambra's big stage to devise ever more complex sets. Hurran actually started out as a dancer in the 1938 show at the King's and eventually became a Howard and Wyndham director. Inspired by a visit to America in 1955, Hurran transformed the Alhambra into 'The Starlight Room' – a Las Vegas-style cabaret lounge for the 1956 *Five Past Eight Show*. The stage was extended over the orchestra pit; there were curving stairs from the circle and everything was moveable – even the orchestra was on a lift to one side of the stage. The back cloths were covered in thousands of twinkling lights and the stars made their entrance down a curving stairway with lights under the treads.

On 3 July 1958 the Alhambra staged Scotland's first Royal Variety Show when the best seats cost a staggering £50 but all the proceeds were, of course, donated to the Entertainment Artists Benevolent Fund and local charities. This enhanced its reputation and soon famous international cabaret acts were booked – the high-stepping Bluebell Girls came from Paris in 1960, and Geraldo's Orchestra was resident during the *Five Past Eight* seasons – but these shows starred local favourites like Rikki Fulton or Jimmy Logan. Sometimes a

Figure 3.30   Frontage of the Alhambra (author collection).

circus ring would be built for animal acts and a glass-fronted swimming pool
with blue water was built for a formation-swimming act. It was used again
when both the Queen and Queen Mother came to the Alhambra for another
royal occasion in 1963. The swimmers were given new trunks before the show
which unfortunately went transparent when wet. It was only when they stood
up to take their bow that this became obvious, so they were quickly ordered
back in the pool from the wings! Fortunately, because of the Alhambra's size,
Her Majesty could not have noticed and afterwards she told staff that the
swimming pool was lovely. The Alhambra was Jack House's favourite theatre.
He recalled:

There was the smell of lingering cigar smoke . . . Although it was a big theatre, it somehow had a cosiness about it . . . I saw my first pantomime there in 1916 and probably visited it more often than any other Glasgow Theatre . . . I recollect being in Paris (in the early 1960s) and going to the Lido on the Champs Elysées. At least half of the Lido programme was composed of acts which I had already seen in *Five Past Eight* at the Alhambra. They were, perhaps, not quite so well presented because the Lido had a comparatively small stage. *Five Past Eight* at the Alhambra brought entrepreneurs from all over the world to see the show. Nothing in London came up to the standard set in Glasgow.[24]

Such perfection came at a high price; audiences expected next year's show to outdo the one before in stars, costumes, big set-piece numbers and settings. The producer of *Five Past Eight* increasingly relied on the novelty of television personalities to lure big audiences.[25] In 1966 Howard and Wyndham sold the King's to Glasgow City Council to generate much needed funds, but costs continued to escalate. The climax of *Five Past Eight* came when the new stars Morecambe and Wise were booked for the 1968 season. Shortly before the first show on 5 June, Morecambe had the first of his heart attacks. The contract had to be cancelled and at very short notice the only other suitable comedian available was Norman Wisdom. Allegedly, his agent demanded that he be paid more than Morecambe and Wise. For the first time *Five Past Eight* was a flop; it had priced itself out of the market. The Alhambra lost so much money over the fiasco that it never recovered and the only solution was for the proprietors to sell the theatre. Its huge capacity, once a tremendous asset, was now a liability. The final show was a concert by Cilla Black on 24 May 1969. Despite the fact that everybody admitted the value of the building, nobody in authority was prepared to do anything about it. A petition was signed by 500,000 people, but the fact that it was then the only listed theatre in the city counted for nothing. It was demolished in 1971 and a property developer replaced it with a characterless office block called Alhambra House. That asbestos-filled monstrosity was pulled down in 1996 and so fortunately lasted only twenty-five years.

THE SAVOY

The **Savoy** was intended to be a luxurious and exclusive rival to Moss's highly popular Empire. Advertised as 'Glasgow's Cosmopolitan House, its twin-towers and ornately tiled exterior in grey and green made it a Hope Street landmark. Designed by James Miller, probably one of Glasgow's best architects of the period, the interior was grandly conceived in Louis XVI style. The double-level foyer had two handsome white-marble staircases which curved upwards to a café, with its own 'Roumanian' orchestra, a stall selling chocolate, cigars and newspapers and even a telephone booth. The walls were clad in dark French-polished marquetry panels, with inlaid mirrors, and the auditorium seated 1,600 in comfortable tip-up seats. The Savoy opened on 18 December 1911, when the American comedienne Nella Webb topped the bill. Luxurious as it was, Glaswegians were unwilling to pay higher prices, especially as the rival Empire already attracted the biggest names. The Savoy never became well established as a variety house and it closed in 1916, unable to secure the foreign acts it needed as a result of the First World War. After some alterations, it was back in business on Christmas Day as the New Savoy Cinema. It eventually became a ballroom and was demolished by the Rank Organisation in 1972 for the speculative development of the Savoy Shopping Centre.

Figure 3.31   Hope Street showing the Savoy (author collection).

HENGLER'S CIRCUS

The story of the **Hengler's Circus** goes back to the early years of the industrial revolution when circuses, especially those with equestrian acts, became popular. It was as a tight-rope walker that 'Monsieur Hengler' made his name in Charles Dibdin's London-based Royal Circus in 1803. The second of Hengler's three sons, Charles, set up 'Hengler's Circus' in 1847 by taking over the family's employers, Price and Powell, who got into financial problems. Hengler was very punctilious – everything had to be spotless and his performers were not allowed to smoke in the street. They were probably quite glad to obey as they could earn 50 per cent more from Hengler's than other circuses paid. When the company visited Scotland in the 1860s, pitching their tent on Glasgow Green, free charity shows were given to thousands of local school children. Such acts of philanthropy caught the attention of the city authorities, and with strict management and an aura of respectability, the Hengler's empire started expanding with more comfortable permanent wood or stone buildings. In 1863 he took a lease on the derelict Prince's Theatre, a cosy little music hall in West Nile Street famed for its pantomimes.

It was a brick structure and had first opened on New Year's Day in 1849 with a performance of Loder's *Giselle*, but was shortly converted into an amphitheatre for equestrian circuses and a horse bazaar run by Edmund Glover, who managed the Theatre Royal in Dunlop Street. Hamilton's diorama, a show in which huge canvases of European landscapes were displayed on a 360-degree loop with effects lighting and music, was tried in the 1850s, but the venture soon fell on hard times. Hengler converted the Prince's to a circus once again. Building on the good reputation of his Glasgow Green shows, he established a tradition in the city that was to survive for sixty years. He enlarged his Glasgow amphitheatre in 1867, and by the 1870s he had a chain of five similar venues all over Britain. As the decade progressed, Hengler's shows became more elaborate and as a result the Prince of Wales brought his family to see the pantomime *Jack the Giant Killer* in London. All Hengler's premises soon sported the Prince's feathers. With royal patronage, his success was assured and Hengler's troupe travelled from venue to venue with month-long stints in each city. In between these visits, dioramas, variety shows, novelty acts or 'scientific' lectures were given.

In 1877 Hengler's usual architect, J. T. Robinson, again rebuilt the Glasgow circus to accommodate water displays. It re-opened on 17 November 1877 with '*Japanese Fête – The Great Fountain of Variegated Waters*, the crystal jets of every hue rising to a great altitude, as played on fête days in the gardens of Japan'.[26]

In 1883 Hengler decided once again to improve his Glasgow circus. It was, after all, his most profitable, but the building was still inadequate for the ever

Figure 3.32   Frontage of Hengler's Circus, West Nile Street (author collection).

larger shows. He sold the property to Her Majesty's Tax Commissioners in 1883 and acquired land in Wellington Street. As J. T. Robinson had died in 1878, Hengler approached Frank Matcham, who was actually Robinson's son-in-law. Matcham produced a large rectangular structure, with pavilions at each corner and a circular amphitheatre with a single balcony. There was a proscenium and fully equipped stage at one end. At the front of house, there were ladies' lounges and a smoking room, while at the back were stables and elephant pits as well as twenty dressing rooms. The building opened on 9 November 1885, in the presence of the Lord Provost and magistrates of Glasgow.

The new Glasgow circus was a great success and the crowning glory of a memorable year for Hengler. He had made a fortune in auctioning his old London circus, and when the new venue opened, his circus was invited to perform at Windsor Castle by royal command. By the time of the Windsor visit in February 1896, Charles Hengler's health was failing; he was exhausted, died in his sleep on 28 September 1897 and left his empire to his two sons, Albert and Frederick.

With public expectation so high, the sons initially had problems outdoing their father's shows. When Hengler's Circus toured Britain in 1891, Albert introduced a 'water spectacular' to their pantomime *A Village Wedding*. It was full of amiable tramps, yokels, old ladies in bloomers stuck up trees and fat policemen falling into the water. Indeed, 23,000 gallons of water were poured into the arena in just 35 seconds and the Glasgow programme warned: 'NOTICE – The Management will not hold themselves responsible for any slight damage that might be caused by the splashing of water during the performance.'

A Village Wedding was a resounding hit, which came at just the right time. 'It paid me better than anything else has ever done,' said Albert Hengler. 'It enabled me nearly to pay for those four buildings . . . which it took my father years of hard and patient work to obtain.' At only thirty years of age, he was the proud owner of a chain of famous circuses. In the 1890s Edward Moss's luxurious Empire Theatres were posing the biggest threat to Hengler's continued popularity and Albert Hengler complained to *The Era* that:

> The jugglers, acrobats, wire-walkers, trapeze artists, the performing animals, the musical clowns and other things are all legitimate circus performances which have been stolen from our business. Every time we open in a town, we are twitted with copying the music halls, with

Figure 3.33 Hengler's Circus, Wellington Street (author collection).

putting too much of the variety show into the performance, whereas the simple truth is the music halls have been stealing from us. The modern music hall is nothing more than a circus shorn of its horses.

It could be of little comfort to Hengler that his Glasgow circus was in many ways a prototype for the Empire Palaces that Matcham designed for Moss. Within the next few years, Hengler more than halved his circus business. All the amphitheatres were sold, except Liverpool and Glasgow, and for the Jubilee season in 1897, he concentrated on devising a more dramatic show using the water spectacle. This was vital in distinguishing Hengler's from a new rival, E. H. Bostock's Scottish Zoo and Glasgow Hippodrome in nearby New City Road, Cowcaddens. The Hippodrome was a huge warehouse-like, iron-framed structure, which not only housed a circus arena and stables for everything from horses to elephants, but also a cinema. Opened on 2 May, it was designed by Bertie Crewe and partly financed by Thomas Barrasford. Although the circus only lasted until 1918, amazingly, the entire structure survives today, housing a supermarket and Glasgow's Chinatown.

While Bostock opened in Cowcaddens, Hengler was busy preparing his new show. Entitled *Siberia*, it would include ice skating, horse riding – *The Cossacks and Their Prisoners: The Escape and Pursuit* – and a sensational finale *The Frozen River: A Desperate Fight for LIFE and LIBERTY*. Of course, it was a recipe for success, so another spectacle about the story of the Red Indians called *The Redskin* was devised as a follow-up. The popularity of Hengler's two new spectacles was enormous; he had invented an extraordinary theatrical device, and inspite of his taking out a patent, it was copied by other managers.

THE HIPPODROME

In the same year the **Hippodrome** opened at 326 Sauchiehall Street in Glasgow. This was a conversion of the unsuccessful Ice Skating Palace by its managing director, the flamboyant South African-born showman, Arthur Hubner. The building had started out in 1882 as a diorama, and was converted for ice skating at the height of the craze in 1885. When this waned, Hubner tried everything to attract an audience, even presenting Glasgow's first ever cinema show in 1896. Everywhere actors, horses and elephants seemed to be tumbling head first into tanks of probably very cold water to excite and amuse hundreds of thousands of theatre patrons. The opening programme declared:

> The provision of a place of entertainment that in its equipment and elegance of design shall be worthy of the Second City of the Empire has been the object aimed at by the proprietors of the Hippodrome . . . The

great steel roof trusses have been covered up with a dome-shaped ceiling of fibre plaster decorated in rich colours, having large cartouche-like panels with spirited drawings of horses and riders in Roman chariots that seem to leap from the clouds, while the old bare brick walls are now clothed in a rich golden covering. The work has been long and arduous, the digging of the huge pit which contains the sinking ring having taken no less than three months to complete.

Situated in the middle of Sauchiehall Street, the city's most fashionable thoroughfare, a handsome canopy of wrought iron work and glass indicates the main entrance to the building and this, being illuminated at night by five unusually powerful arc lamps, makes a land mark which there is no possibility of mistaking. The vestibule, beautifully decorated in rich, warm colours, affords access to the stalls and balcony . . . Once inside, the amphitheatre has seating for over 1500 . . . and the ring in front of the proscenium is 142 feet in circumference . . . by an elaborate mechanical contrivance [this] can be converted within one minute into a huge lake of water. This is contained in a tank composed of steel boiler plates held together by no less than 9,000 rivets. This tank, which when full holds 100,000 gallons of water and weighs 400 tons,

Figure 3.34   Interior of the Hippodrome, Sauchiehall Street (author collection).

rests on a framework of steel girders and dwarf concrete walls. Inside the tank is fitted a rising and falling platform constructed of eight steel girders, each weighing some ton and a half. This platform, on which the performance takes place, is raised by a powerful hydraulic ram and pumps.

The building is lighted throughout with a complete system of electricity, and provision has been made for illuminating and decorative lighting on a large scale. Great care has been paid to the musical part of the entertainment. In the orchestra are twenty skilled performers, who, under the capable direction of Mr W. Milne, will provide a programme of the highest class. The architect from whose plans the building has been constructed is Mr James Miller of Blythswood Square, who was the architect for the Glasgow International Exhibition in 1901, the most successful exhibition of modern times.

Miller was ideally suited to the job. His exhibition pavilions had been remarkably flamboyant and theatrical with great domes and Indian motifs, but he was also technically very proficient, designing everything from churches and banks to Glasgow subway stations.

Meanwhile, the lease on Albert Hengler's Wellington Street premises expired in May 1900 and he believed he had lost the backbone of his business. In fact, the lessor, the Post Office, had written to Hengler telling him that they were not ready to proceed with their redevelopment of the site, but remarkably the letter had been lost in the post. The Glasgow circus was abandoned and within a few years as their leases expired one by one, Albert Hengler had lost all his other venues. He was then forced to collaborate with his former enemies, the variety magnates Moss and Stoll, who had built their own Hippodromes with water displays throughout Britain. Then, Hengler had some good luck. Arthur Hubner did not have the expertise to make a success of his Hippodrome, so he agreed to lease it to Hengler, who took it over on 5 December 1904. Hengler's final period in Glasgow lasted a memorable twenty years. Many of his touring shows were included in the programme, so a new generation of Glaswegians had the opportunity to thrill to the spectacular *Siberia* and *The Redskin*. A new epic, *The Balkans*, was premiered in 1912. The *Glasgow Herald* reported:

It has a bearing on the present war in the Near East. There are shown wild mountain passes, up which horsemen canter, live sheep and bullocks are driven, and peasants pipe and gather for war. There is a love interest in it with the exciting finale of the Turkish Pasha tying his daughter on a horse's back and making the animal plunge headlong into the lake beneath his castle, which she had led the Balkan peasants to attack in order to rescue her peasant lover. The bold youth escapes from his cell at the right moment, dives from a dizzy height and rescues the girl. Then there is the bursting of the floodgates up the mountains and the stampede of oxen, horses, men and women, the wild plunge and the exciting swim for life. The piece is excellently staged and goes through with a swing.

Productions were certainly the last word in originality, being both newsworthy and technically sophisticated as they had to compete with lavish rival cinemas like the Salon or La Scala a few blocks away. Between the long circus seasons, Hengler now found profitable use in running his own premises as a cinema. Rows of seats were fitted over the arena so that an audience of more than 2,000 could watch. An article in *Milden Miscellany* recalled:

Several flights of steps divided by brass and iron handrails led up to the entrance hall which was painted bright red. The stone corridors had a peculiar smell, not unlike that of a tenement close after it had been washed and pipe-clayed. But there was also an essence of something essentially Hengler's. In the off-seasons, children trooped to Hengler's from all parts of Glasgow on Saturday afternoons to pay their penny admission and climb up to the gallery, where wandering eyes paused momentarily at the site of voluptuous ladies reclining against gilded cornucopias on the frescoed heights. The screen was on a wooden frame and could be lowered and raised like a kitchen pulley.

During the First World War, the popularity of cinemas soared and with circus acts conscripted away, Hengler's found the post-war era tough going. The final circus season in Glasgow was in 1924, but four weeks in, the company was threatened with a bankruptcy petition. Albert Hengler closed his last circus and retired to Hove on the south coast. After an unsuccessful spell as a ballroom, Hengler's Circus was radically rebuilt as the Regal Cinema. It is now the ABC, and folk climbing Scott Street can still see brick fragments from the old circus in the cinema's side wall. Inside, the remains of animal pens can be seen below the cinemas.[27]

THE OLYMPIA

In the Edwardian period a last generation of large theatres was developed in densely populated suburbs, peripheral to the city centre. To attract every section of the local community, these theatres presented both variety and touring productions of plays, operas and concerts. Architecturally, they were much larger than the older city-centre theatres and were often more lavishly decorated, the idea being to lure patrons away from some of the older (but well- established) music halls in the centre. Grandeur came at a high price, however, and within only a few years of opening, they were facing tough competition from the many newly opened cinemas, which were much cheaper to operate. For many, going to the theatre was something one only did on a special occasion. Soon, they all went over to films.

The former **Olympia Theatre of Varieties** still dominates Bridgeton Cross with its imposing red-sandstone facade; above the corner entrance lofty Ionic columns and, along the main wall, slim pilasters flanked by rusticated ends, rise over three storeys to an imposing dome. The bulk of the theatre was designed by Airdrie-born George Arthur. He was a distinguished man who designed many of the burgh's fine public buildings before being elected Provost in 1893. Producing a large modern theatre must have proved too much of a challenge though, as he wisely sought the advice of Frank Matcham's expert firm to design the interior.

Throughout, the decor was much more restrained than in Matcham's Victorian theatres. The foyer was circular with a high domed ceiling and curving stairs with marble balustrades leading to the circle. There were elegant lounges, and the two-tiered auditorium, which was at a 45-degree angle, was decorated in two shades of cream with gilding, red drapes and upholstered seats for 2,000. The plaster work was a heavy interpretation of the French Renaissance-style with garlands on the balcony fronts and heavy cornices around the panelled ceiling, which had a sliding roof to let the smoke out. The curtains were partly festooned with the crest of the City of Glasgow on either side.[28] Altogether, it was quite a contrast with the grimy streets of Bridgeton and the sordid local cinemas which vied for its audience. In its early days it was advertised as 'The Clean, Comfortable Family Resort . . . Disinfected with Jeyes Fluid in the Interest of Public Health'. Special mention was made in the opening brochure of the 'Cinematograph chamber and electricity box', from which all the lighting was controlled – a sign of the technology to come! The building was soon converted to a full-time cinema, so the fact that there was already a projection box from the outset was ominous for its future as a theatre.

The theatre opened on 18 September 1911 and was run on the traditionally popular 'twice nightly' basis, the first manager being Samuel Lloyd, who was well known from stints at other Glasgow theatres. *The Era* reported:

> On the afternoon of 18 September, a large invited company was welcomed by Provost McMillan, of Greenock, who was chairman of the directors. At both houses [that evening], the Olympia was given a grand send-off, the place being filled to capacity.

Figure 3.35   Frontage of the Olympia Theatre of Varieties, Bridgeton
(author collection).

Chief place on the programme was given to the Eight Welsh Miners, who appeared in full rig-out of colliers, with lamp and pick-axe, working down the pits. As vocalists, they demonstrate their ability to do full justice to such concerted pieces as *The Soldiers' Chorus*.

Gradually, cinema shows played an increasing role in the Olympia's bills, especially when most theatres were closed for the summer it showed films instead. In 1924 it was sold to Scottish Cinema and Variety Theatres. Even such a modern variety house was not entirely suitable as too many of the seats had an angled view of the screen, so the old interior was ripped out in 1935 and replaced with a modern cinema auditorium, run by ABC. Largely unaltered since, the Olympia still entertains Bridgeton folk as a bingo hall.

THE EMPRESS

Harry McKelvie, later of the Olympia, began his career as a manager at the

West End Playhouse, a lavishly planned theatre in St. George's Road, by Maryhill. The theatre was designed by W. B. Whitie in Louis XV style for opera and melodrama. It had a splendid symmetrical red-sandstone exterior, five bays wide, topped by a weighty parapet. There were extensive foyer spaces and a restrained baroque interior with two balconies and two boxes flanked by pilasters on either side, seating only 1,300 in a very commodious auditorium. Although launched with great bravura on 4 August 1913 by the Carl Rosa Opera, being located in a working-class district well away from the centre, with a staff of fifty and such a small capacity, it was probably doomed to failure. Sure enough, it closed within six months and the directors declared bankruptcy.

With a reduced staff and more modest programmes, it was relaunched as the Empress Variety Theatre and Picture Playhouse on 30 March 1914, under Harry Goodwin. In its early days Empress programmes had a strong Irish and American influence, with dancing and newly imported films on the 'American Bioscope'. George Urie Scott, who ran a primitive cinema round the corner and was later a director of the Pavilion, took charge in 1933 and the Empress became a variety house, copying the Olympia with films only during the summer and a long panto season, sometimes lasting until Easter. Donald McKenzie was a regular customer:

> I stayed in Maryhill at the time, so it was easy to get to the Empress. Fancy having a palatial theatre just round the corner! Anyway, it was a lot cheaper than in the city centre, a shilling I think for really good seats. Of course, the audience was more down to earth. I remember seeing Tommy Morgan there and laughing my head off. Suddenly, an arm with the biggest clenched fist you ever saw appeared in front of me from the row behind and a low voice said 'Shut it, son, or I'll smash your face.' You wouldn't get that in the King's! I remember going with friends to see a variety show with a turn who played all sorts of horns and saxophones. I recalled seeing him before and he was grim, so we all bought lemons and threw them into the horns of his instruments from the front stalls so that he couldn't play. It was better entertainment than if he had done his act and everyone thought it was hilarious, except the ushers but they were outnumbered anyway.[29]

Having avoided fire for over forty years, the Empress met the customary fate of so many Glasgow theatres on the night of 13 March 1956. The blaze started in the upper balcony, probably as a result of hot ash falling from the carbon-arc spotlights. The seating, ceiling plaster work and much of the flooring and structure of both balconies were badly damaged by fire and water, and the theatre cost £40,000 to restore. A lighting box was built to prevent a recurrence, seating was reduced to 697 and the ceiling simplified before the Empress re-opened for the autumn season.

In 1960 the theatre was sold for only £32,500 to the Falcon Trust, a charity which intended to develop an arts centre and youth theatre presenting serious drama. This failed miserably, and when Glasgow Corporation refused to become involved, what was by then known as the Falcon Theatre closed. Following the fire which destroyed his venerable Metropole in Stockwell Street, Alec Frutin purchased the Falcon and it opened once again on 15 November 1962 as the **New Metropole** with a traditional variety show, *Scotland Calling*. The old Metropole had been renowned for its 'tartan spectaculars', and the stars, like Grace Clark and Colin Murray and the Alexander Brothers, all transferred to the new venue. Sadly, the financial success of the old theatre was more elusive.

Alec Frutin retired and a highly appropriate saviour came in the person of Jimmy Logan, whose show-business family had first found fame in Frutin's old theatre. Logan was now the nearest thing Scotland had to the Hollywood film stars and he loved to dress stylishly and act like one. He later recounted:

> When I was a wee lad of seventeen, we played the Dunfermline Opera House, a lovely old theatre which was then for sale at £7,000. I wanted to buy it! I had always, always wanted to own a theatre and when Alec gave up his Metropole, I had my chance. I wasn't a such a businessman as Alec, of course, but I thought I knew as much about the variety business as anyone – I suppose I had youth and some arrogance! The former Empress was a very beautiful theatre and so I paid £85,000 for it and spent a good deal more on renovating the foyers and fitting new bars. It really looked grand. All the big Scottish stars were booked – good friends like Stanley Baxter, or Jack Milroy. Before the show we'd drive round the front and see how big the queue was. If it went round the block, we'd go off for a meal in a good restaurant and if it didn't, we'd get a carry-out of fish suppers![30]

Jimmy Logan's Metropole had several notable box-office successes and his ownership was certainly marked by ingenious programming. Alongside the old-time family shows, there were musicals like *Hair*, complete with its notorious on-stage nudity and swearing. This was made possible because the long reign of the Lord Chamberlain as censor of plays, since 1737, came to an end in 1968. After a sell-out West End season, the show arrived at the Metropole and had been seen by over 200,000 patrons when it closed on 28 March 1971 after a run of thirty-eight weeks. It was the Glasgow production that helped establish Cameron (now Sir) Mackintosh's career as a producer. Unfortunately,

Figure 3.36   Frontage of the Metropole, St. Georges Road.

Jimmy Logan's brave attempts to make his Metropole a success were constantly thwarted by officialdom. He was refused permission to open a restaurant, which would have been a money-making attraction as the theatre was well away from the city's main dining and drinking areas. Glasgow's planners, meanwhile decided to blight the St. George's Cross area: by smashing their crass urban ring road through the densely populated Cowcaddens and Woodside areas, effectively isolating it from the city centre. They determined that Anderston, with its brutalist shopping arcades (since demolished) was to be Glasgow's new entertainment focus – a ridiculous notion.

Understandably, after so much hard effort, Jimmy Logan became very dejected when, as a result of this, audiences started to dwindle, but his loyal staff still had to be paid.

> The Metropole became a real worry and a burden. We tried everything, but the city planners were having all the streets around it pulled down.

Folk don't want to go out to the theatre and have to pass skips of rubble and dereliction, so I really don't blame them for staying home as it was a heartbreaking sight. Reo Stakis wanted to buy a big chunk of St. George's Road for a hotel and casino. He said he'd also build a new theatre for me, so all the agreements were made and they put in for planning permission. It was refused and the Metropole was instead listed. When far more important buildings were still being demolished, this struck me as being very odd. Without an audience, I was forced to put the shutters up. It really was the worst situation.

Figure 3.37   Auditorium of the Metropole.

Having effectively sealed the Metropole's fate, the Corporation now refused to buy it and it lay in a state of increasing dereliction for the next fifteen years. The interior was damaged by a fire in 1982, and the abandoned building subsequently became a popular roost for thousands of pigeons. In November 1987 the Metropole, by then an eyesore, was demolished for a housing development. It was a pity to lose such a fine and solid building, which could so easily have become a live music venue, or even a theatre once again especially as, not three years later, in 1990 Glasgow became 'European City of Culture' and all the performance spaces that could be found were urgently required.

THE LYCEUM

Then an independent burgh, now a district of Glasgow, Govan is synonymous with shipbuilding. The local yards, Fairfields, Stephens, and Harland and Wolff, were the core of the local economy, employing tens of thousands. In 1877 we find the first attempt to establish a legitimate theatre in the area; William Kidston, the proprietor of the Prince's music hall, opened in 1862, applied to local magistrates for a licence, but this was refused as the Prince's was 'down a filthy lane opposite a public house and any large gathering might

Figure 3.38 Govan Road showing the Lyceum Theatre (author collection).

result in trouble'. Govanites had to wait until 1899, when Rich Waldon (of the Royal Princess's) and Ernest Stevens opened their magnificent **Lyceum Theatre** on 14 November.

The building, designed by David Barclay, at once became a favourite local landmark with its flamboyant red-sandstone corner entrance projecting from the surrounding tenements of Govan Road and rising as a corbelled tower, topped by an onion-dome. Inside, the foyer was clad in dazzling white marble with crimson drapes, while the two-tiered auditorium was decorated in the Italian Renaissance style, with gilded plaster work and statues on either side supporting a richly frescoed ceiling in the form of a saucer-dome. There was seating for 2,300, and room for a further 700 standees, making the Lyceum the largest theatre in the Glasgow area at that time. In front of the auditorium, there were elegant lounges for circle patrons with buttoned plush settees and tapestry rugs. As an added attraction, there was a billiard room in the basement with nineteen tables, which was said to be the largest outside London.

In 1902 'animated pictures' were presented in Govan for the first time at

*Figure 3.39   A sketch of the interior of the Lyceum from
an old theatre programme* (author collection).

the Lyceum. Although opera, musical comedies and drama remained popular, they were expensive to stage, so the Lyceum became a music hall around 1912. Gradually cinema shows played a larger role in its success, and it was leased to George Urie Scott for cine-variety in 1923. By the 1930s it was a full-time cinema, so the proscenium was removed and the seating extended into the stage with one large balcony in 1932. This was but a brief interlude, as the old Lyceum burned down on the night of 23 October 1937 and was replaced by a modern purpose-built cinema of the same name.

NOTES

1. *Glasgow Herald*, 16 April 1817.
2. In November 1845, the *Illustrated London News* reported on the proliferation of show booths around Glasgow Green.
3. Miller was fined £100 for performing plays without Letters Patent. Sympathy lay with him and the fine was paid by public subscription.
4. Hamilton's output from 1802 in Glasgow included Hutchison's Hospital, the Royal Exchange (now the Gallery of Modern Art) and the portico of the Union Bank in Ingram Street, later re-used on Her Majesty's Theatre.
5. Coatbridge-based architect. Also designed King's Theatre in Edinburgh.
6. Prolific Glasgow-based designer of serious classical buildings, including St. Andrew's Halls, Kelvingrove Parish Church and Kelvinside Academy, which makes his light-hearted approach to the design of this one-off theatre all the more interesting.
7. In 1867 Bayliss opened the Royal Colosseum and the Scotia was run thereafter by his wife, Christina.
8. Father of Stan Laurel.
9. The Frutins also ran a chain of large suburban cinemas around Glasgow, including the New Bedford, Granada, Tudor and Oxford. These all had full stage facilities and successful performers from the Metropole were sent to entertain the audiences between the films.
10. Interview with Derek Sugden.
11. Interview with John Fairley.
12. Ibid.
13. Information supplied by Ronald Singleton, son of George Singleton.
14. From an extensive description in the *Glasgow Herald*, 4 April 1897, and opening brochures in the Baillie's Library Collection located in the Mitchell Library's Glasgow Room.
15. Recalled by Jack House in his regular column in the *Evening Times*, 2 May 1978.
16. Author's conversation with Johnny Beattie.
17. Interview with Donald McKenzie.
18. It has been suggested to the author that the rebuilt Tivoli did not have enough capacity to pay for the rebuild and, being outside the city centre, was forced to charge lower prices of admission – a miscalculation on the part of its owners.
19. Information on the Pavilion's later career supplied by Bob Bain of the Scottish Music Hall Society and one of the Pavilion's staunchest supporters.
20. Various articles in the *Glasgow Herald* between 7 October 1977 and 5 January 1978.
21. Lord Provost Sir John and Lady Ure-Primrose and Edinburgh's civic chief, Sir Robert

Cranston, were guests of honour at the opening of the King's. Messages of good luck were sent by top actors of the day performing in London's West End such as Henry Irving, Beerbohm-Tree and J. L. Toole. The opening attraction was *The Cardinal*.

22. See Brian Walker, *Frank Matcham: Theatre Architect*.
23. See Jack House, *I Belong to Glasgow*, p. 22.
24. See the *Evening Times*, 17 September 1976.
25. The *Glasgow Evening News*, 12 May 1965, reported that the new *Five Past Eight* production was 'The Biggest and Best yet . . . Jack Radcliffe is joined this year by Jimmy Logan, an experiment so tremendously successful in the comedy sense. The highlight? Jimmy Logan as Churchill being interviewed within a huge TV cabinet. This is a triumph . . . *Five Past Eight* could run almost indefinitely.'
26. See Sean McCarthy, *Hengler's Circus: A History and Celebration 1847–1924*.
27. At the time of publication, the ABC is up for sale and may shortly be demolished to enable a new retail development to be built.
28. See the *Glasgow News*, 18 September 1911.
29. Interview with Donald McKenzie.
30. Interview with Jimmy Logan.

PAISLEY

Paisley, an industrial town to the south of the Clyde was famed for its weaving mills and fine municipal buildings. Before the industrial revolution brought growth and prosperity, the theatre had already been established; from around 1800, plays were given in a converted barn, known as Higlet's Hayloft, near Seedhill Bridge on the River Cart. Access was up an outside wooden staircase, and it is said that the young Edmund Kean once acted Shakespeare there before he found fame in London. Later, about 1822, a hall attached to the Saracen's Head Inn was fitted up as a theatre. Two years after, the ballroom adjunct to the Tontine Inn in Bank Street was similarly converted. About the same time, a derelict building in New Smithmills became yet another primitive theatre with a wooden interior and Kean, who evidently gained many admirers in Paisley, returned to play *Richard III* there in 1832. Kean Jnr also performed there, aged only eighteen, and admission prices were 2s to 6d with a surcharge of 1s when a London company was performing. These buildings were obviously rather makeshift, but they paved the way for two larger venues. In 1840 the Exchange Rooms in Moss Street were converted with a proscenium stage and run as the Theatre Royal. When the second Paisley Theatre opened in 1890, the Theatre Royal became a music hall called the Empire, owned by J. H. Savile with an American circus performer Delino Fritz as manager. It closed in 1904 when Fritz returned home.

An old factory building in Abercorn Street was converted to the first Paisley Theatre, but facing pressure from local Kirk Sessions alarmed at the growth of so many seedy rivals, the Paisley magistrates ruled that it could not open more than 120 days a year and prices had to be a minimum of 6d. A Mr Adams was manager, reputedly bringing excellent companies from Glasgow.

The first properly equipped theatre in Paisley was the Royalty, opened in 1845, and there was soon keen competition between it and the Theatre Royal in securing the best touring companies. Unfortunately, the Royalty was destroyed in a disastrous fire in 1887, but its place was soon taken by the much larger Paisley Theatre.

The Paisley Theatre in Smithfields Street was built for Henry T. Brickwell, a Londoner who had run the Royalty for its last seven years. His new venture was an early collaboration by two young London architects, W. G. R. Sprague and Bertie Crewe. Each went on to become a theatre designer of brilliance. Crewe later produced dozens of opulent variety houses the length of Britain, including the Pavilion and Palace in Glasgow, while Sprague perhaps achieved even more status by designing a clutch of superb Italian Renaissance-style theatres in London's prestigious West End. Wyndham's, the Albery and the Strand are some of the finest theatres ever erected in Britain. Their early work together lacked such architectural fireworks, although the modest Paisley Theatre was advertised as 'the first entirely fireproof theatre outside London', being built entirely around iron frames. What was not envisaged was the need to place duck boards in the dressing rooms as when the Cart was in spate, they flooded and throughout its long career there was a constant smell of damp with fungus growing on the ceiling.

It opened on 23 October 1890 with the Paul Jones Opera Company playing selections to a crowded audience of 1,200. After lukewarm reviews in Glasgow, the company gave a first-rate performance at the new theatre and got a long standing ovation. No wonder everyone was in festive mood that night for Brickwell's new playhouse was indeed very well appointed. It had a modest red-brick frontage with stone dressings and gas lanterns on the canopy, but the auditorium, with two rectangular tiers and four stage boxes, was grand, being in the French Renaissance style favoured by Crewe. A report in the *Paisley and Renfrewshire Gazette* records that the seating was 'deeply upholstered in crimson Utrecht velvet . . . the hangings in the boxes being of peacock blue Roman satin with fibrous plaster decorations in shades of gold, set off by wall-paper of a rich, warm colour specially designed by Messrs Cowan and Stewart of Paisley.'

For a spell around 1916, the theatre was managed by J. H. Savile, the local impresario who had previously owned the Empire. In 1921 control passed to E. H. Bostock, the showman whose Scottish Central Theatre Company controlled four other theatres across the Central Belt. In 1934 the Victoria Circuit became lessees and after the Second World War William Galt took over, renaming Paisley Theatre the Victory.

Jimmy Logan, who had many successes there, recalls its post-war phase with affection:

> I left school at sixteen, and being in a theatre family, I was glad to get
> a job as assistant manager at the old Paisley Theatre, earning £2 a

week. I suppose I was a big strapping lad, and it was just as well as the job description was actually a euphemism for 'chucker out' when drunk patrons created trouble. Later in the early fifties, I was appearing on stage there when a young producer called Trafford Whitelock spotted me and got me to appear on a new radio series called *It's All Yours*, which was a top programme before the telly came along. Galt also ran a well-known agency in Glasgow and there is a lovely old story about a pole-vaulter who came in looking for work. Nobody ever saw Galt himself, you were greeted instead by Nellie Sutherland, his assistant. After being told that there wasn't work anywhere, he asked her 'What about Paisley?' And Nellie replied, through her loose teeth, 'Ah've telt ye 'fore – yer poles too big for the stage at Paisley,' and then slammed her wee reception window shut.[1]

Although the gallery level was closed during the 1950s, such was the populariy of the Logan family's shows that it had to be brought back into use when they performed. In 1957 Andy Stewart appeared for a successful season of his Scottish song and dance show, but with falling patronage it was shut during the summer. Johnny Beattie headlined the 1958 spring revue and customers were told to look out for a 'Grand Re-opening' after the long summer recess, but the theatre stayed shut until 19 December and the pantomime *Cinderella*. On 10 January 1959 the Victory closed with *The Boy Scouts' Gangshow* and lay derelict until 1967 when Smithfields Street was unsympathetically redeveloped with brutalist commercial blocks.

On 15 October 1906 the Hippodrome, a brick amphitheatre for variety and circuses, opened on a site previously occupied by showman's caravans at Old Smithfields, near to the theatre. Run by E. H. Bostock, this was a single-storey building with a wooden single-span roof to give patrons a clear view of the ring, however it was short-lived for the roof caught fire on 29 February 1916 and the building was destroyed.

CLYDEBANK

The first purpose-built theatre in Clydebank was the New Gaiety. Located on the corner of Elgin Street and Glasgow Road, it sat 1,400 in stalls, pit, dress and upper circle. A drama policy was tried from the opening on 29 January 1902 'for the improvement of Clydebank's minds', according to a newspaper report. The Gaiety received a poor response; after working in heavy industry, most customers wanted light entertainment to relax, not to be improved! The Gaiety became a music hall instead, with a Friday-night talent contest, which ended in a tug-of-war competition for audience members on stage.

On 14 September 1908 the Gaiety came under the aegis of the flamboyant and eccentric showman A. E. Pickard, who styled himself 'A. E. Pickard Unlimited of London, Paris, Moscow and Bannockburn'. Having introduced picture shows at his Panopticon in Glasgow, he placed advertisements in the local Clydebank papers to the effect that 'Pickard's Perfect Cinematograph Pictures, known throughout the Empire, are coming!!!!' These were supple-mented with some of the bizarre variety turns from his Glasgow theatre – 'Polly, the Mysterious Hairy Lady, Winona, the Champion Lady Aerial Shot of the World, the Brothers Ferguson, Midget Champions in Wooden Shoes and Alf Warner, Novelty Musician and Raconteur'. The theatre closed on 9 June 1917 with a revue appropriately called *Cheerio*. After a renovation, it opened again eight weeks later as the Bank Cinema and was sold to ABC in 1927. It narrowly avoided being hit in the Clydebank Blitz during the Second World War, but, being rather a ramshackle building, was closed finally in 1961 and demolished. The Palace of Varieties in nearby Graham Street was less fortunate. It was a corrugated-iron music hall on one level with a twin-towered stucco facade. Having included the Bioscope in its billings over many years, it became a full-time cinema, but took a direct hit from a bomb in 1941.

Amid the celebrations of Hogmanay in 1914, the Empire Theatre in Glasgow Road opened its doors. By George A. Boswell, a Glasgow architect who also produced churches and cinemas, it was electrically lit with seating for 800 in the stalls and circle and 500 in the gallery. Some of the more outlandish performers at the Empire were Elroy, 'the armless wonder whose feet perform the actions usually delegated to the hands'; Cora Corina, the quick-change artiste; and Lena and Lewis, billed as 'the black and white comic duo'. The Empire was an original member of John Maxwell's Scottish Cinema and Variety Theatres circuit when it was formed in 1917. It became a full-time cinema with one balcony after 1928 and was destroyed by fire overnight on 21 June 1959.

The fourth addition to Clydebank's music halls opened on 29 December 1919. The Pavilion in Kilbowie Road was a member of George Urie Scott's Glasgow-based circuit of theatres and cinemas. Again with an ornate twin-towered frontage in Louis XVI style, it was an elliptical stadium-type hall with a thirty-foot-square stage projecting into the auditorium like a kind of amphi-theatre. The 2,000 oak seats were made by disabled soldiers. Clydebank's civic heads attended the opening, when juggler Pauline Mars and a comic singing troupe called the Five Jocks headed the bill, and the Bioscope, which became a popular feature of Pavilion programmes, appeared alongside music hall, pantomime, plays and talent evenings.[2]

At the outbreak of the Second World War, many benefit nights were held in the Pavilion to raise money to help the war effort. Ironically, it was not a German bomb, but a fire which destroyed the building on 8 October 1942.

The resort towns on the beautiful Clyde coast were all connected with Glasgow by a network of steamer routes and the suburban railways. When the

Victorian quest for self-improvement through better health made seaside holidays in bracing fresh air popular, these towns expanded rapidly. A profusion of ornately decorated Victorian buildings – from richly tiled urinals to grand hotels – were built, as well as some excellent theatres and pavilions. During the Glasgow Fair holiday, many hundreds of thousands of Glaswegians sailed down the Clyde; most theatres in the city were closed for the summer and instead a carnival atmosphere prevailed in the resorts, with their waterfront illuminations and holidaymakers dancing to the latest hits by the bandstands. All the favourite comics and entertainers featured in colourful summer shows and such indoor entertainment was highly popular due to the notorious west of Scotland climate.

GREENOCK

Sailing past the Inverclyde conurbation of Port Glasgow, Greenock and Gourock, one would have seen shipyards and basins full of ships, lofty ware-houses and the landmark customs building rising behind. Basing its wealth on trade and engineering (a famous son was James Watt, improver of the steam engine), Greenock was a prosperous town by mid-century.

Towards the end of the eighteenth century, theatrical performances were given in a hall at the eastern end of Cathcart Street. Later, in 1809, the actor-manager Stephen Kemble erected a theatre in Mansionhouse Lane. It was initially popular, attracting companies led by Kean and Macready. Following its closure in 1854, the *Greenock Telegraph* recorded that it was latterly 'in such a state of dirt, disrepair and discomfort and the representations have been of such a mediocre description, to speak mildly, that we think its decline and fall will not be deplored as a public loss ... In days of yore, it was nightly frequented by the beauty and fashion of Greenock, but of late years, its state of disrepair ... has lead to its total desertion by the better class.' Kemble's Theatre was converted to a store, but all trace of it has long since vanished.

On 27 December 1858 Edmund Glover, the well-known actor-manager of the Theatre Royal in Glasgow's Dunlop Street, opened a magnificent newly built Theatre Royal in West Blackhall Street. It was designed by Joseph Potts, a Sunderland architect and was thought to be one of the finest provincial theatres of the period. The facade had niches which contained statuary of the great dramatists, removed from Glover's Theatre Royal in Glasgow. Entrances to the pit and gallery were at either end, and between was the circle foyer, with a floor of black and white marble slabs and a gas chandelier. The *Greenock Advertiser* described its lavish appointments. 'The proscenium is framed by Corinthian columns with an elliptical arch above. The decorations are white and gold and the ornamentation is extremely chaste and elegant. The fronts of the boxes are adorned with scrolls, alternated by medallions, containing groups of figures in bas relief on a blue ground, while the roof above the pit will be covered by a painting of the Muses . . . The pit is nearly twice as large as that of the Glasgow Theatre Royal and the whole house contains 1,600 persons.' Next door to his theatre, Glover built a concert hall called the Western, which opened on 16 May 1860 with 700 seats and murals of opera scenes on the walls.

Under different managers, notably the brothers J. J. and Alex Wright, the Theatre Royal provided Greenock folk with high-quality drama and opera for almost half a century until a new theatre, the Alexandra, opened almost next door. The Theatre Royal was redecorated to emerge on 28 August 1905 as the Palace Music Hall, run from Glasgow by George Ashton, with Captain Woodward's Trained Seals as the top attraction. It was briefly renamed the Pavilion, before becoming the Hippodrome in 1908, leased by a local man, Harry Skivington. It passed to a local syndicate when he died, but in 1920 Greenock went dry when the council voted for prohibition. All the nearby pubs closed and the Hippodrome suffered badly. Then, the authorities decided to widen and straighten West Blackhall Street and the Hippodrome closed on 1 December 1923 for demolition. The famous statues were removed from the facade and sold by auction. Presumably they now languish in a country-house garden somewhere.

It was James Moss, father of Edward, who was later to found the Moss Empires circuit, who introduced music hall to Greenock in 1873. Travelling with his diorama show and appearing as a comic singer, he rented the Mechanics' Institute in Sir Michael Street. His alliterative posters promised that 'Moss will introduce mirth making merry musical morsels for melancholy moments and mimics of men and manners.' His shows had a strong Irish influence with clog dancing and singing, something which his son continued in his Empires.

Despite its name, the Empire in Manse Lane had nothing to do with Moss, but was developed by an anonymous local syndicate, whose names its secretary refused to reveal even to the licensing committee. Greenock's premier variety theatre opened on 16 March 1903 to the design of Thomas Kennedy, a Glasgow architect. The *Greenock Telegraph* enthused that 'the little thoroughfare presented a lively appearance just prior to the opening of the doors, the effect being heightened by the brilliant light from the large electric lamps over the entrance'. The theatre, though compact, was well appointed. The red- sandstone frontage had pavilions at each end with steeply pitched roofs and there was a large window between, fronting the airy circle lounge. Being cleverly built on a downward slope, with excavation, it was possible to build the pit 'downstairs' with only a short flight of steps to the circle. The auditorium was decorated in the French Renaissance style with plaster garlands around the tiers and fine ceiling paintings.

The Empire was soon a favourite with Greenock folk, but not for long as it was leased to the B.B. Picture Company from March 1910. B.B. stood for 'bright and beautiful' and was the trademark of J. J. Bennell, a Scottish cinema pioneer with halls showing films across the country. The era of pictures supported by variety acts lasted until 1926, when twice-nightly variety shows were reinstated. The Empire was reputedly a rough house, and allegedly, acts who failed to entertain were frequently given a tirade of abuse, and netting was fitted over the orchestra pit to protect the musicians from the rivets sometimes thrown by disillusioned shipyard workers.

It was sold to the brothers David and George Wooley in 1933. The Wooleys were in the licence trade in Greenock and during their tenure, the Empire continued with popular variety. It was extensively renovated in 1954 in response to the public's higher expectations but these improvements were short-lived. The Empire had hosted many amateur productions, but the new Arts Guild Theatre, opened in 1955, took these away. After a spate of summer closures and shortened engagements with twice-nightly performances restricted to Friday and Saturday, the Empire staged its last show on 14 May 1957. Sold to the council the following year, it was leased as a furniture store and auction room for a further ten years before demolition in October 1968, to make way for town-centre redevelopment.

Built as a replacement for the neighbouring Theatre Royal at the junction of Kerr Street and Grey Place, the Alexandra was to be Greenock's lavish new venue for touring opera and drama. Expertly designed on a fan-shaped site by the Greenock architects Boston, Menzies and Morton, the curved landmark frontage, with art nouveau overtones, was capped by a large dome and lantern. Lines of leaded glass windows lighted the circle and gallery bars. The *Greenock Telegraph*'s reporter was obviously impressed by the town's new theatre, opened on 10 August 1905:

> The opening of a new theatre in a provincial town, unlike London where they spring up like mushrooms, is one of the events of a lifetime, and tonight the formal opening of the magnificent Alexandra will be done by Sir Hugh Shaw Stewart Bart, who will unveil a memorial stone in the Grand foyer... The house has accommodation for 1,900 persons and has two tiers... there are in all ten private boxes, two of them being on the pit level, four on the dress circle level and the rest in front of the gallery. The outstanding internal decorations are of fibrous plaster in cream and gold with touches of cameo here and there to emphasise the ornament, which is French renaissance in character. Special notice must be taken of the allegorical painting in the ceiling dome representing comedy and tragedy. The boxes are draped with tastefully stencilled art canvas curtains, the floor of the orchestra stalls

being covered in a rich green Axminster carpet, the entire seating being tip-up and upholstered in old gold velvet.

The following day, a wonderfully evocative description of the opening night described how 'the brilliantly lighted interior was filled with an immense throng of gaily dressed ladies and gentlemen in evening dress, making up a picture that will never fade from the minds of those who were privileged to be present . . . When all had assembled, the drop scene, itself a work of art, was raised, disclosing the immense stage, daintily set off. Miss Marie Nilsson, in a soprano voice of exquisite quality, sang a verse from the National Anthem, which the audience, upstanding repeated with loud enthusiasm.' Finally, R. C. Buchanan, the managing director of the owning firm, and Mr Alex B. Wright, the manager (who had guided the Theatre Royal in its final years), made speeches.

It was renamed the **King's** Theatre in 1910 and continued as a top touring theatre with occasional local amateur shows until taken over by E. H. Bostock in 1926. The King's was next leased to Sydney Friedman, a London-based cinema pioneer from the era of travelling shows, who spent four months converting the King's to a cinema, which opened on 6 August 1928 with the silent epic *Dawn*, accompanied by a full orchestra. It became Greenock's premier

Figure 4.1 The King's and Hippodrome, Greenock (author collection).

'talkie' house in January 1929. The King's made a brief return to stage shows during the Second World War when a number of shows were produced for servicemen in the district.

Bought by the Rank Organisation in October 1955, the upper circle, boxes and stage were stripped away, dressing rooms removed and the auditorium extended to the back wall, before re-opening as the Odeon in January 1956. Although the facade remained, the interior bore no resemblance to the once palatial theatre. It was closed in October 1969 and after a compulsory purchase order was served, it was demolished in April 1973. A crowd gathered as the still grand facade was sent tumbling down by a pole demolisher. While the youths cheered at the spectacle, older folk who remembered the building in its heyday looked on with sad faces as Greenock lost yet another fine landmark to the developers.

Originally St. Michael's Church in Argyle Street, a new music hall, the Argyle, with 1,000 tip-up seats was opened on 1 October 1928. Advertised as 'Greenock's Cosy Corner' featuring Ellis Drake and Dr Walford Bodie among early attractions, it was not a success and became a boxing arena. The Mechanics' Institute moved in when its Tobago Street premises were blitzed in 1941 and the building, with its tell-tale fly tower still stands as a furniture emporium and pool hall.

DUNOON

The attractive resort town of Dunoon had minarets on its magnificent steamer pier and a waterfront fairground. Immediately behind in Castle Gardens was the **Pavilion,** a very imposing all-purpose theatre, concert and dance hall with a great circular auditorium behind a restaurant with a view over the busy river scene. Having squabbled and fretted over specifications, the council finally gave the go-ahead and the Pavilion was opened by the Duke of Argyll and HRH the Princess Louise on 17 August 1905. It was designed by William Fraser in a style similar to some of the pavilions at Glasgow's great exhibitions.[3]

Sadly, this exotic building was destroyed by fire early in the morning of 3 April 1949. This was a terrible blow for Dunoon at the start of the summer season, so two portable military hangars were bought as a temporary replacement and it was another nine years before its modern replacement opened in nearby Pier Road. A commodious, if now somewhat decrepit, building in 1950s style, the Queen's Hall still entertains with everything from pensioners' tea dances to rock concerts.

ROTHESAY

Beautifully located in a wide, sheltered bay, Rothesay, 'the Madeira of Scotland', is still the doyen of Clyde resorts. For the thousands arriving by steamer

Figure 4.2   The Pavilion, Dunoon (author collection).

through the decades, its principal landmark is the **Winter Gardens Pavilion**. Standing proudly in the middle of its immaculately maintained waterfront lawns, the Winter Gardens started life in the 1890s as an open-air bandstand. Later, in 1911, it was replaced by a larger structure with a seated amphitheatre, which was leased to Fyfe and Fyfe, the Glasgow entertainment firm. On its stage, colourful Pierrot shows entertained the holidaymakers, but the sometimes wet climate persuaded the authorities to enclose the structure. An order was placed with Walter Macfarlane's famous ironworks in Glasgow's Possil district for a commodious new hall to cover the entire site. It was designed by Macfarlane's own team, with a local architect, Alex Stevens, supervising construction. Macfarlane's were experts at iron structures, and their fine work can be found all over the former British Empire (their Rothesay building has a more angular sister at Ryde on the Isle of Wight). In 1924 the parts for the new structure, costing £7,000, were floated down the Clyde on barges. It was an unusual but elegant design with art nouveau details, corner towers, and wide curving windows, looking out over the bay. Its wide, gently domed roof was held up by an ingenious system of exposed curving iron beams, which were both elegantly shaped and functional. There was seating for 1,100 with comfortable tip-ups in the first ten rows and long benches to the rear.

Lessees of the 1,200-seat hall for over twenty years were still Fyfe and Fyfe, who presented Gordon Inglis's Rothesay Entertainers twice nightly during many summer seasons. The group, with local accordionist Ella Wilson, continued to give music and humour until 1971 when declining tourist trade was brought about by cheap package holidays to sunny Spain.[4]

During the late 1970s and early 1980s the Winter Gardens fell into a terrible state of dereliction, something which exacerbated Rothesay's decline as a resort. After much lobbying by local amenity and architectural heritage concerns, it was finally decided to rebuild in 1987 with a multi-use hall, cinema and restaurant. It was completed in May 1990. The work was very successful and has helped to transform Rothesay's fortunes. After a few scares with flooding and early financial problems, the Winter Gardens has once again become a firm favourite with residents and visitors alike, its ceilidhs being a big attraction.

In 1936 the Winter Gardens got a rival when the Pavilion, a sensationally streamlined hall and restaurant complex, was built further along the promenade. It was designed by James Carrick and was heavily influenced by Eric Mendelsohn's De La Warr Pavilion at Bexhill-On-Sea. Not centrally located, it only hosted occasional variety shows, but survives today as a conference, concert, dancing and exhibition venue.

The Palace theatre was less fortunate. It stood to the rear of an imposing Louis XV-style tenement block with steep mansard roofs in East Princess Street by the harbour and was originally Rothesay's public hall of 1879. It had one tier with long slips, decorated with egg and dart moulding and a lofty barrel-vaulted

Figure 4.3 Rothesay Winter Gardens (author collection).

Figure 4.4   *Rothesay's Open Air Theatre with Pierrot Show.*

Figure 4.5   *Rothesay Waterfront showing the Palace* (author collection).

ceiling. A proscenium arch was built in 1909, when it became a music hall, run by local entrepreneurs James and Robert Duncan. Eventually a cinema, run by Caledonian Associated Cinemas, it was flattened by a landslide in the mid-1970s, although the tenement in front remains.

NOTES

1. Interview with Jimmy Logan.
2. Born within sight of the theatre, Lex McLean made his professional debut there as a pianist in the orchestra. Scott realised he had comic talent and sent him touring round his theatres and cinemas in Glasgow and Lanarkshire. By the 1950s McLean had become one of Scotland's favourite comics.
3. The summer 'Cowal Carnivals', presented at the Pavilion in the 1930s, were typical seaside shows with casts of fifteen, including dancers. An arrangement was made with Glasgow Corporation Parks Department for concert parties to visit the Dunoon Pavilion for week-long stints after their tours of the city's bandstands.
4. After the Second World War, Fraser Neal became lessee and highlights from the 1950s were Francie and Josie from the King's in Glasgow, Lex McLean and Jimmy Reid.

BURNS COUNTRY

AYR

In his *Recollections of Ayr Theatricals from 1809*, James Morris writes that in 1809 a former soap works by the gates of Dalblair House was being run as a theatre 'with a surprisingly good company headed by Mr Beaumont'. The works had been owned by a Mr Gibb, who built Dalblair, expecting to marry into a wealthy family. The marriage did not take place and Gibb went bankrupt. Consequently, the theatre closed and until 1812, performances were given in a hastily converted hall in Content Street. In 1815 a new purpose-built theatre was erected at the junction of Fort Street and Wellington Square. The Theatre Royal was developed by the lessee of Ayr's previous theatre venues, H. E. Johnston. A modest building of undressed sandstone with a simple stucco facade in classical style, it attracted the highly regarded Edinburgh companies of Henry Siddons and William Murray. Unfortunately, the drama was not sufficiently popular in Ayr to support a legitimate theatre. Morris wrote of a performance of *The Moor of Venice* with Edmund Kean as Othello. As the great tragedian was about to address the Senate in the hushed auditorium, a bored voice from the pit called out 'Whane wull the ferce begin?' The Theatre Royal became the Queen's Hall for concerts in the 1860s and, later, the Ayr Baptist Church. The interior was gutted in the conversion, although the facade remains intact.

The future of the theatre in Ayr was in light entertainment. During the 1800s temporary canvas theatres or 'geggies' were a common feature of the entertainment scene in Scotland's market towns. One such geggie, owned by the local partnership of Pierce and Bolton, stood just off Carrick Street in Ayr (Fred Bolton's daughter, Lily, became the first wife of the comic Will Fyffe). By the turn of the century it seemed to have attained some degree of permanency, becoming a wooden structure advertised as the Caledonian Theatre, but it was soon replaced by a substantial new theatre, built on land directly in front.

The **Gaiety**, which during an eventful career became one of Scotland's favourite houses of variety, was first opened on 1 October 1902, designed by a local architect, J. McHardy Young. Outside it had an unremarkable frontage of red brick. The interior, for 1,200, had two tiers and cost £9,500 in total. At the opening ceremony there was a concert and R. A. Oswald, the county convenor, declared it open and it was not until the following Monday that a play was performed for a full house. Excitement ran so high that a sketch entitled *Hogmanay* was almost entirely drowned out by the boisterous behaviour of the 'gods'. The enthusiasm did not last and despite strong touring casts, Ayr folk seemingly preferred pictures at Green's and the Electric to the Gaiety's opera and drama. In 1904 the auditorium was badly damaged by fire, and was remodelled by Alexander Cullen who designed the ornate baroque fibrous plaster work, the quality of which later helped to save it from demolition. The proscenium arch only reached the bottom of the boxes at gallery height because the existing fly tower was low and the space above was filled with painted panels.

Reverting unsuccessfully to drama, the Gaiety's management next tried films, run by a local firm called Ayr Picture Palaces, but even this eventually failed as there were many more suitable purpose-built cinemas in town (including the firm's own Palace in Burns Statue Square) and, notwithstanding Ayr's prominence as a popular summer resort, the Gaiety began to make losses.

Figure 5.1   Ayr Gaiety Theatre as built (author collection).

Figure 5.2 The Pavilion, Ayr, when first completed (author collection).

Ben Popplewell, a Bradford-born impresario and performer who had once featured in the Pierrot show at Clacton-On-Sea, was the unlikely saviour of both the Gaiety and Ayr's other white elephant, the Pavilion by the promenade. After spells running shows in Blackpool and in his native Bradford, Popplewell became a stockbroker. He maintained a financial interest in the theatre which took him to Ayr to find out what was going wrong with an investment he had in the company which leased the Pavilion from the local authority. He must have liked the town, for aged forty-three years and with a wife and family to support, he abandoned his career in finance and moved to Ayr to take personal charge of the Pavilion in May 1913. A public venture, it first opened on 23 May 1911, having cost rate-payers £8,000. With space for over 2,500, it was a multi-purpose hall with a horseshoe balcony and was designed by J. K. Hunter. Outside there were tall, slender Italianate towers at each corner.

Popplewell lost no time in bringing the biggest names in variety – like George Formby, Florrie Forde and Dr Walford Bodie – to the Pavilion, which he billed as 'The House that Rocks with Laughter'. It was a great success, but in November 1918, the lease ran out. Tired out and with his sons doing national service, Popplewell went home to Bradford and the Fred Collins circuit took over for a time.[1]

In May 1922 Ben Popplewell and his sons, Leslie and Eric, returned to Ayr and the Pavilion – this time for good. In 1925 the family bought out its rivals,

Ayr Picture Palaces. Their Palace cinema was leased out to become the Bobby Jones Ballroom, but, for Ben Popplewell, the Gaiety obviously had great potential as a variety theatre. Having brought most of the best-known music-hall stars from all over Britain to the Pavilion and the Gaiety, in 1930 the Popplewells decided to use the theatre for a lavishly produced summer revue show with 'A Powerful Cast of Thirty Brilliant Artistes', compered by J. H. Wakefield, hired specially from the prestigious London Palladium. What became 'The Gaiety Whirl' in its second year was an outstanding show with beautiful costumes, music and scenery. It was acknowledged as the best summer show on the Clyde and did much to bolster Ayr's popularity as a resort. The Pavilion was relinquished and became a dance hall at the same time. The Gaiety was refurbished in 1935 with more comfortable seating, suitable for its status as a top-class variety house, and a modernised facade. A great improvement, it had the smart look of a modern cinema with cream and black faience tiles, neon lights and a bold, vertical sign.

Each summer, the Popplewells devised new line-ups of top entertainment, presenting Will Fyffe, Sir Harry Lauder, Flanagan and Allen, Tommy Lorne, Harry Gordon, the Logan family and many others.

Ben Popplewell died in 1950, and his sons, Leslie and Eric, continued the enterprise with pantomimes around the festive period, the summer 'Whirl', and variety in between packing the theatre. On 2 August 1955 the stage was gutted by fire, but mercifully the iron curtain was down so the auditorium escaped unscathed. After much thought, it was decided to rebuild the stage and the Gaiety was back in business with the 'Whirl' the following July. Insurance only covered half the cost of £60,000 and the Popplewells had to dig deep into their finances at a time when television was an ominous threat. In 1963 Eric Popplewell joined the board of the Glasgow Pavilion and this bolstered both theatres at a time when variety venues were closing everywhere. With their enthusiasm, the Gaiety kept up high standards, nurturing new talent, like the young Johnny Beattie, who made his debut there in the 1958/9 winter show. He later starred in many 'Whirls' and pantomimes, becoming known as 'the comedy king of Ayr'. He wrote the first of his own pantomimes, *Wee Willie Winkie*, for the Gaiety. As a respected star of the stage and television in Scotland, he was later to be instrumental in saving the Gaiety from destruction and redevelopment.

In 1965 the Gaiety was bought outright by Glasgow Pavilion Ltd, from which Eric Popplewell finally retired in 1973. Profit margins became very slender as admission prices could not keep up with the overheads of hiring musicians, costumes and big-name stars, many now used to generous television wages. The *Ayrshire Post* of 24 November 1972 carried a sensational front- page story – the Gaiety's owners in Glasgow had sold out to a property company to make way for a retail development. Perhaps Ayr folk had taken its survival for granted, instead of paying regular visits to guarantee its future. Long-serving members of staff and performers, like Johnny Beattie, who stayed loyal to the theatre, were appalled. He recalls:

> Of course the Gaiety was very, very dear to me. I probably owe my career to it, but there was more than sentimentality. When you're in 'the business', you have to have places to perform, and we all watched with dismay as old favourites like the Metropole, the Empire [Glasgow] and the Palladium [Edinburgh] were pulled down . . . the Gaiety was a really special place with the warmest, friendliest audience . . . you felt like you could reach out and touch them all from the stage . . . that was the rapport you had in there, and there was also the golden plaster decorations, well you just can't make something like that in a modern place, not the same. These old houses had such an atmosphere at panto time, even before the curtain went up. The Gaiety had to stay and it would only have taken a wee subsidy to make it pay.[2]

A committee was formed in December 1972 to save the Gaiety. Johnny Beattie and other stars threatened to chain themselves to the front doors to stop the bulldozers. Behind the scenes, the Gaiety was surveyed by Scottish Office inspectors and because of its fibrous plaster decoration, was given grade B-listed status. Ayr Town Council was finally persuaded to buy the Gaiety in November 1973 for £72,000. The developers were thwarted and it has been delighting audiences ever since. In 1995 it was fully refurbished with a mediocre new extension to house offices, dressing rooms, a new box office and a highly popular café. There are now regular theatre workshops for school children, which should attract a new generation to the Gaiety. As a result, the building is full of activity throughout the day.

Ayr has managed to retain both of its Edwardian pleasure palaces, although the recent history of the Pavilion has been more controversial. After a number of short leases, it fell into disuse in the 1970s, but was later revived to house disco events. More recently, it has been used for pensioners' tea dances and as a venue for raves called Hangar 13. This made national headlines when some unfortunate young clubbers died outside the hall from the effects of taking ecstasy pills. Its entertainments licence was temporarily revoked while security was improved, but soon both the Gaiety and Pavilion were once again busy entertaining Ayrshire folk, offering very different types of pleasure. Today, Ayr has three theatre venues. Apart from the Gaiety, disused church buildings have been converted, one to Ayr Civic Theatre, hosting amateur productions, and another as the home of the innovative Borderline Theatre Company.

DUMFRIES

Dumfries is a prosperous market town on the banks of the River Nith. The Dumfries Theatre in Shakespeare Street was opened on 29 September 1792 during the reign of George III. Until then, strolling players had used the old Assembly Room in the nearby George Hotel for their shows. However, in 1790, Mr George Stephen Sutherland, an actor-manager who had been playing with a company at the Assembly Room, approached various people in Dumfries and its environs to raise money for a proper theatre in the town.

Robert Burns, writing from Ellisland to his friend William Nicol in February 1790, said:

> Our theatrical company, of which you must have heard, leave us this week. Their merit and character are indeed very great, both on the stage and in private life, not a worthless creature among them; and their encouragement has been accordingly... there have been instances of sending away six and eight and ten pounds a night for want of room. A new theatre is to be built by subscription... three hundred guineas have been raised by thirty subscribers and thirty more might have been got if wanted. The manager, Mr Sutherland, was introduced to me by a friend from Ayr; and a worthier or cleverer fellow I have rarely met with.

Plans, by Thomas Boyd, said to be based on the Theatre Royal, Bristol, were submitted to the magistrates, but once construction began the money was quickly used up and £500 was eventually needed to complete the theatre.

It opened under the management of Mr Williamson, from the Theatre Royal in London's Haymarket, assisted by Mr Sutherland. The event was reported in the *Dumfries Weekly Journal*, which stated 'the united elegance and accommodation of the house reflected equal honour on the liberality and taste of the proprietors, and design and execution of the artists, and conspired with the abilities of the performers in giving universal satisfaction to a crowded and polite audience'.

The front of the theatre was in classical style with a portico of four Doric columns. The interior consisted of a pit, excavated into the ground, a horse-shoe-shaped dress circle, the rear of which consisted entirely of boxes, and above that the gallery. Each box, which was divided into pens containing a number of seats, was entered by a baize-covered door with an oval glass panel in it, and was draped with crimson curtains. According to a reporter, it was then 'the handsomest provincial theatre in Scotland'. No expense had been spared, to the extent that Alexander Nasmyth, who had painted a famous portrait of Burns five years previously, was commissioned to design some of the scenery, and one of his sketches, showing a palatial drawing-room setting, is now in the National Gallery in Edinburgh.

Not long after its opening, a riot nearly occurred in which Burns was involved. This was a period of high political tension. The French Revolution had broken out in 1789, and by 1792 the government was afraid that revolutionary ideas might be gaining ground in Britain. Some Scots had initially welcomed the revolution as the beginning of a new liberal age, but as its reign of terror progressed, their opinions became bitterly divided. Dumfries was a fashionable place, the winter retreat of prosperous families from all over the south of Scotland. They were avid patrons of the theatre and on 30 October 1792 there was a gala performance of *As You Like It*, for the gentlemen of the Caledonian and the Dumfries and Galloway Hunts. The distinguished audience included the Marquis of Queensbury and his party. When 'God Save The King' was called for after the play, there were counter calls from the pit for 'ça ira', the song of the French revolutionaries. Scuffling and shouting broke out, which was quickly suppressed and drowned by the singing of the National Anthem, although it was noticed that Robert Burns remained seated, which was thought a scandalous act of defiance when public feeling was running high against the French.

In June 1810 the *Dumfries and Galloway Courier* carried a notice stating that the Theatre was 'Patronised by Her Majesty, First Time these Seventeen Years', a reference to its being granted Letters Patent, for it was advertised for the first time as the **Theatre Royal** during the next season. In 1815 it was leased to John Macready of the Theatre Royal Newcastle for £40 a year. His son, William Charles Macready, was a well-known actor-manager, reputedly very fond of Dumfries, who, at the height of his fame in 1845, played Hamlet, Shylock and Richelieu there. The stage was enlarged in 1830 before Miss Jarman from the Theatre Royal Covent Garden played in *Rob Roy*.

In 1876 a radical renovation of the theatre was carried out to a Charles J. Phipps design. A new facade was added and land was bought next door for more dressing rooms. The most radical change was to the auditorium with enriched Corinthian pilasters and painted panels framing the proscenium. The dress-circle front was of stylised metal leaves and both tiers were supported by slender iron columns. There was room for over 1,000 patrons and the alterations cost nearly £3,000. The Theatre Royal was re-opened in September 1876. A vivid description of a benefit performance in the latter years of the nineteenth century is to be found in *The Greenwood Hat* by J. M. Barrie, who spent some years of his youth in Dumfries and was a keen member of the Theatre Royal's audience.

From the turn of the century, increased interest in the cinema led to the Theatre Royal being leased to Messrs Peter and John Stobie, local auctioneers, who opened the Theatre Royal as a cine-variety venue. About 1920 the pit was

Figure 5.3   Interior of Theatre Royal, Dumfries, after rebuild by Phipps
(courtesy Billy Jardine).

decked over with a maple floor for roller skating with a basement underneath. Phipps's auditorium was soon heavily altered for cinema use and the only remnant of his design was the metal circle front, straightened and reused in the new balcony. It was renamed the Electric Theatre and continued as a picture house until 1954, known locally as 'The Scratcher'. It lay derelict until April 1959 when the Dumfries Guild of Players, a highly dedicated amateur dramatic group, formed in 1913, purchased the historic building and began a renovation, masterminded by their director, Percy Hopkin. It had suffered water penetration, so the roof and ceiling had to be repaired and a new stage and rehearsal spaces were built.

After a formal re-opening by Sir Compton Mackenzie, the first Guild production was *What Every Woman Knows* by J. M. Barrie in October 1960. The Theatre Royal has continued to play an important part in the cultural life of south-west Scotland ever since. It celebrated its 200th anniversary in 1992 and Scotland's oldest working theatre looks set to continue to entertain well into its third century.[3]

The Lyceum at the south end of the High Street opened in December 1912. Designed by George A. Boswell of Glasgow and built with one level on the stadium plan, it was a cine-variety house run by a local enterprise, whose directors, Robert Oughton, George Russell and Matthew McKerrow, were a restaurateur, a bank agent and a solicitor. Its narrow stage hosted variety stars as great as Harry Lauder and Will Fyffe, but it was outmoded by the 1930s and demolished for a new Lyceum.

It was the work of Alistair G. MacDonald, a noted cinema architect and

Figure 5.4   Exterior of Theatre Royal, Dumfries, after rebuild by Phipps
(courtesy Billy Jardine).

the son of Ramsay MacDonald, the Labour Prime Minister. Construction was delayed when a storm caused the collapse of the exposed steel frames, but the Lyceum finally opened in October 1936. Modest on the outside, it had a striking art deco interior with illuminated shells lighting the side walls, modelled on the New Victoria cinema in London. The new Lyceum had stalls and a balcony with a commodious stage and dressing rooms, and under the direction of the cinema magnate, Alex King, it continued to give top variety shows as well until it was pulled down in January 1970 for a shopping development.

KILMARNOCK

Kilmarnock's first theatre was probably 'Bricket's Hall' in Fore Street, dating from around 1820. Edmund Kean appeared there in a touring company, but in 1852 it was dismantled and replaced by the Commercial Bank building. Also in the 1820s there is documentary evidence that a stable on King Street was fitted with a wooden interior of one tier with boxes and functioned as a theatre until 1835, when it was sold as lumber for £5. A temporary replacement for Bricket's Hall was built under railway arches between Wellington and Bank Streets, but the noise from passing trains must have made it a most unpleasant venue for plays. Its owner, Jock Simpson, was apparently a local character who ran all aspects of the hall and amused his audiences by performing over-the-top dying scenes, and if he was applauded enough, he repeated the death several times to great laughter and applause.

Kilmarnock's first respectable theatre was the Opera House at the foot of John Finnie Street, opened in March 1875. It was designed by James Ingram of Glasgow for a company promoted by John Gilmour, a local entrepreneur. With two tiers and 1,050 seats, it was reputedly well appointed, and being run by William Glover and George Francis of the Theatre Royal, Glasgow, it would have got many high-quality productions. After a few good years of touring drama and opera, interest waned and it was converted to a United Free church in 1885. After different uses, including an auction sale room and various nightclubs, it was gutted by fire in April 1989, although its fine three-storey listed facade has been retained.

Faced in red sandstone and costing £19,000, the imposing **King's Theatre** in Titchfield Street opened on 1 October 1904 with a concert attended by Provost Hood. Telegrams wishing good luck were sent from London by the actors Sir Henry Irving and Beerbohm-Tree. It was a ponderous 2,200 seater, with two tiers and eight boxes in French Renaissance style, designed by Alex Cullen of Hamilton and soon proved to be a giant white elephant. Financed by local businessmen, it was promoted by R. C. Buchanan and Ernest Stephens. The latter ran several theatres and music halls in England.

During the opening week, a production of *Miss Elizabeth's Prisoner* by

Figure 5.5 King's Theatre, Kilmarnock (author collection).

Lewis Waller's company was enthusiastically attended as people were curious to see the decorative wonders of their new theatre. The soaring facade, lit with electric lanterns, was symmetrical and capped by twin turrets with steeply pitched roofs. There were shop units either side of the entrance and high up there was a colonnade with opening windows for patrons to smoke during the interval. Martin Harvey, Frank Benson and Edward Compton were among the distinguished names to tread its boards early on. Notwithstanding the lavish praise heaped on the King's by Compton in his prologue, who 'did not recall so handsome a temple of Thespis in a similar sized town or in most towns of twice Kilmarnock's population', the owning company went into liquidation in 1908.

After six months' closure, it was acquired by John Cummings, lessee of the nearby Corn Exchange hall and later passed to R. C. Buchanan in 1916 for a mere £5,400. Not wanting to risk running it as a theatre again, Buchanan added the King's (which had shown its first film in 1913) to his growing circuit of picture houses. John Maxwell's Scottish Cinema and Variety Theatres acquired it with some other Buchanan properties in 1920. Maxwell's company showed films as well as variety turns but from 1925 silent pictures with orchestral accompaniment became the norm. On 29 May 1929 the King's became one of Scotland's first provincial cinemas to be wired for sound, showing Richard Barthlemass and Betty Compson in *Weary River*. 'Talkies' were complemented by occasional variety nights until 14 April 1934, when the King's closed with a show starring Sir Harry Lauder.

It was drastically rebuilt as the Regal, a 1,853-seat super cinema, with a modern interior by Charles J. McNair. Apart from faience tiles added to the ground storey, the facade was unaltered and the building was split with bingo in the stalls and films upstairs in 1973. After a small fire in 1975, it was converted to three incredibly spartan cinemas, which are open today as the ABC. Little evidence remains of its past as the King's Theatre front of house, but dressing rooms and connecting corridors remain backstage. With a new Odeon multiplex cinema recently opened, the former King's must face an uncertain future.

The imposing Corn Exchange, whose red-sandstone Italianate tower, by James Ingram, dominates the cross at London Road and Green Street, was opened on 16 September 1863 as a multi-use concert hall. One of the first performances featured the Kilmarnock Philharmonic Society with Handel's *Judas Maccabeas*. It became the Palace Theatre in 1903, when a stage was built, but like many such conversions from public halls, it suffered as the balcony faced the proscenium squarely and was isolated from the action on stage by blank side walls. The Grand Agricultural Hall was added to the Palace complex in 1927, and was one of the last commissions for James Miller, a prolific Glasgow architect. This was also fitted with a stage in 1929 and was used as a concert room while the Palace found success as a theatre.

In the 1920s and 1930s, the Palace alternated between cinema and theatre, run by William Cummings, John's son, sometimes showing documentary films like *The Sinking of the Lusitania*. In 1947 a gift of £5,000 meant that the Palace could be converted to Kilmarnock's civic theatre. After £30,000 of work, it opened in 1951 as the Exchange Theatre, but there was not enough money left to pay its running costs and shortly it closed again. On 3 September 1956 the recently formed Kilmarnock Arts Guild, headed by Fred D. Neilson, an amateur actor and one-time tour manager for Duncan Macrae, moved in. While some locals regarded the old Palace as a lost cause, the enthusiastic newcomers began a repertory season there. The council slashed the rent by two-thirds, and the theatre became well established with an annual pantomime and touring shows to supplement the amateur dramatics.

Sadly, the interior was destroyed by fire in 1979. It lay unused for a time, but eventually the council decided that Kilmarnock should once again have its own theatre, and having spent £190,000 on the first stage of refurbishment, the Palace opened its doors again on 31 August 1982. Exactly three years later, and with more spent to improve the foyers and backstage facilities, Billy Connolly came to declare the theatre open. He told the audience, which included Provost Tom Ferguson who had supported its reinstatement, 'I love the way you change the theatre every time I come here. I've never seen this place the same twice.' The comfortable modern auditorium of the Palace today may be relatively small and undistinguished for a theatre of Victorian origin, but it continues to be a great asset for Kilmarnock folk, who support it well.

NOTES

1. See John Moore, *Ayr Gaiety*, for a more detailed description of the theatre's complex career.
2. Interview with Johnny Beattie.
3. Information on the recent history of the Theatre Royal and the Guild of Players supplied by Billy Jardine.

According to Kennedy's *Annals of Aberdeen*, on 13 May 1580, during a royal visit by King James VI, citizens were instructed by the city magistrates to show their joy by making 'glaid the Kynges Majestie with farceis, playes, historeis, antikis, &c'. In 1601 the King invited Queen Elizabeth to send her company of players to Edinburgh. This was a distinguished group, managed by Lawrence Fletcher, which may have included Shakespeare himself. The King sent the Aberdeen magistrates a letter instructing them to allow the company to perform. With royal approval, they were not only warmly welcomed by large audiences, but also treated to a banquet at which they were paid 32 merks and granted the freedom of the town.[1]

Occasional visits by itinerant companies continued until the period of instability leading to the 1745 uprising. Companies were despatched to Aberdeen from the Canongate Playhouse in Edinburgh in 1746 and 1751. On both occasions they were refused permission to perform as both Kirk and magistrates were deeply suspicious of the theatre. This was not surprising as the Playhouse manager, David Beat, had been a vocal supporter of the Pretender. From 1768 the authorities felt secure enough to allow no less than three rudimentary theatres to open. William Fisher's company performed in the New Inn, a hostelry at the junction of Castle and King Streets. Later, John Jackson from Edinburgh erected a wooden theatre in Shoe Lane. In 1780 a more solid hall was built at the back of an inn in Queen Street. The price of admission was half a crown in the pit and one and six in the gallery. Oddly, a high chair was fitted in the middle of the gallery benches for the exclusive use of an eccentric schoolmaster, known as 'Mad Sinclair'. His 'task' was to orchestrate the audience, who, at his signal either applauded and cheered loudly, or drowned the actors with shouts of abuse. It only lasted until 1789 when the Reverend Chandler had it converted to a church. Meanwhile, yet another little-known theatre had appeared in Chronicle Lane, known as 'Coachy's Playhouse' (its proprietor was a coachman) and the drama continued. Companies were regularly despatched from Edinburgh under the auspices of Jackson, and, in the late 1770s, by West Digges.

THE THEATRE ROYAL

In 1795 a house in Marischal Street, belonging to merchants called Brebner and Gibb, was turned into a theatre, managed by Stephen Kemble, a fine actor who had previously managed theatres in Edinburgh, Glasgow and many English cities. In Aberdeen, the drama had obviously made an impression on some wealthier citizens, but only twenty-four dared take out subscriptions. Each paid Kemble £25, expecting a 5 per cent return and free admission. Investors were strongly discouraged by the Kirk, which was then an all-powerful voice, so the theatre had to be built very economically. Kemble already owned a wooden circus amphitheatre in Edinburgh, which he had converted to a theatre, so he ingeniously had this redundant structure dismantled and transported on wagons to Leith docks, from where it was shipped to Aberdeen. Kemble employed his usual Edinburgh-based architect, Charles Dodd, to convert and furnish the new theatre. It opened under Letters Patent in October 1875. Surprisingly, after so much effort, Kemble did not retain the lease for long and from 1799, a succession of less-known managers struggled to make it pay. In 1815 both Edmund and Charles Kean performed in the Theatre Royal. William Charles Macready visited the theatre, playing *King Richard the Third*. There, the distinguished young actor met a girl called Katherine Aitken, who was the daughter of the theatre's scene-painter. Macready revealed in his memoirs how he fell deeply in love with Miss Aitken. Although his sister thought that the naive, penniless and little-known Aberdeen lassie was a most unsuitable partner for him, they eventually married in 1824. John Philip Kemble performed there a year later. Visits by famous actors from the south such as Kean and Macready were rare, however, and the Theatre Royal instead became known instead for home-grown drama.

In 1817 its fortunes improved when Corbet Ryder took over management. Both Ryder and his wife, Mrs Pollock, were reputedly fine Scots actors and the former is said to have been a great *Rob Roy*. Their connection with the Theatre Royal in Aberdeen was long lasting – Mrs Pollock had joined the company aged fifteen years and continued to be involved until she retired in 1862. Subsequent managers, McNeil and Price both married her daughters, so the family link was maintained. Aberdeen was considered remote and inaccessible and visits by Edinburgh companies were a treat for the cities play-goers, but Londoners rarely got beyond the Scottish capital. The Theatre Royal in Marischal Street was very creaky and uncomfortable, so there was little prestige in performing in what was still thought (so far as taste in drama was concerned) a backward outpost. The work of new writers like Byron, Robertson and

Halliday had yet to find favour in Aberdeen, although Byron had lived there as a child. Not only were pit and gallery patrons unruly, there was also a serious language barrier for English performers to overcome! The audience even heckled in broad Doric! According to the historian Keith Angus, writing in 1878, they would shout choruses of 'Up wi' the hippin'!' to demand the raising of the curtain ('hippin' being a rude phrase also used to describe a baby's nappy). During a dramatic silent pause in *Hamlet*'s soliliquy, a voice from the pit said in a loud whisper a Doric version of the next line 'Ech! Conscience mak's cooards o' us a'!' Gallery patrons tore their programmes into strips, which they joined together to make streamers, while many folk ate meat pies, drank ale and smoked their clay pipes. The atmosphere inside the Theatre Royal Aberdeen must have been foul. Edwin Waugh, the Lancashire poet, gave a terse description of a visit to the premises in the 1860s:

> When we got to the theatre we found that our first impression was right. The check-taker looked like a worn-out bum-bailiff; the woodwork of the interior looked as if it had been made out of old orange boxes and ruined market stalls. The tragedy was a farce; the comedy was down-right murder; and the music sounded like an accompaniment to tooth-drawing. But the scanty audience, chiefly sailors, evidently enjoyed the whole thing . . . we had a good view of one of the side wings, and *Ambriar The Barbarian*, after taking a long swig of something in a pitcher, was rehearsing his countenance for the agonies in the next scene before we came away.

Commercially, Aberdeen was increasingly prosperous thanks to textile production, a booming fishing industry, and the fertile farmland that surrounded it. The Aberdeen railway to Forfar was completed in April 1850 and the city rapidly become a bustling trading centre, thankfully without much of the polluting heavy industry found in Scotland's Central Belt. Architecturally, it had been transformed into a handsome modern city of lofty granite buildings that was focused on the grand boulevard of Union Street. In 1872 a superb new theatre called Her Majesty's Opera House was completed. The old Theatre Royal was closed and replaced with, of all things, a church.

Aberdeen's new wonder-theatre could not have been more different from its ramshackle predecessor. On a compact site in Guild Street, conveniently opposite the railway station, a syndicate of local businessmen and civic dignitaries began its construction to designs by Charles J. Phipps and James Matthews, who later became Provost of Aberdeen. Her Majesty's was a strikingly beautiful little theatre with an imposing three-floor Venetian Gothic frontage in granite and polychromatic stone (the work of Matthews). Concrete was used for the first time in a Scottish theatre to frame the side and rear walls, but the real wonders lay within. The gracefully curved auditorium accommodated 1,744 patrons in six boxes and two tiers. The circle had high-backed plush benches, while gallery patrons had to squat on the steppings. There was exquisite gilded low-relied plaster latticework on the balcony and box fronts typical of Phipps's best interiors of the period.

On the evening of 19 December 1872 Guild Street was blocked by sightseers and carriages conveying dignitaries to the grand opening ceremony. Robert Arthur, the managing director, was a Londoner who controlled a chain of theatres in England, and one in Dundee. He recited a prologue and after the National Anthem, his company performed *The Lady of Lyons*.

In 1897 Frank Matcham was called in by the owners to improve the theatre with extra fire exits and redecoration. The theatre was reputedly well run with good housekeeping and a comfortable, well-ventilated interior. Audience behaviour seems only to have improved marginally; although smoking and drinking were strictly banned, the farmers, fishermen and their families who filled the pit and balcony were still a fearsome and vocal challenge for the actors and musicians.

Delighted with the success of Her Majesty's, in 1906 Robert Arthur's syndicate completed another, much larger, theatre, His Majesty's. The older venue however was a superb building and its intimate interior made it ideal as a variety theatre. Two months after the Alhambra was closed, Her Majesty's did indeed re-open as the **Tivoli** Music Hall in May 1910.

Frank Matcham had once again been engaged to carry out an extensive rebuild and it is the attractive results of this work which gives the building its delightful character today. The existing frontage was thankfully retained. The 1909 rebuild cost £10,000, and involved the replacement of all but four of the iron supporting columns with cantilevers. The balconies were deepened, leaving just four boxes flanking the proscenium. The upper pair were given elaborate curved cowls, topped with cartouches in front of recessed conch shells. The whole auditorium was covered in voluptuous and deeply modelled baroque plaster work so typical of the period. The ceiling and tympanum, with their richly frescoed panels, are particularly wonderful details which survive even today.

As a music hall run by the great variety impresario Fred Collins, the Tivoli was second to none; not only was it an outstandingly beautiful building which was well located to attract lively audiences, it also became the favourite venue for northern 'turns'. Twice nightly houses started with an overture by the grand orchestra, led by Jack Shepherd. Among the early acts was W. C. Fields, who appeared in the Tivoli's fourth programme as a comedy juggler in his pre-Hollywood movie days. Local 'Strathspey King' James Scott Skinner was one of many traditional fiddlers who led rousing sing-alongs in the Tivoli.

Figure 6.1   The Tivoli Theatre (author collection).

There, top-quality acts with a Scottish (preferably north-east) flavour seem to have been most in demand. Will Fyffe made his first appearance there in 1917, followed in the 1920s by Tommy Lorne and Dave Willis. Of course, Harry Lauder was a huge attraction, as were a less well-remembered speciality act of comic tumblers, the Three Aberdonians. The Tivoli was extensively redecorated in 1938, and during and after the Second World War seems to have enjoyed greater success than ever before with queues stretching down Guild Street in both directions, night after night.

The style and shape of Tivoli shows changed after the war when weekly engagements of variety bills became the exception and touring revues with comic anchormen like Jack Anthony or Alec Finlay began. Robert Wilson, the fine Scots tenor, broke Tivoli box-office records with his White Heather Group in 1953, while versatile Andy Stewart was another favourite Scottish performer. The Aberdeen comic Harry Gordon never appeared there, but then he did run the rival Beach Pavilion. The Tivoli passed to the William Galt Theatrical

Syndicate in January 1954. Galt's was based in offices adjacent to the Glasgow Empire and controlled a small but interesting group of highly popular and typically Scottish variety theatres, of which the Tivoli was the jewel in their crown and is happily the only survivor today. By the late 1950s, the strain of increasing costs was beginning to show. To attract the necessary capacity audiences essential to the atmosphere of a variety theatre, prices had to remain competitive, and consequently the orchestra was reduced to five and resident revues continued to account for the greater part of the Tivoli's output, now managed by Andrew Foley. Johnny Victory and the inimitable Lex McLean fronted the highly popular comedy, song and sketch shows that were still given twice nightly. In its last decade as a theatre, some big London names even made it to the Tivoli – the stylish top hat and tails crooner Frankie Vaughan, ebullient Billy Cotton and the eccentric comic Tony Hancock. Many of these shows were arranged by the much-loved Gaelic singer Calum Kennedy, who, at a time when many variety houses were closing, took on the role of impresario, persuading London's finest to come to the Tivoli. Kennedy was only postponing the inevitable: the Hancocks and Cottons were being lured away by television and the Tivoli closed on 2 April 1966.

Figure 6.2 The interior of the Tivoli, Guild Street (author collection).

The building was sold to the Perth-based bingo specialists, Top Flight Leisure, who have run it ever since. Ignoring the fact that the old theatre with its many steep and twisting stairs could never be ideal for older bingo players, the Tivoli has been beautifully maintained and still looks and smells like a theatre. The maroon plush benches of the gallery remain – now peppered with old saucers to use as ashtrays. It is quaint and charming. Unfortunately, the National Lottery seems to have had a catastrophic effect on such smaller private bingo clubs. The Tivoli has long been a listed building and, as a theatre, is Scotland's sleeping beauty. The building was put up for sale in 1997 and Jimmy Logan has proposed that it become a youth theatre, a wonderful idea for which the Tivoli's 29- by 27-foot stage and modest 800 seating capacity would be ideal. If National Lottery money could be used to set up such a project, it would be a worthy atonement for the demise of bingo. The Tivoli is a rare and precious survivor of the highest quality and a real asset to the city of Aberdeen. It must be protected accordingly.

The Alhambra,[2] on the corner of Guild and Exchange Streets, was converted in 1881 from the Trinity Chapel of Ease (known locally as the 'Tarty Kirk') with William McFarlane, later manager of Her Majesty's, in charge. The Livermore brothers (who then also ran the Palace) operated it as a downmarket 'try-out' venue for new talent. They were forced to make it their main venue when the Palace burned down in 1896 (see later). On 28 September that year, the Alhambra was the venue for Aberdeen's first cinema show, using Lumière equipment. Latterly it housed a waxworks and a menagerie and even a cinematograph. From 1907 it was leased to an animal trainer called John Sinclair, who owned a small summer zoo by the beach. Sinclair decided to make his attraction all year round, so the Alhambra became his 'Winter Zoo', with popular cinema shows. The Alhambra's end came in May 1910 but the building still exists as a supermarket.

In 1888 the Equestrian Circus magnate John Henry Cooke acquired yet another site for his well-known travelling show when he bought the natural depression between Bridge Place and Crown Terrace that almost 450 years before had witnessed Aberdeen's first recorded staging of drama. On this ideally shaped site, Cooke built his wooden amphitheatre. In January he placed typically flamboyant advertisements in the *Daily Free Press*:

JOHN HENRY COOKE'S
ROYAL CIRCUS

Delighted Thousands Nightly testify by cheers and laughter their high appreciation of the MORAL instructive artistic and World Famous Equestrian Company. Enthusiastic Reception last night of all the Comic

Clowns with new and original funniosities, the highly trained Goats and Donkeys and the wonderful leaping dog 'Waverley'. By Special Request the charming Infant Artiste LITTLE VIOLET will again appear in her delightful act entitled 'Beauty and the Birds', introducing her Flight of Trained Doves.

Prices: 3/-, 2/-, 1/-, and 6d Children under 10 Half Price to all parts except the gallery

Although well loved by Aberdonians, the logistics of transporting increasingly complex shows by rail from their Edinburgh base finally put paid to Cooke's venture and, in 1891, the amphitheatre became the Jollity Royal Vaudeville Theatre, run by trustees and leased to the splendidly titled showmen Baron Zeigler and Major Wieldman. Over £1,000 worth of alterations and improvements were made to the building. Two years later, the Livermore Brothers took over and called it the People's Palace. They quickly purchased it outright to replace it with a more robust and fireproof theatre. Meanwhile, its manager, Ernest Sheldon, not only put on top-class variety programmes with lavish scenery including waterfalls, which culminated in a grandly conceived spectacular, *The Gathering of the Clans*, with a cast of hundreds, bagpipes and Sheldon himself singing 'Mary of Argyle'.

Disaster struck the People's Palace during a performance on the evening of 30 September 1896. Just after comedians O'Conner and Martrey had completed the second act, a red glare was seen through the drop-scene. Fire had broken out when the top of the flies had come into contact with one of the gas lights, and in no time flames shot between the curtains and through the roof, igniting the wooden interior and frames. The fleeing audience was hampered in the rush for the exits by other patrons sitting in the aisles and narrow passages. There were no fire escapes and the doors did not have panic locks, so seven people perished as the People's Palace was engulfed in flames, while many more were maimed by burns, falling timbers and slates. The destruction of the amphitheatre was one of the worst fires Aberdeen had witnessed, and even the Lord Provost and Baillie Edwards, the Fire Committee Convenor, joined in to help to dowse it. The next morning, only the granite facade was left standing with smouldering ruins behind. Undaunted, the Livermore Brothers quickly had the site cleared to build their new Palace Theatre.

The imposing new, fireproofed and electrically lit theatre opened on 24 October 1898. It cost £15,000 to build and the *Bon Accord* newspaper considered it 'absolutely the handsomest theatre in Scotland'. The architect, John Rust, who had previously been employed by the city authorities, used the Venetian Gothic style. The Palace had a lofty, if slightly crude facade – the local granite did not lend itself to carved ornamentation. The hallway was

Figure 6.3   Frontage of the Palace Theatre as a cinema (author collection).

lined with Japanese paper and glazed tiles with the name 'Palace' set into a
mosaic floor and wide marble steps to the grand circle. The commodious
interior was arranged on two tiers with seating for 1,800 in crimson plush.

At the opening ceremony, the Livermore brothers were, not surprisingly, at
pains to emphasise all the safety features of the new theatre. Interestingly, the
last bill on the opening night was 'Moving Pictures on the Electrographe' – yet
another name for the cinematograph. The spacious stage was crossed by the
young Charlie Chaplin on three weekly engagements when he was in Fred
Karno's comic troupe. From the 1890s until the 1920s, a succession of other

famous stars came to the Palace, and in 1959 George Hay, then in his eighties, wrote about them for the *Press and Journal*:

> N. C. Bostick and George Ripon were two of the best comics of the day, although they are forgotten now. People like Harry Lauder and Florrie Forde also came to the Palace. Toleration was a word unknown to audiences at that time and on one occasion, when a benefit was being held for the manager, some amateur artistes on the bill didn't come up to standard. They were immediately showered with coins and other more horrid things by the 'pitties'. Dr Walford Bodie, the hypnotist, was also an accomplished ventriloquist as he came to the Palace with twelve different dummies. Bodie was indirectly involved in a fire scare at the Palace one night in 1902. He was about to begin his act, which consisted of putting a young lady in a trance, when a drunk began to shout as he was being thrown out by the management. Some women screamed and a shout of 'fire!' went up from another part of the house. People started to make for the doors, but to his credit old Bodie, calm and commanding, came forward to explain the problem, asked everyone to return to their seats, complimented them and went on with his act.

According to Leo Small, a 'lime' boy who operated the spotlights at the Palace around 1910, who was interviewed in the 1950s:

> If you went regularly to the stalls, you were well advised to take out an insurance policy beforehand for it was not unknown for bottles, full and empty to be dropped from the gallery and once I remember an outsize gobstopper hitting the conductor on the head. Classical music was definitely non-U at the Palace, the patrons expressing their disapproval by hissing, or by showering coins on the unhappy artist who left the stage as quickly as possible to make way for the stage hands who raced to collect these 'winnings' after the curtain fell.
>
> Up in the gallery there were frequent disturbances and several dozen people used to be thrown out at every performance, special attendants being kept for the purpose. The gallery doors opened to Crown Terrace, which was not paved at that time, and the mostly drunk patrons who had been ejected would retaliate by digging stones from the road and aiming them at the attendants.

In 1904 an up-and-coming young Liberal MP, Winston Churchill, in his tile hat and tail coat addressed a packed political rally in the Palace, telling his audience 'We are an island [laughter]. What makes an island rich? Is it what comes into it or what goes out of it? We free traders say it is what comes into it that makes it rich! [cheers].' This was obviously a swipe at the Labour and Communist candidates. The escapologist Harry Houdini also visited the theatre, having been put into a strait jacket and padlocked sack and pushed into Aberdeen's Albert Dock as a stunt to promote his performances at the Palace.

In 1911, after a succession of owners and leases, the Palace was taken over by Fred Collins, who also ran the nearby Tivoli, and films were introduced for part of the programme. In 1925 Arthur Hinton took over management with a policy of melodrama in which his wife, Peggy Courtney, usually played the brave heroine and triumphed over the 'villains'. It was a short interlude, for the Edinburgh-based cinema magnate Jack Poole bought the theatre in 1929. As with many another, it was closed for a radical rebuild, emerging in 1931 with one large balcony in an undistinguished modern interior. Both Poole's Aberdeen cinemas – the Regent and Palace – passed to County Cinemas in June 1936, and later went with that circuit to Odeon Cinemas Ltd. The Palace was converted to a Top Rank Ballroom in 1959 with a big band on stage, and has been a nightclub since 1976. It is still known as the Palace, but only the Bridge Place frontage and shell of the old theatre remains.

HIS MAJESTY'S THEATRE

Perhaps the finest view of **His Majesty's Theatre**, close by Rosemount Viaduct, is from Union Bridge. Between the decorative leopards and heraldic beasts adorning the balustrade and across the grand ornamental gardens of Union Terrace, you can glimpse this magnificent theatre with its imposing facade of Kemnay granite glinting in the sunlight.

Following the great success of Her Majesty's (later the Tivoli), Robert Arthur decided to give the rapidly expanding city of Aberdeen an even finer theatre to attract the best touring companies in the country. So, at a cost of £35,000 he built His Majesty's on what must at first have seemed an inappropriate site for a theatre – by a viaduct above a deep valley through which ran the Den burn. In fact, it proved ideal, for not only was it one of the most conspicuous in the city, but also its slope enabled the front entrances to be located on the viaduct approaches, while the stage door was deep in the hollow behind. The railway line from Aberdeen ran alongside the gardens and stopped at a little station called Schoolhill, a few yards from the rear of the theatre, a big help as scenery and props could be moved direct from the trains.

The architect was, of course, the great Frank Matcham. Matcham had first submitted plans for His Majesty's in 1901. He had intended a symmetrical design, but due to difficulties in obtaining the granite stipulated by the authorities, construction did not begin until 1904. By then, the design had been completely revised. The site, adjacent to the imposing court house and church, called for

Union Terrace Gardens showing H. M. Theatre, Aberdeen

Figure 6.4   His Majesty's Theatre and Union Terrace Gardens
(author collection).

a monumental approach. Although the elements which make up the design – giant pilasters, rusticated arches and a dome – have awe-inspiring intention, as assembled by Matcham, they fail to be so. Maybe he felt that overbearing architecture was not appropriate to entertainment. The facade is none the less handsome in a free adaptation of early Georgian, which was then becoming fashionable. The dome, plonked without much finesse on the right, was intended to balance that of the church next door.[3]

Inside, Matcham used the steeply sloping site to advantage; the foyer leads directly to the dress circle and the stalls are down a flight of marble stairs. His Majesty's has some wonderful front-of-house spaces with finely grained Italian marble, polished woodwork and elegant plaster mouldings; the tone is much more refined and spacious than in most of his previous theatres. Most noteworthy is the superbly carved circular bar with a marble counter behind the dress circle. The auditorium was also beautifully handled, although it too was uncharacteristically chaste for Matcham. Its solid classicism is emphasised by massively composed tiers of boxes between the ends of the three, wide balconies and the marble-framed proscenium. The tympanum contains a fine frieze in low relief depicting the Roman 'Goddess of the Drama' and her

Figure 6.5   Interior of His Majesty's (David Trevor-Jones).

acolytes. Below, the curtains were originally gold with an embroidered repro-
duction of *Les Fêtes Venetiennes* by Watteau. The crimson- velvet pelmet had
a crown in the centre and King Edward's cipher on either side. The ceiling has
solid-looking moulded beams and rectangular panels and even the off-white
colour scheme is remarkably restrained. The overall effect is very elegant and
in harmony with Aberdeen's severe granite architecture outside.

His Majesty's opened on Monday 3 December 1906 under the management
of Harry Adair Nelson, from Bath. Aberdeen had rarely witnessed a celebration

like it. Every seat had been booked for weeks in advance, and by five o'clock crowds began to gather for the first show. Not only was there a large body of policemen to control the crowds, but even Chief Constable Anderson was present on horseback to escort the dignitaries as their carriages drew up at the brilliantly lit entrance. The gentlemen were in full evening dress, while the ladies were in long dresses and bejewelled. The first production was the operatic pantomime *Little Red Riding Hood*, which played to packed houses for four weeks. The *Gazette* advertised it as 'having special scenery, new and elaborate costumes, a chorus of forty trained voices, children's ballet and Poppyland Troupe Dancers'.

His Majesty's was not only a sumptuously appointed theatre for audiences, but was also technically advanced with good dressing rooms and a big 56-foot-deep stage. It became so popular within the acting profession that it was reputedly easy to book it with stars of this calibre a year in advance. Audiences were usually sedate and appreciative, but writing in the 1970s, Elizabeth Adair, the first manager's daughter, recalled one unfortunate incident:

> Although my father, Harry, was a strict disciplinarian, both at home and in the theatre, he was immensely popular . . . I remember his habit of standing during a performance at the little balustraded platform to the right of the dress circle . . . surveying the audience like a captain from his bridge. I even saw him take out his handkerchief and wipe imaginary flecks of dust from the handrail. So, you can imagine what he felt on a 'Student Night', a feature of the Aberdeen University annual production when the audience was composed entirely of students. A riotous section of the crowd, carrying hockey sticks and other weapons, heckled the poor actors mercilessly and scattered pease meal from the 'gods' over the red plush seats and carpets. They invaded the bar and smashed all the glasses. The orgy of destruction was indescribable and was ended only on the arrival of the police. Next day the student representatives made abject apologies, but my father put a ban on student nights and it was many years before permission was again granted.

In 1923 Robert Arthur, now associated with Howard and Wyndham, decided to sell His Majesty's. Walter Gilbert, the manager of the Tivoli, took control and continued to uphold the established high standards of the theatre. The continued growth in popularity of the cinema in the early 1930s was, however, having its effect, and theatre audiences declined. Gilbert died in August 1931 and the theatre was again put up for sale by auction. The national reputation which His Majesty's had carefully built up was in danger of vanishing. The famed impresario C. B. Cochrane was so incensed at its possible closure that he offered to bring his current West End hit, Noël Coward's *Bitter*

Sweet, from London at his own expense. The crisis was such that application was made to the Stock Exchange for permission to deal in shares. A subscription list was opened in December 1931 and the Aberdeen Theatre Company offered 30,000 £1 shares. This well-meaning venture came to nothing and the few investors were reimbursed.

All was not lost, however, and salvation came in 1933 when James Donald, a famous local entrepreneur, councillor and cinema tycoon, purchased His Majesty's for £35,000. A three-month closure followed the purchase when a £10,000 refurbishment took place. A projection box was fitted to the rear of the upper circle and a revolving stage was installed to enable a quick change from film screen to variety orchestra. His Majesty's was back in business that August, and alongside its regular programmes of pictures and variety, touring plays and musicals made occasional visits. Donald died in 1934, but his sons, James and Peter, continued to ensure that the theatre remained at the forefront of Aberdeen's entertainment scene.

After the Second World War, the Donald era continued with a third generation of Donalds, when James F. Donald became manager at his father's death in 1971. In 1975 His Majesty's came under civic control when it was sold to Aberdeen Council for £250,000. The authorities realised that having successfully guided the theatre for so many years, it would be foolish to dispense with the services of the Donald family. A unique arrangement was made whereby J. F. Donald (Aberdeen Picture Palaces Ltd) would manage His Majesty's on their behalf. Over the years this proved successful, but during the late 1970s and despite healthy audiences and profits, all was not well with the now venerable

Figure 6.6 Auditorium of the Capitol (author collection).

theatre. New government safety legislation made it essential that a substantial rebuild be carried out if the theatre was not to close for good. With much trepidation, but faith in the future, the council allocated in 1979 over £3 million for a thorough renovation.

On 17 September 1982 His Majesty's witnessed another glittering occasion when the kilted and smiling HRH Prince Charles attended the gala re-opening. The show featured the Scottish Ballet, impressionist Janet Brown, Scottish baritone Bill McCue and the three brilliant Aberdeen satirists of 'Scotland The What?' Being local comic heroes, they got the loudest cheers for their witty parodies of life in the north east. The restoration was immaculate; the frontage had been cleaned and the interior returned to its cool, pristine white splendour. Thanks to the close proximity of Balmoral Castle, a favourite royal retreat, royal visits to His Majesty's have become a regular occurrence. The theatre continues magnificently to serve Aberdeen as a touring venue for productions of all kinds. Long may it continue!

Aberdeen's old Beach Pavilion was a basic wooden structure with a corrugated roof, dating from the 1880s. On 4 May 1928 a more solid replacement opened as part of the beach development scheme, which also included the promenade. The new hall seated 750, and the locally born comic Harry Gordon fronted its first summer show. This consisted only of Gordon, four Tiller girls and a piano accompanist. He had an innate gift for portraying Aberdeenshire wifies (most often without teeth) and the characters in his fictitious village, Inversnecky.

Although owned by the Iles family (they also owned Dreamland in Margate), Gordon took charge of booking the Pavilion, which became a popular variety hall. He paid as much as £200 a week to secure big names such as Flanagan and Allen during summer seasons in the 1930s. When the Second World War began, it was closed and the Admiralty moved in. Happily, the 1950s saw a flurry of activity again. The Beverley Sisters, Dick Emery, and Morecambe and Wise entertained there, but summer shows quickly became uneconomic and the Pavilion closed in 1961. It was converted to a restaurant two years later and is now the Mediterranean-style Café Continental.

Aberdeen still has two superb traditional theatres in His Majesty's and the dormant Tivoli, but mention must also be made of the **Capitol**, an incredibly sumptuous super cinema in Union Street, which regularly put on stage shows and an annual pantomime from its opening in 1933 until the 1960s. Presently out of use, the Capitol is still owned by the Donald family and until recently hosted occasional rock concerts in the auditorium with a bar in the former café. Designed by Alexander Marshall MacKenzie, it is one of Scotland's art deco gems and of equal importance to Aberdeen's other surviving theatres.[4]

Figure 6.7   Foyer of the Capitol (author collection).

NOTES

1. See Keith Angus, *A Scotch Playhouse, Being the Historical Records of the old Theatre Royal, Marischal Street, Aberdeen.*
2. Photographs of Aberdeen in the 1890s show a rather small, crowded city, mainly clustered around the harbour and the Union Street area. Fitdee, Torry and Woodside were separate communities, although the prosperous tenements of the 'granite city' around Union Street were starting to take shape. The twisting cobbled streets around the Alhambra were crowded with folk and horse-drawn traffic. Numerous pubs and the close proximity of the harbour must have made the Alhambra's location ideal as a vaudeville house.
3. See Angus McPhail, *The Story of His Majesty's Theatre, Aberdeen* (document in Aberdeen Central Library) and Brian Walker, *Frank Matcham: Theatre Architect.*
4. The full history of the Capitol is recounted in Michael Thomson, *Silver Screen in the Silver City.*

In 1805 the first purpose-built theatre opened at the junction of Castle Raat and Inglis Street. The latter was renamed Theatre Lane and is now Hamilton Street. Early records show that it was managed by a Tom Ryder, but was not a success and was converted to shops in the spring of 1827. A variety of halls were subsequently used for intermittent performances, but the widely held notion that going to the theatre was somehow sinful persisted for a time.

In 1882 the *Inverness Advertiser* observed that 'the want of a proper place for theatrical entertainment has long been keenly felt . . . Several gentlemen have formed a company and asked the local architect, J. H. Gall, to produce a suitable and commodious design.' Building work began that spring on a site in Bank Street, next to the *Advertiser*'s offices. In October 1882 Andrew Macdonald, representing the company, appeared before the Justices of the Peace in the Castle to ask for a theatre licence. The building was inspected and all but one, Dr Mackenzie of Eileanach, were in favour.[1]

The New Theatre Royal, as it was at first known, had a grand opening on 6 November 1882, attended by 'the principal townsmen and their families and several of the county aristocracy'. After the National Anthem, Charles Barnard's company performed *Les Cloches de Corneville*. The theatre, curiously described as being in 'the Glasgow classic style', seated 750 with two tiers, supported by hollow iron columns, which, ingeniously, also served as ducts for fresh air. The first of the Theatre Royal's many successful pantomimes was staged in February 1883, when William McFarland, lessee of the Dundee Theatre Royal, presented *Aladdin and his Wonderful Lamp*. Drama and opera were performed by visiting companies, and, later, touring productions of revues, with top comics like Sir Harry Lauder, a great favourite in Inverness, and Will Fyffe topping the bill. Mrs Isobel Macdonald recalls seeing Lauder as a teenager in the late 1920s:

> Harry Lauder's show had queues along Bank Street both ways. I remember him as a really cheery, outgoing wee man. He had a crooked

walking stick, which he used to conduct the audience, singing the chorus of 'Roamin' in the Gloamin'.' His highland dress was also exaggerated with a big glengarry, kilt and sash. He had this cheeky, knowing smile and would stop the band to tell wee stories about wee lassies he knew. It was clean and innocent fun and everyone enjoyed it.[2]

In the summer of 1930 the Theatre Royal was thoroughly renovated and redecorated. Sadly, it was not to last. During a week's run of *The Will Fyffe Show*, early in the morning of 15 March, the theatre burned down. The fire brigade pumped water from the river and managed to prevent the blaze spreading to adjacent buildings, but the roof collapsed 'in a furiously raging sheet of flame'. Fyffe's considerable wardrobe of props and costumes was also lost in the devastation, but in the best traditions of the stage, the Inverness Light Opera Company loaned replacements and the show went on the next day at the Central Hall Picture House in Academy Street.

In Scotland, as has been seen, the distinction between 'cinemas' and 'theatres' was often blurred. Many theatres were converted for the movies, but only the **Central Hall Picture House** went the other way. The building had first opened on 20 December 1912, the work of a local architect, Alister Ross. Its incongruous, but imposing twin-towered frontage with steeply pitched pavilion roofs was an exotic mixture of Hanseatic and art nouveau elements, which somehow resembled a hunting lodge in the German alps. Inside, it was richly ornamented with plaster swags and medallions. The single large balcony ended with small boxes.

It was the comic Tommy Morgan who persuaded Sir Alex King, the cinema tycoon who booked films for the Central's owners, Caledonian Associated Cinemas (CAC), to try regular variety shows in Inverness. CAC also ran La Scala, the Playhouse and Palace cinemas in the town, so in the spring of 1934, the Tommy Morgan Show was booked at the Central.[3] It was such a success that the cinema was closed for the summer, fitted with an enlarged stage and dressing rooms, before re-opening as the Empire Theatre on 17 September 1934. For the next thirty-six years it housed opera, revue, variety, pantomime, plays, amateur productions, highland dancing competitions and even occasional wrestling matches. Appropriately for a highland theatre, it was two Mod gold medallists, Alasdair Gillies and Calum Kennedy, who made the greatest impact; in fact the Stornoway-born Kennedy, a fine Gaelic singer, holds the record for the highest number of seats sold during a week at the Empire.

The theatre's gala final night was attended by over 1,000 on Saturday 28 November 1970. It was given a splendid highland send-off with baritone Bill McCue, accordionist Will Starr and Muir of Ord comedian Johnny Brogan, many local groups of singers and dancers and the orchestra, conducted by John Worth, who had managed the Empire during its last twenty years. It must have

*Figure 7.1 The Picture House in Academy Street, later
the Empire Theatre* (author collection).

been a poignant occasion, for everyone knew that the owners had sold out for
a speculative office development. The Empire was shortly torn down and its
replacement was a sadly dull and characterless concrete high-rise block.

Live theatre later returned to the Highland capital in 1976 when the controversial Eden Court complex, a striking modern theatre and conference centre
designed by the Dunbar-Naismith Partnership, was added to the former
Bishop's Palace of 1878.

Notes

1. See James Miller, *The Magic Curtain*, pp. 7–11.
2. Interview with Mrs Isobel Macdonald.
3. Information supplied by Mrs Xandra Harper, daughter of Sir Alex King.

8 DUNDEE AND ARBROATH

DUNDEE

In August 1734 the 'Edinburgh Company of Comedians', with which the poet Allan Ramsay was connected, visited Dundee. They were well received and 'acted frequently to the entire satisfaction of the gentlemen and ladies . . . they played for the entertainment of the Ancient and Honourable Society of Freemasons, the grand master patronising the same by assembling all the masons at his lodge, and marching at their head to the playhouse in their proper apparel, with hautboys and other musick before them.' The 'playhouse' described was actually the Town House. Gradually, the Kirk persuaded magistrates to veto plays, but the actors got round this restriction by advertising 'concerts of musick', costing a shilling, with a free play during the interval. The Trades Hall, erected in 1778 at the end of the High Street, was a popular venue for these 'concerts'. Sadly, ludicrous superstition combined with the Kirk's preaching that the theatre involved devil-worship led a deputation of fishermen from Broughty to petition the town council to have a group of actors thrown out of the town, claiming that since the arrival of the company, all the fish had left the river. In 1784 the magistrates resolved to stop John Jackson, the energetic manager of the Edinburgh Theatre Royal, from performing in Dundee. Jackson had both popular opinion and the law on his side, but it was not until 1787 that his company was finally allowed to visit the town. It was a big success; nevertheless, for the next thirteen years, plays were rarely seen in the town because there was no suitable venue.

On 23 July 1800 Messrs Moss and Bell opened a wooden theatre at the end of Yeoman Shore, later the site of the now-demolished West Station. Moss was said to have been outstanding as Shylock, but he lost a lot of money in the Yeoman Shore Theatre and died in poverty. A production of *The Merchant of Venice* was given by Moss's stock company at its opening. John Kemble and Edward Kean occasionally performed there, but it must have been too rudimentary a building ever to enjoy success.

On 27 June 1810 the handsome, sandstone-built Theatre Royal in Castle Street was opened, initially under the management of Henry Siddons and, six years later, William Murray (both famed for their stints at the Theatre Royal, Edinburgh). The Theatre Royal was designed by Samuel Bell and had a restrained entrance hall with stone steps to the circle and balcony and an intimate auditorium with painted panels on the fronts of the tiers. Unusually, there were no seats in the stalls, and most of the audience of 1,200 actually stood. In view of this, it was not surprising that it too received poor support in Dundee and was opened only at fitful intervals. Although opening a theatre in these circumstances was obviously risky, in July 1841 the Thistle Hall in Union Street was rebuilt as a theatre; after only two weeks' rivalry with the struggling Theatre Royal, the newcomer closed for good.

The Theatre Royal, by now an all-seated venue, enjoyed its first success in the 1860s. By then Dundee was into the throes of the industrial revolution as its position by the Tay made it an excellent site for a port and as industry prospered, it grew rapidly into a modern city. Edward Lyons was now its skilful manager, and shortly, large touring companies were visiting the city. In 1877 the music hall impresario, William McFarland took over the management.

As an enterprising young man, McFarland had been linked with the origin and advancement of music-hall entertainment in Dundee. In 1870 he took over a wooden amphitheatre near the site of the East Railway Station, which had been used by Sanger's Circus, and renamed it the Alhambra Music Hall. His first notable production was a £600 pantomime *Little Red Riding Hood*, which was, by all accounts, very successful. Hamilton's diorama, a show in which large paintings were rolled across the proscenium to a musical accompaniment, was also featured at the Alhambra in addition to locally based variety turns. Shortly, the theatre closed, being considered a danger to public safety. McFarland was then asked to take over the running of the music hall in Castle Street, a sordid hall adjacent to an inn, which had been running since the 1860s and was probably Dundee's first music hall. He must have realised the limitations also of the old Theatre Royal, for he acquired a large site on Seagate to build a new theatre.

In 1885 Her Majesty's opened in Seagate. The Theatre Royal was temporarily closed, but once the new theatre was established, McFarland re-opened it again with variety. Having enjoyed seventy-eight years without a fire, the Theatre Royal was burned down in 1888. Only the restrained facade remains today, fronting offices, a bust of Shakespeare on the pediment recalling that this was once the site of a playhouse.

The day of 19 October 1885 heralded the opening of the 1,700-seat **Her Majesty's Theatre and Opera House** in Seagate. This magnificent theatre, designed by the prolific Dundee architect William Alexander, had a grand foyer with marble staircases and a fireplace with a carved oak mantelpiece and glazed tiles depicting scenes from the works of Sir Walter Scott. The auditorium

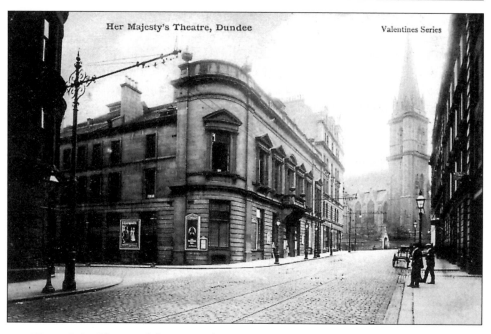

Figure 8.1   The grand frontage of Her Majesty's as the Majestic Picture Theatre
(author collection).

had two elegantly curved serpentine tiers, with no less than ten boxes and slim Corinthian columns with enriched shafts. There was an ornate circular pan-elled ceiling and the gilded proscenium was hung with voluptuous crimson drapes. At the opening the Caste Company gave the first performance of an obscure play called *Birth, or the Legend of the White Lady*, and singers loaned from the Carl Rosa Opera performed arias. Her Majesty's was run at first by McFarland, who financed its £12,000 cost with a public subscription of £10 shares. This was oversubscribed, but McFarland sold out in a deal with the Robert Arthur Theatre Company and Howard and Wyndham when he retired in 1891. They had the expertise and financial backing to bring the best touring companies, such as Carl Rosa and D'Oyly Carte's operas, to the theatre.

In 1919, unable to secure enough touring companies as a result of the First World War, it was restyled Her Majesty's Picture Theatre, billed as 'Dundee's Luxury Kinema'. Renamed the Majestic in 1930, it was only to last until 1941 when it was destroyed by fire. In 1956 the Dundee cinema magnate, J. B. Milne built his new Capitol cinema on the site, incorporating the rear wall of the partially demolished wreck of the Majestic. This is still in use today as the ABC cinema.

In 1891 the Livermore Brothers took over an old circus building in Lochee

Road and turned it into a music hall. Two years later, they moved to a larger hall, the Palace in Nethergate. It too had previously served as an indoor circus for twenty years and the obsolete circus ring was covered over by the stalls, but the other original interior decorations lasted for the rest of the theatre's long career. The theatre also retained its original dull frontage of undressed sandstone, but what it lacked in architectural grandeur was made up for in raucous atmosphere. The young Harry Lauder was booed, and despite the Palace's proprietors claim to be 'pioneers in refinement' and that the Palace was 'the only place where you can safely take your wife and families', Monday houses were notoriously tough for less experienced performers. According to the *Dundee Courier*, shouts of 'Awa' for a can!' greeted the efforts of one unfortunate English singer. It was a directive bellowed at apprentices in the jute mills when tea was required, or they were expected to make themselves scarce. The singer appealed to the restive elements in the balcony, reminding them that singing was his bread and butter. They heard him out, but at the second house, when he thought all would be well, a voice roared from the gallery 'Here's your bread an' butter!' as a loaf was flung at the stage, skimming his ear.

The Palace became a cinema in 1912, an early member of John Maxwell's Scottish Cinema and Variety Theatres circuit, but the advent of Green's palatial

Figure 8.2 The auditorium of Her Majesty's (author collection).

Playhouse cinema further along Nethergate probably caused the owners to revert to variety shows, twice nightly, in 1938. The William Galt Agency, based in Glasgow, added the Palace to its chain of halls in 1952. After a brief foray into bingo in 1962, Grampian Theatres Ltd, a company founded by the entertainer Calum Kennedy, bought the building, and opened it as the Theatre Royal in 1965. Rikki Fulton and Jack Milroy played to full houses as *Francie and Josie*, while singers Frankie Vaughan, Lena Martell and Moira Anderson were also star attractions. When the former State cinema, which had started out in 1928 as the short-lived Alhambra Theatre, was converted back to house amateur shows in 1972, the Theatre Royal was shut. It became a nightclub, which burned down in 1977 and was demolished.

The Gaiety Theatre of Varieties on Victoria Road first opened on 13 April 1903 by a company associated with Thomas Colquhoun and Bernard Armstrong, who also ran the Queen's and Tivoli theatres in Glasgow. It was a two-tiered house with a tall, narrow sandstone frontage, designed by McCulloch and Fairley. The manager, James Creighton, had a liking for illusionists and dramatic speciality acts, such as the 'electric wizard' and hypnotist Dr Walford Bodie and his assistant, La Belle Electra.

In 1910 the Gaiety was enlarged with a bigger stage and improved front-of-house spaces, designed by William Alexander. At the same time, a projection box was added to the rear of the balcony. When it re-opened as the **Victoria Theatre**, run by R. C. Buchanan, twice-nightly variety was interspersed with film shows. Gradually, films came entirely to replace the live element and in 1935 it became known as the Victoria Cinema. The boxes were removed and the stage was incorporated into the auditorium. During the 1980s it was run by the Poole family, who began to notice alarming cracks in the building's fabric. In 1989 it was condemned by the authorities and demolished.[1]

In 1904 the Empire opened in Rosebank Street up in Hilltown. It belonged to a local company, managed by James Mollison Kidd. As with the Gaiety, it began with variety twice nightly, but in 1911 it became a cinema and was sold as such to Richard Singleton, a Glasgow-based cinema entrepreneur, in 1927. It became a full-time cinema and was sold with Singleton's other interests to Odeon in September 1936.[2] At the same time, Odeon also bought Singleton's modern Vogue in Strathmartine Road, and as that cinema took the Odeon name, the old Empire continued unchanged until it burned down on the night of 30 October 1957. It lay derelict until 1962 when the site was cleared for redevelopment with flats.

The **King's Theatre** in Cowgate, dating from 1909, was perhaps the most outstanding of Dundee's theatres. It was designed by a local architect, James Thomson, who had previously designed the imposing classical edifice of the Caird Hall.[3] The King's was commissioned by a syndicate of local businessmen,

Figure 8.3   The Victoria Theatre (author collection).

styled United County Theatres Ltd. If the exterior presented dour red sandstone
solidity, inside the King's was very bright and spacious. The foyer had a marble
floor with handsome oak panelling and high, panelled ceilings. The auditorium
was opulently decorated with gilded plaster mouldings on a cream background
and dark crimson upholstery. Following contemporary American practice in
theatre design, the balconies faced the stage almost square on with the single
sets of boxes isolated between decorative panels on either side. This was entirely
practical, as from the outset, it was intended that the King's should be able to

present the cinematograph and everyone would have a good view. It was a lush and beautiful space, which must have been the great sight of Edwardian Dundee; the plaster work appeared deeply sculpted; the decorative treatment of the tiers was continued as friezes round the sides; there was a superb domed ceiling with frescoes and a fine marble proscenium arch.

The opening ceremony was conducted in grand style, naturally the Provost and magistrates arrived in carriages, wearing evening dress, and Bransby Williams, a successful actor of the period, gave the prologue. From then until 1921, the King's was run as a high-class variety theatre with performances by, among others, Harry Lauder, Florrie Forde and Marie Lloyd, twice nightly. In 1919 it was renovated with comfortable seating replacing the benches in the balcony. When Her Majesty's became a cinema, the King's took over all the touring productions of musical comedy, opera and drama, but from 24 September 1928, the theatre was run by Provincial Cinematograph Theatres (PCT) as a cinema. PCT was a London-based firm who ran, mainly purpose-built, luxurious cinemas all over Britain. Its Dundee venture was such a success that it later bought the building. Capacity was reduced to 1,500 seats and an organ was fitted, the pipes being hidden behind grilles in the disused boxes.

Figure 8.4   Exterior of the King's Theatre at night (author collection).

Figure 8.5 The auditorium of the King's (author collection).

During the Second World War, the King's was known as the Garrison Theatre, and both live shows and films were given to entertain troops. By this stage, PCT was owned by Gaumont British and the King's was renamed the Gaumont in May 1950 with an extensive, but sympathetic, refurbishment. From 1955 London theatre companies were permitted to use the Gaumont for only six weeks every year. This brought many successful productions to the city, including Sadler's Wells Ballet (today known as the Birmingham Royal Ballet), Sadler's Wells Opera (now English National Opera), *Peter Pan*, *Wedding in Paris* with Evelyn Laye and annual productions by the Dundee Operatic Society.

By 1961 the Rank Organisation, which controlled Gaumont and Odeon, was embarking on many destructive alterations to their older cinemas, and that year, the Dundee Gaumont was gutted. The proscenium was dismantled and a new screen erected on the rear wall. The balcony was dismantled, a new false ceiling installed and every vestige of the remaining ornate plaster decoration was covered up. It was precisely how not to treat a well-loved and historic theatre. It later became an Odeon, and operated as a bingo hall from 1983. This too has closed and the building was sold to a developer.

Meanwhile, an enthusiastic local campaign was started with the backing of the London-based Theatres Trust to have the King's restored to its former glory. The group's chairman, Stephen Fraser, correctly argued that it was a disgrace that a city of Dundee's importance does not have a single traditional proscenium theatre, only a couple of small, modern venues. The city loses out as it cannot even host touring West End musicals. For reasons best known to themselves, and notwithstanding expenditure cutbacks, elements within the city council instead backed their own proposal to build a brand-new leisure complex, incorporating a theatre. At the same time, changes to the King's auditorium were stripped back, and much of the original decoration, including the ceiling dome, was again revealed. Although the council are gradually being won round to supporting the restoration of the King's, they may be too late as a parallel proposal has been submitted to convert it into a theme pub. Having lost so many of its important buildings to fires and insensitive redevelopment, it is to be hoped that the King's, a building rich in theatrical history, will eventually be restored to its original splendour.[4]

ARBROATH

On 21 May 1793 the Arbroath Theatre in Horner's Wynd (now Commerce Street) opened with *King Lear*. It was evidently purpose built, making it one of the first provincial theatres in Scotland. Although a remarkable achievement for Arbroath, it was short-lived, closing in 1815 to be altered to stables for the neighbouring George Inn. A hall located opposite the inn and entered through a tenement was then converted to a replacement theatre. It attracted many of the leading actors of the era who frequently stayed in Arbroath for extended seasons, perhaps due to the difficulty and expense of transporting companies and props so far north for short runs.

The Trades Hall, built in 1815, was used as a theatre from the mid-1820s. It was reputedly well appointed with a balcony and a large stage house, equipped with an overhead gangway, from which the scenery was controlled, and a trap door in the floor. It was rebuilt as Arbroath's Sheriff Courthouse in 1886.

In 1901 the Arbroath Theatre and Music Hall Co. bought the abandoned Inverbrothock Free Church, converting it to the second Arbroath Theatre with a mixture of drama and variety shows. It had become the Palace Cinema by 1910. The present theatre in the Webster Memorial Hall dates from 1867, when, known as the Public Hall, it opened as a venue for touring plays and vaudeville. At first, it was poorly supported but was rescued by the Webster family, flax manufacturers, who gifted it to the town in memory of their son who was killed in the First World War. In the 1930s its summer shows, the *Arbroath Follies*, became very popular. Further renovations in 1951 and an extensive enlargement of the stage and auditorium in 1970 have transformed the hall into a successful theatre and cultural centre.

Notes

1. Information from Eddie Poole, who now runs the Playhouse cinema in Galashiels.
2. Interview with the late George Singleton, proprietor of Singleton Cinemas Ltd.
3. Information from Gertie and Trixie Thomson, daughters of the architect.
4. Interview with and information supplied by Stephen Fraser.

9

PERTH

From around 1616 the Perth Grammar School doubled up as the St. Anne's Lane Theatre. At that time, anybody known to have visited a theatre was deprived of church privileges and pupils were berated by the clergy for neglecting their studies in favour of performing with the visiting companies. Even as late as 1780, several people were taken before the Kirk Session for daring to see a play. One elderly lady rebuked the religious kill-joys, writing 'a wheen narrow-minded loons wad attempt on account of their jimp brains, sour stomachs and bad temper to spoil the daffin' o' weens and braw lads and bonnie blushing lassies, forbye the fun o' auld folk, by their skirlin' an' roarin that tae dance or lauch, or aiblins gang tae the pantomime is a mortal sin.'[1] During this harsh period, the theatre was run unofficially, but eventually opinions relented and on 2 May 1810, it was formally opened to the public as a full-time theatre, fitted with a balcony and boxes. Mrs Glover, from the Theatre Royal, Covent Garden, starred in a comedy, *The Jealous Wife*, on the opening night and performed in four different plays during the following week, although a local critic was 'considerably mortified by the thinness of the houses'. Business improved later, and in 1813 Henry Siddons (of the Theatre Royal Edinburgh) took a lease on the theatre. In 1817 Corbet Ryder became manager, and in June 1818, the St. Anne's Lane Theatre was filled on consecutive nights with Scott's dramatisation of *Rob Roy*. Ryder left for Aberdeen in 1821, and the theatre fell into disuse. It became a joiner's store and workshop, but sadly came to its own dramatic end in 1824, when it burned to the ground overnight. Fortunately, the 2nd dragoons of the Royal Scots Greys and the Perthshire militia were quickly called to prevent the fire from spreading to surrounding houses.

By 1824 there were other theatrical venues in Perth. During the early years of the eighteenth century, the Guild Hall had been used as a theatre. Later, the Glover's Hall in George Street, built in 1786, was fitted up as a temporary theatre. George Street became the fashionable street in Perth, contemporary etchings showing the 'dandies' of the time parading in front of the hall.

Unfortunately, just as interest in the theatre was picking up, a terrible accident happened in 1809 when the balcony of the Glover's Hall collapsed, during a crowded performance of *Macbeth*. Macbeth was on stage, looking at his bloodied hands and exclaiming 'This is a sorry sight' when in an instant the wooden supports gave way, and the whole came down with a thunderous crash to the floor. Patrons in the pit scrambled on to the stage, where ghosts, witches, Lady Macbeth and the audience stood terrified and bleeding. It was a miracle that no one was killed, but one local representative of the Kirk reported that 'the play had been representing the Day of Judgement, and the fall of the gallery was a judgement on them!' No more plays were given that year, but plans were soon being prepared for a new theatre.

THE THEATRE ROYAL

The success of Corbet Ryder as manager of the St. Anne's Lane Theatre encouraged him to return to Perth and develop a new, larger building. A subscription raised £2,625 and he acquired a corner site at the junction of Atholl and Kinnoull Streets in the handsome and prosperous Georgian new town. As part of the former Blackfriars Monastery, this was historic ground where several Scottish Parliaments had been held, and where King James I of Scotland had met his death in 1437. When workmen began the excavations for the new theatre, they reused part of the foundations of the monastery in the new building.

Ryder arranged the formal opening of his Theatre Royal for 28 August 1820 and announced with great pride that he had secured at great expense the famous William Macready, an actor at the top of his profession, to appear for six nights in *Macbeth*, *King Richard the Third*, *Coriolanus* and *Romeo and Juliet*. While performing at the Theatre Royal, Macready first met Catherine Atkin, a beautiful young actress whom he later married.

Long before the doors opened, a large crowd had gathered in the spacious streets around the theatre, and when the curtain was raised, there was much cheering, indeed the play had to be halted several times to let the audience calm down after Macready's dramatic soliloquies. The performances were highly praised but the theatre itself, a sombre-looking building with both frontages in dressed stone and three arches in the facade leading to the pit, circle and boxes and gallery, was said to be 'very neat and elegant but not very commodious . . . The space between the walls being too small to admit proper lobbies and dressing rooms, too small for its purpose when the leading companies visit . . . it is too large for the ordinary run of business', sentiments which have a familiar ring with theatre managers even today.

In 1825 the theatre was fitted with gas lighting by new managers, Messrs Jones and Mackay, but three years later, audiences declined when an illegal

rival theatre opened in a rickety building in Canal Street. A collapse of its
balcony did not deter patrons, but the magistrates were not amused and it was
raided by town officials on the evening of 18 February 1828. The Theatre
Royal now enjoyed a revival, beginning its spring season with *The Fair Maid
of Perth*, which, not surprisingly, was a tremendous success. On the first night,
a large piece of plaster suddenly fell from the roof into the pit. Some people
feared that the building might be collapsing and made for the exits, but most
kept their seats and the play continued. The explanation was that a boy had
broken in from the roof of a neighbouring building by one of the ventilators
in the theatre's roof. When passing along to the opening to the gallery, he put
his foot through the plaster work. After short periods of closure in the 1830s
as new leases were negotiated, changing public tastes and the need for greater
comfort hastened the demise of the Theatre Royal. In 1845 the 'old' City Hall
was opened, and as it had better facilities, most visiting companies performed
there. After lying deserted even during the Perth Hunt Race Week, the theatre
was sold to John Jamieson, a clothing manufacturer and converted to a factory.
It later became a stationer's and a bakery, but is now a restaurant but still
recognisable outside as a Georgian playhouse.

PERTH THEATRE

It was not until 1900 that Perth folk once again could visit a proper theatre in
their town. On Thursday, 6 September, the new **Perth Theatre** opened in the
High Street, almost hidden behind a towering red-sandstone tenement facade.[2]
Only an ornamental iron and glass canopy advertised its presence, but in spite
of this, it was one of the most beautiful and intimate in Scotland. Designed by
William Alexander, a Dundee architect, the two-tiered auditorium was reached
by climbing stairs through the tenement to an airy conservatory-style foyer
with a glass roof in the back court. The cosy 950-seat theatre (managed, and
later owned, by John H. Savile, of the Paisley Theatre) had florid rococo
plaster mouldings in cream and gold and richly draped boxes in dark red. The
ceiling had a saucer-shaped dome, painted to resemble a sky with puffy clouds
and a border of wreaths and flowers, where the names of great masters of the
musical world were spelled out in gold leaf.

The first performance was *Maritana*, given by the Turner Opera Company,
and the Perth Theatre became a popular addition to the touring theatre
companies venues, with both plays and opera. All went well until the morning
of 28 April 1924 when the theatre was badly damaged by a fire which started
in the balcony. Although the firemen faced a roaring inferno when they broke
the doors open, within three quarters of an hour the fire was subdued. Both
tiers were badly damaged by burning and water and repairs were to cost
£5,000.

Figure 9.1   The unassuming facade of the Perth Theatre (author).

Savile promised that the theatre would soon re-open, but after the fire, his health deteriorated and he died in June 1924. A strike by joiners compounded its problems, but it was finally back in business on 22 September 1924 now managed by Savile's widow and daughter, with Bromley Chancellor and Enid Cooper in *When Knights were Bold*. Although most of the interior was restored, the ceiling was much simplified and it is in this form that we see the theatre today.

In 1935 Marjorie Dence and David Steuart founded the Perth Repertory Theatre, which has made its home in the Perth Theatre ever since. The indefatigable Miss Dence steered the Perth Theatre from the 1930s until her death in 1966 and built an enviable reputation for Perth Theatre with seasons of plays to suit all tastes. The start of the first season was encouraging, but as the winter advanced, audiences fell off. However, a small nucleus of regular theatre-goers formed themselves into a club to promote the interests of the theatre in any way they could, even arranging lectures, recitals and talks. In spite of these faithful friends, money was so tight that all staff nobly offered to cut their wages. Many thought that the new venture would not see its third season, but after a public subscription of £500, its fortunes changed for the better and during the following decades, many fine actors gave memorable performances in the Perth Theatre. Sir Alec Guinness, John Gregson, Donald Pleasance, Edward Woodward, Roddy Macmillan and Una McLean all made early appearances there. During the summer, the Perth Theatre hosted revues, often led by the jovial comedians and singers, Grace Clark and Colin Murray.

In 1946 the theatre passed to a local committee, formed under the chairman-ship of Sir George McGlashan of Auchterarder, and funded by the Scottish Arts Council. Dence became its artistic director and the theatre enjoyed a welcome period of stability. The arrival of television had a devastating effect on atten-dance at provincial theatres throughout the country, but this only made the management of the Perth Theatre more determined to combat the threat with top-class acting and high production values amid comfortable surroundings. The Perth Theatre retained its loyal following; numerous generous offers to purchase for redevelopment were rejected and it continued as a theatre.

In 1968 Joan Knight became its artistic director, and, like Dence before her, proved an outstanding leader. She persuaded Jimmy Logan, always popular in comic roles, to 'go straight' in the drama *Harvey*, which was highly acclaimed, and during her first seven years, audiences continued to increase.[3] After decades of hard usage, the Perth Theatre was starting to look decidedly shabby so a wide-ranging programme of improvements was commenced under the architectural direction of the Gordon and Dry Partnership.

Between May and December 1981 the auditorium was completely re-seated and redecorated; a coffee bar, restaurant and workshops were erected. Later renovation of the backstage areas commenced and even now improvements continue to be made.[4]

After suffering poor health for some time, Joan Knight retired in 1993 and died in 1996. Thanks to her, and Miss Dence, the Perth Theatre has prospered to become Scotland's most successful repertory venue, playing on average to 90 per cent capacity, a wonderful legacy. It is a joy to visit, being a model of good housekeeping with gleaming brass and well-polished woodwork and is bustling with activity throughout the day.

Figure 9.2   The Alhambra, Perth (author collection).

THE ALHAMBRA

The **Alhambra Theatre** in Kinnoull Street was developed by a local entrepreneur, James Currie as a rival to both the Perth Theatre and the few cinemas in the town. Currie had been an electrician who joined the BB Picture Company in the early days of cinema to help with its travelling cinema show around central Scotland. The architect, A. K. Beaton, designed a lavish interior with marble stairs and marquetry panels in the foyers and a spacious auditorium with 1,010 seats. There was one large balcony and stage boxes, all covered in ornately gilded plaster in the Louis XVI style. There was a large stage with twenty dressing rooms and the screen could be hoisted into the fly tower. The exterior was less successful, being a lumpish mixture of brick and stone dressings.

The Alhambra opened on 15 April 1922 and as it had such ample back-stage facilities it had an edge over the Perth Theatre when large opera companies visited the town, but once 'talkies' arrived in 1929, live performances became less frequent. The Alhambra joined the Motherwell-based Thomas Ormiston cinema circuit and later passed to the Rank Organisation, through its take-over of Gaumont British, which by then controlled the Ormiston company. The Alhambra became the Gaumont after a thorough rebuild in 1956. The interior was completely demolished and a new modern design of dubious appearance in orange, green and purple replaced it. It became an Odeon in 1962 and later ran as a nightclub for ten years before an arsonist destroyed it late in the summer of 1993.

NOTES

1. Quoted from Roy Boutcher and William G. Kemp, *The Theatre in Perth*.
2. See ibid.
3. Interview with Jimmy Logan.
4. Interview with staff during visit to Perth Theatre.

10

FIFE AND
CENTRAL SCOTLAND

DUNFERMLINE

From the 1790s Dunfermline's town green was used by visiting animal menageries and circuses. An account, written later by a former resident, recalls:

> Youngsters from all the ends of the town and from the coast towns and villages, and the mining villages inland spent long hours watching the preparations and the raising of the tent . . . There was a parade of animals through the town, led by the elephants . . . In 1815 Mr Howatt, an actor of considerable local distinction, leased the site on the east side of the Green for a theatre [this was presumably a wooden temporary construction]. He conducted his 'house' with great spirit, and gave the town folk good value for their money. His most constant patrons were the miners, whose partiality for 'the play' was unmistakable. Mr Howat was a capital stage manager as well as a capable actor. One of his pantomimes I witnessed would have done credit to a metropolitan theatre, all the more creditable because of the limited stage accommodation at his command.[1]

Howat's theatre was extended and improved many times, and finally traded as the Victoria and Albert Theatre. Even so, it was reputedly cold and draughty, and also a fire-risk.

By the 1850s Dunfermline folk wanted a public hall, so a long row of property on Guildhall Street was acquired by a local entrepreneur and inventor, William Clark. He was a publisher's son who first trained as an engineer, and using these skills he drew up ambitious plans for a complex containing three halls. The main hall at first accommodated 1,400 and was fitted with a proscenium stage. Later, galleries were added, giving it a capacity for 2,000. Below, a smaller hall was intended to be used by the Corn Exchange, but this became a venue for plays by touring companies, while in front there was a meeting room for 600. At first, locals thought that the new building was unsafe and the Dean of Guild Court was petitioned. After inspection, it was passed and opened on 30 December 1852. The main hall was intended for meetings and events of all kinds, but its main use was as a variety theatre, known as the Music Hall. This was entered through a narrow porch between existing properties down a side street, known as Music Hall Lane. Artists were booked from Glasgow and Edinburgh theatres to perform plays and give recitals, and touring companies from London made occasional visits. In 1868 the smaller hall was closed as a theatre and became a rehearsal room and dancing academy. Towards the end of its period as the Music Hall in the 1870s, evangelism became popular in Dunfermline, and many religious meetings were held there. Doubtless owing to the success of Clark's venture, a fine new public hall, St. Margaret's Hall, was constructed in St. Margaret's Street. While the Music Hall was tucked behind existing properties, this was a grandly designed venue with a fine organ. It also contained billiard rooms and a lending library. Many of the companies who had performed at the Music Hall moved to the new and more salubrious venue, and the old hall became a fully fledged variety theatre with religious meetings on Sundays. In February 1888 Professor D. Beaton, billed as 'the champion scientific swimmer of the world', and Miss Anne Beaton, the champion lady, performed various feats under water in a large glass tank, erected on the Music Hall's stage. In this tank, the Professor and his daughter performed several acts, which included eating, drinking, smoking, writing and music-playing, all under water.

In 1889 a panorama show was presented to a full house, but time was running out for the Music Hall. It had been neglected for many years, and in its final year it was plagued by a leaking roof, so much so that the well-known dramatist, W. T. Rushbury, moved his company to St. Margaret's Hall during the middle of a run in Dunfermline.

In November 1898 the *Dunfermline Journal* newspaper, run by William Clark's father leased the building as a printing works. In 1912 the newspaper moved to new premises and left the heavily altered old Music Hall abandoned. A new era in entertainment now began in Dunfermline, for the Music Hall was extensively rebuilt as the La Scala Picture Theatre, described as 'the most luxuriously equipped and up-to-date picture palace in Scotland'. It was fitted with electricity and comfortable tip-up seats for 800, and was run by R. C. Buchanan, the Edinburgh councillor and Scottish theatre impresario. Buchanan realised that in smaller towns like Dunfermline, cinemas, not theatres, were the future, and soon many of his playhouses across Scotland went over to films. In 1922 it was further rebuilt, opening in April that year as the New Scala, but it was not to last. On 13 April 1924 the cinema burned down overnight. The fire, which raged for seven hours, was thought to have started in an adjoining furniture warehouse, but the former Music Hall was totally destroyed and its ruins were demolished. St. Margaret's Hall also succumbed to fire, being destroyed in 1961, after years as a dance hall.

In 1903 two enterprising local builders, the Anderson Brothers, built a new theatre for Dunfermline, designed by a local architect, Roy Jackson. Opening on 11 September, the **Opera House** was originally a modest theatre with a plain, three-storey frontage on Reform Street, flanked by little Pavilions. The auditorium had two balconies with stage boxes, supported on slender iron columns and a domed ceiling, all softly lit by gas lanterns. The Opera House had cost £6,000 to build and the *Dunfermline Journal* praised it as a 'tidy, compact and cosy little opera house'. Unfortunately it was not a success and the theatre closed in 1910 and lay vacant for two years.

Salvation came in 1912 when the Opera House passed into the ownership of Henry Hare. He already ran the Olympia in Canmore Street. This was a

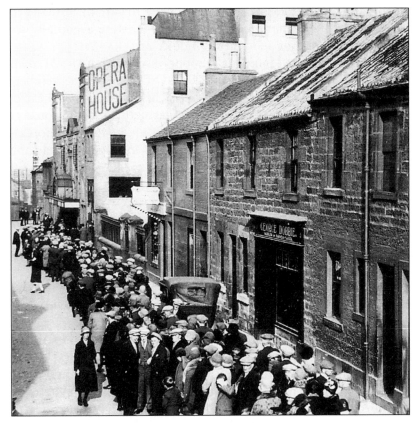

*Figure 10.1   Reform Street, Dunfermline, with queues for
the Opera House* (author collection).

former roller-skating rink, which he had rudimentarily converted in 1911 to a combined cinema and music hall. Top price at the Olympia was 6d, compared with 2/6 at the Opera House. While the Olympia attracted large audiences with a mixture of pictures, singers and local comics, the Opera House re-opened on 30 December with a touring version of the recent London hit operetta, *The Chocolate Soldier.*

With many cinemas opening in Dunfermline, it was clear that the theatre would have to be thoroughly modernised to keep up to date. Once the First World War building restrictions ended, Hare employed J. D. Swanston, the architect of the King's Theatres in Edinburgh and Kirkcaldy, to design a new interior for the Opera House. Swanston's scheme substituted fully cantilevered balconies and completely changed the form of the ceiling, boxes and proscenium. He added a new, taller fly tower and a projection box, in case the Opera House should also become a cinema. The boxes were flanked by fluted pilasters and a scrolly broken pediment topped off the crimson and gold stage curtains. The new interior was one of the finest in a provincial theatre in Scotland and the sumptuous plaster decorations in, Louis XV style, were eventually to be its saviour, although the facade remained nondescript.

Re-opened as the Opera House and Hippodrome in August 1921, ownership passed to a local company, chaired by Mr J. O'Driscoll, in September 1935. The theatre was now run by Horace Collins, who also had the Theatre Royal in Edinburgh's Broughton Place. With his expertise, the Opera House enjoyed continuous success with queues stretching to the foot of Reform Street, especially during the pantomime season and the Opera House was appropriately marketed as 'Fife's Premier Theatre'. During the early 1950s the future of the still internally beautiful Opera House became less secure and soon after celebrating its jubilee, manager Robert Walker felt it necessary to restrict twice-nightly performances to Saturday with only one house during the week. As attendances continued to decline, closure loomed and the final show was a traditional Scottish song and dance show, starring Joe Peterson, George Cormack, Irene Sharp and Andy Stewart on 26 March 1955.

The Opera House became a furniture and electrical goods warehouse, a fate which saved it from demolition. The superb interior was badly neglected – but not wilfully harmed. When a nationwide survey of surviving Victorian and Edwardian theatres was carried out in 1981, the splendours of the long-abandoned Opera House auditorium were again discovered and the building was given a well-deserved grade B listing, although it remained derelict. In April 1982 a fire began in the grand circle seating, but fortunately, this was quickly controlled with only superficial damage to the theatre, even so its future looked bleak. Happily, Professor (now Sir) James Dunbar-Naismith, brought his architecture students from Heriot-Watt University to survey the theatre with a view to its restoration. But the local council was anxious to be rid of what was externally an eyesore especially as its site was needed for redevelopment. Under Dunbar-Naismith's guidance, the interior was carefully dismantled and all the ornate cornices, wall panels, friezes, carved box fronts, proscenium and ceiling arches were carefully cut out and labelled before the demolition men moved in. Even the pediment stone from the facade was rescued and put in storage. 'It really was completely unnecessary to demolish it,' recalls Sir James Dunbar-Naismith. 'It would only have cost peanuts to retain it but nobody at that time felt there was a future for it. Yet the similarly-sized Perth Theatre shows how successfully it could have been renovated.' What followed was remarkable and totally unexpected.

Half way across the world, in Sarasota, Florida, a new performing arts complex was being prepared and the designers recognised the attraction that a traditional, intimate, curvaceous and plush theatre would be. They purchased the entire auditorium plaster work from the Opera House in Dunfermline for half a million dollars and had it despatched in containers to the United States.

Dunfermline's loss was Sarasota's gain and after spending $15 million, with sponsorship from Burt Reynolds, the auditorium was duly restored to its former brilliance as the main auditorium at the heart of the new Asolo Centre for the Performing Arts, opened on 27 January 1990. The dimensions of the original were modified slightly to suit modern requirements, even so every effort was made to replicate the original decoration and curtain design.

Figure 10.2   Interior of the Opera House as re-created at the Asolo Centre for the Performing Arts (courtesy Bob Bain).

With a clutch of cinemas, the Olympia and Opera House theatres, Dunfermline, was certainly a hub for entertainment, but in 1924 an even larger theatre, the **Alhambra,** was built at the junction of Canmore Street and New Row. The theatre was developed by a syndicate of local businessmen, headed by Henry Hare of the existing Opera House, and designed by John Fraser. Construction had started in 1921, but due to materials shortages it was not ready for opening until 4 August 1924. The theatre was entirely clad in English red facing brick and had a small frontage with stone dressings facing Canmore street, with the massive auditorium and battlements on its castle-like fly tower

Figure 10.3 Frontage of the Alhambra, Dunfermline (author collection).

Figure 10.4 Interior of the Alhambra as a bingo hall (author collection).

rearing up behind. While hardly beautiful, it was solidly constructed and conceived on a grand scale. The foyer was double-height with pay boxes on either side and massive Doric columns. The auditorium had one immense fully cantilevered tier of seating, which was split with the 'gallery' immediately behind the 'dress circle'. The *Dunfermline Press* emphasised 'the enormous stage . . . with sufficient accommodation in every way to stage grand operas, pantomimes or spectacular plays.' Shortly before opening the Alhambra, the management had a rethink and perhaps wisely decided that Dunfermline could never support two theatres, so the new building started out as a luxury super cinema, with the screen set back in the stage and surrounded by specially painted scenery. It opened with the D. W. Griffith film *White Rose*, followed by *The Wembley Exhibition – The Eighth Wonder of the World* with orchestral accompaniment. There were later occasional visits by theatre companies, but after the advent of the 'talkies', the Alhambra became a full-time cinema. It is now extremely well preserved as a bingo hall with its extensive stage put to good use as the no-smoking section.

COWDENBEATH

Once known as the 'Chicago of Fife' when twenty coal pits worked within a three-mile radius of the town, Cowdenbeath had its Empire Theatre, opened in

1899, to entertain its miners and their families. The Empire was a solid stone building, designed by J. D. Swanston, with one balcony and stage boxes. Although small, it was very popular and Harry McKelvie's prestigious pantomimes transferred there from their base at the Royal Princess's Theatre in Glasgow – an April event eagerly anticipated throughout Fife, especially when comedian and penny-whistle player Sam Thomson was principal. Cowdenbeath was then on the tram system, and special late cars to Lochgelly, Kelty, Crossgates and Dunfermline were laid on after each performance. From 1914 the proprietor, George Penman, ran cine-variety and the professional acts were replaced by twice-weekly talent contests for locals during the First World War. The Empire became a full-time cinema in 1922.

METHIL

On the coast, Methil was another important town in the Fife coal field. Despite its close proximity to Kirkcaldy, the **Gaiety Theatre** opened there on 27 December 1907. Also designed by Swanston, this most attractive little theatre was built behind an existing terrace in Denbeath; with the 'orchestra stalls' and 'circle' foyer converted from a disused post office, it had a large glazed canopy on iron columns lit from within in a blaze of electric light. This was panelled

Figure 10.5   Entrance to the Gaiety, Methil, in use as a recruiting office during the First World War (author collection).

with mahogany dados and white marble stairs led to the auditorium. The pit and balcony were reached through doorways further along the street. The theatre had two tiers with stage boxes and baroque-style plaster decorations in cream with gold leaf and shading.

During the First World War, the Gaiety served as Methil's army recruiting office, the tragic consequences of so many brave men signing up being visible today on Methil's war memorial. In the 1920s it became the Denbeath Theatre of Varieties, and later a full-time cinema called the Western with shows at seven and nine. The cinema closed finally in 1973 and the gutted building is now Rick's Nightclub, although the fly tower is still very visible.

LEVEN

With the exception of the Second World War years when it was requisitioned by the army, the Beach Pavilion in Leven was a successful venue for summer revues, advertised as concert parties, from 1929 until 1965. Leven was Fife's favourite seaside resort and shows at the Beach Pavilion were hosted by comedians Ian Maclean and Ballard Brown, or later the lanky Tommy Hood. Doubling as a cinema and dance hall, the Jubilee Theatre was a conversion of the town hall which also staged occasional variety shows during the holiday season. After the 1951 summer revue, the Jubilee reverted to being a dance hall. It was demolished in 1973 for a road development.

LOCHGELLY

In Lochgelly, the Reid's Hall opened on 26 December 1908. Although it had a large stage and hosted many variety 'turns' to entertain the miners, its simple interior with a barrel-vaulted ceiling and one balcony looked more like a contemporary cinema. Quickly renamed the Opera House, it was sold during the early 1930s to J. B. Milne's cinema circuit and is now a bingo hall.

KIRKCALDY

Although plays were given by touring companies in the town's Corn Exchange, Kirkcaldy's first theatre was the Theatre Royal in Kirk's Wynd, opened in 1887. Notwithstanding its grand name, it was a basic building, whose interior was made almost entirely of wood. It had previously been a flax warehouse and was leased from John Hunter, a local farmer.

Early in the morning of 30 December 1888, the theatre was found to be on fire, and as there was an armoury in the building next door, it was crucial for the fire brigade to stop the flames from spreading in case there were explosives. While the fire-fighters dowsed the adjacent roofs, the wooden theatre burned out and only the blackened stone walls were left. At first the cause of the fire was a mystery as the theatre had been closed for some time, but it was insured and it soon became apparent that it was arson to defraud the insurers. In March 1889 George Clark, John and Andrew Torrance appeared before Lord Younger at Dundee Circuit Court, charged with wilful fire-raising and attempting to defraud the Federal Insurance Company Ltd. Clark, who had been in Edinburgh at the time of the fire, pled not guilty, but it turned out that the Torrances had been left the theatre in a trust-deed. Without any skills in theatre management, they had run up heavy debts and John Torrance was given a five-year jail sentence for his attempt at fraud.

The new **King's Theatre** opened on 14 November 1904 having been developed by R. C. Buchanan at a cost of £20,000. Designed by John D. Swanston, the Kirkcaldy architect who had already produced the larger King's in Edinburgh, the King's was entered through a handsome row of red-sandstone tenements (by William Williamson), with a bay window and pediment above the entrance. The lofty Edwardian elegance of the foyer, in white and pale green with two grand marble staircases with torch-bearers at the foot set the tone. Flooring was of linoleum – a product for which Kirkcaldy is famous. Patrons entered the incredible baroque auditorium through heavy mahogany doors. As at Edinburgh, Swanston again produced towering ranks of boxes, eight on each side, and it seems that again the balcony fronts were slammed into these in an arbitrary fashion. Doubtless, because the King's was beside the sea, a nautical theme was chosen for the trompe l'oeil panels and domed ceiling above, which had mermaids and whales, in gilded wavy frames. The King's seated 2,000

Figure 10.6 The frontage of the King's theatre, Kirkcaldy (author collection).

Figure 10.7 The elegant foyer of the King's (author collection).

with railings around the backs of the two tiers for a further 500 standees. Lighting was by gas chandeliers and to prevent it getting unbearably hot, the middle of the ceiling could slide open during the interval.

At first the King's was a touring theatre with drama, opera and musicals. This policy was misguided, and having accumulated debts, Buchanan's syndicate sold the King's to the showman E. H. Bostock in 1908 for only £7,000. Bostock renamed it the Hippodrome and presented pictures and variety, especially circus acts. In 1916 it became the Opera House and was sold to John Maxwell's Scottish Cinema and Variety Theatres in 1928, but was the wrong shape for films, especially when 'talkies' arrived. Maxwell had the theatre rebuilt in 1937 as a modern cinema with a streamlined interior by Charles J. McNair, the Glasgow cinema specialist.[2] The building has since been split into three screens and is still entertaining Kirkcaldy folk as the ABC.

The **Palace** in Whytecauseway was a smaller 1,100-seat variety theatre, also designed by John D. Swanston and opened on 10 May 1913 by Bailie James Wright, a shareholder in the local firm that ran it. Outside, it was an interesting building of colour-washed cement blocks in debased art nouveau style; the large leaded windows at the first floor fronted the circle lounge. In the corner tower there was a tea room, which was open air in good weather. The Palace had one balcony with comfortable red tip-up seats throughout and

Figure 10.8   The magnificent auditorium of the King's (author collection).

the auditorium was decorated in shades of cream with gilding. The stage was 30 by 50 feet and had a full set of scenery for variety turns but being outside the established circuits, the Palace found it hard to book the best acts, and it soon became a cinema. The stage was dismantled to increase seating, and as with the Opera House, it passed to Scottish Cinema and Variety Theatres in 1928. The nitrate film spools of the time were highly flammable, and it was thought to be one of these smouldering overnight that made the building burn down on 28 December 1946. Due to war-time restrictions, it was never rebuilt.

BO'NESS

The **Hippodrome** was intended as a venue for the frequent visits by circus

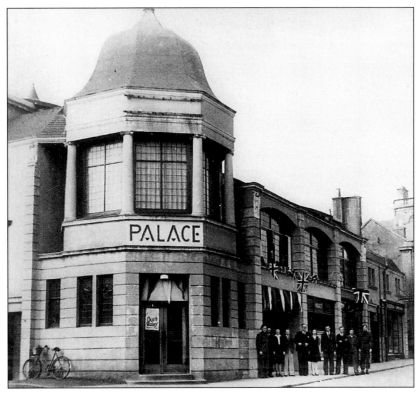

Figure 10.9   The Palace, Kirkcaldy (author collection).

troupes to Bo'ness, with variety and cinema shows between. It was designed by
Matthew Steele for the showman Louis Dickson and declared open by Provost
Grant on 11 March 1912. It was an interesting circular structure in the Scottish
art nouveau style with harled walls, a shallow domed roof and entrance porti-
cos at each end. Within, there was a small amphitheatre with a ring in the
middle and a proscenium at one end. Almost immediately after opening, the
Hippodrome became a full-time cinema, which it remained until the 1970s
when bingo took over. Following a spell of dereliction, the historically rare and
interesting structure was rescued and partly restored by the Bo'ness Heritage
Trust. Unfortunately, it has not found further use and has since continued to
deteriorate.

FALKIRK

In the eighteenth century, Falkirk folk went to a wooden theatre in Callender
Riggs for their entertainment. When Vicar Street was redeveloped in the 1900s,

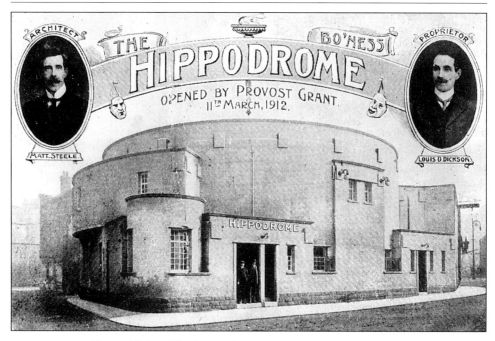

Figure 10.10   The Hippodrome, Bo'ness (author collection).

R. C. Buchanan bought land on which he developed the impressive **Grand Theatre and Opera House**. The Grand was designed by one of its directors, the Hamilton architect Alex Cullen, who also produced the handsome art nouveau tenements fronting the street behind which the theatre stood with side entrances cut through existing properties on neighbouring Princes Street. It was a vast enterprise of operatic grandeur with room for over 2,200 and complications in its construction made it seem that it would not be finished on time. However, the builders worked round the clock for a month as there were penalty clauses in the contract and eventually it was ready just one hour before a private reception for the Provost and magistrates on 24 December 1903.[3]

It had three tiers with no less than fourteen private boxes, four on each side of the stage and three at the circle sides. The circle fronts had gilded plaster garlands and stencilled foliage on a cream background. There were statues of nautch girls between the boxes and painted panels above the proscenium and on the ceiling dome depicted the art of music. Thirsty patrons were well catered for in the Grand's five bars.

The Grand opened to the public on Christmas Eve with the W. W. Kelly's company from the Princess's Theatre in London in *A Royal Divorce*, a play about the Battle of Waterloo. The first season of plays and opera was well attended and at their annual general meeting, the directors paid dividends of between 6 and 12 per cent to shareholders. From 1907 the theatre was opened during the summer holidays with variety shows with a visit by the Anglo-American Bioscope Company drawing particularly good audiences. That out-fit showed topical films, including footage of the Prince and Princess of Wales's visit to Glasgow, shot only five days earlier. By the First World War variety programmes became more common and with many cinemas opening and travel restrictions affecting touring companies, cine-variety was introduced for a short time in 1917. When peace returned, the Grand was redecorated and con-tinued to host many London companies touring Buchanan's theatres. These high-quality productions seem to have had little appeal to Falkirk audiences and Mrs Elspeth Clark recalled that 'The Grand was thought to be a bit posh and special. We went to the pictures every week nearly, but the theatre was something you saved up for and got dressed up nicely to go with your parents. The only time there were big queues at the theatre in Falkirk was for pantomimes and pictures.'[4]

The Grand was sold to the Stanley Rodgers Circuit in 1920. Faced with declining audiences, matinees were abandoned for some shows and on 29 December 1926, the Grand passed to Henry Hare to become a cinema with occasional variety acts. John Maxwell's ABC took it over in 1929, and in need

Figure 10.11   The Grand Theatre and the Salon Picture House face each other across Vicar Street, Falkirk (author collection).

of redecoration, Maxwell decided that it would be better to demolish and build a new cinema of the latest design. The Grand closed without ceremony in April 1932. The auditorium and a row of two-storey properties on Princess Street were demolished and on their site the Regal cinema, designed by Charles J. McNair opened in October 1934, the original access to the Grand Theatre becoming the entrance to the cinema café. Apart from sections of one auditorium wall, which were incorporated in the new cinema, the still elegant facade is all that remains of the long-lost Grand Theatre. The Regal still enjoys success as the ABC.

While the Grand with its heavier productions was failing, Falkirk's other theatre, the Roxy was thriving with its cheerful diet of films and variety. Originally the Erskine Church in Silver Row, after a spell as a roller-skating venue, it was converted to the Electric Theatre in 1910 by Teddy Atkinson, who spent £2,000 on the conversion. At first silent films were shown, but by Christmas 1913, the Scots character comedian Donald Mackay and the Balmorals musical group were at the Electric, accompanied by a resident orchestra, led by the exotically-named Otto Zeblock. In 1921 the stage was enlarged and the theatre became the Empire.

In 1938 it was completely gutted and a new art deco-style interior was built with central heating and comfortable seats. The theatre was now the Roxy – named after Samuel 'Roxy' Rothafel, a legendary New York showman who ran two of the world's biggest cinema-theatres, the Roxy and Radio City Music Hall. The comparatively modest Falkirk Roxy re-opened in October 1938 (still a theatre) with 'Britain's King of Swing' Billy Mason and his orchestra. It became a favourite haunt of soldiers from Grangemouth barracks, and in 1943 the young Max Bygraves got a start there, singing and doing a sketch for fellow troops, when serving in the RAF.

The Roxy closed down in 1958, the management claiming it was not only a victim of television, but also CinemaScope – the wide-screen format fitted to rival cinemas. It was pulled down in 1961 and replaced by a hotel.

STIRLING

Up the hill opposite the railway station, within the shopping arcade, was the Arcade Theatre. It opened in 1882, designed by John McLean, who also built the elegant surrounding arcade. The theatre was reached up a stairway with the pit at first-floor level. It had two U-shaped balconies, supported on iron columns, with a vaulted ceiling of painted panels. It seated 1,200 and had a chequered start with various short leases. It was sold to William Crawford in 1912, who ran variety twice nightly, renaming it the Alhambra Music Hall: Films also proved popular and it passed to Stirling Cinema and Variety Theatres in 1930 as a full-time cinema, but stage shows returned by the end of the decade. Because of safety concerns about its restricted access, the Alhambra closed as a fire risk in 1939 and was partially converted to a shop. It is now abandoned, but the deserted interior still contains fragments of the theatre – an ornate twisting staircase in the entrance, fragments of plaster decoration and the form of the old auditorium, boxed in under layers of shop fittings.

Close to the Alhambra in Murray Place was the rival Olympia, a former roller-skating hall which became a variety and picture house in 1911. It burned down in a spectacular fire ten years later.

NOTES

1. From an article by 'An Old Fifer Abroad' in the *Dunfermline Journal*, 8 September 1862.
2. See Allen Eyles, *ABC: The First Name in Entertainment.*
3. See the *Falkirk Herald*, 24 December 1903.
4. Interview with Mrs Elspeth Clark.

11

LANARKSHIRE

COATBRIDGE

The discovery of ironstone in 1805 sealed the future of Coatbridge as Scotland's iron burgh. By mid-century a grim industrial panorama of belching chimneys and furnaces stretched as far as the eye could see along the Main Street. The smoke, heat, light and noise went on twenty-four hours a day, seven days a week. 'Hell with the lid off' was how one correspondent described the town. The industry brought great wealth, which was reflected in the town's impressive municipal architecture. Large numbers of Scots came there off the land, as did the Irish, and by the 1870s the population of Old Monkland Parish (which included the neighbouring burgh of Airdrie) exceeded 40,000. These folk needed to be entertained, so in 1873, work was started on the **Theatre Royal**. When finally it opened on 1 September 1875 on a commanding site at the east end of the Main Street, and opposite the sprawling Phoenix and Clifton Ironworks' forest of chimneys, the splendid new theatre, designed by W. R. Quinton of Glasgow, was a much needed addition to the town. It was lofty and commodious, with seats for 2,000 and could then claim to be the finest theatre in Scotland (it pre-dated the mighty Edinburgh Theatre by three months). *The Era* was duly impressed:

> The circle is luxuriously upholstered in crimson utricht . . . The gallery – supported on two rows of iron pillars, one row in the centre and another in front, the front pillars being painted in marble with gilt Corinthian capitals – is very comfortably seated. The decorations are . . . very attractive. The large ornamental domed ceiling strikes the eye the moment one enters, being elaborately frescoed in Pompeiian style. The proscenium walls are laid out in panels which are filled with portraits of the following eminent authors: Shakespeare, Scott, Burns, Goldsmith, Sheridan and Goethe – all of whom were largely employed

Figure 11.1   Interior of the Theatre Royal (author collection).

in the development and the cultivation of the modern drama . . . The stair cases are wide and spacious and no fewer than nine fire exits have been provided, so that the utmost safety of 'Lovers of Drama' is assured.

In January 1907 the Theatre Royal was sold to R. C. Buchanan's rapidly expanding chain of provincial theatres. After the pantomime season, it was closed for a month to be fitted with electricity and entirely redecorated, in time for a visit by Mrs Brandmann-Palmer, a well-known Shakespearean actress who brought her London company to the Theatre Royal on 28 February to perform Schiller's tragedy *Mary, Queen of Scots* and *Jane Shore*. The Theatre Royal had become notorious for the drunken behaviour of some of its audiences, and occasionally police assistance was needed. Buchanan was obviously determined to improve matters, so it was now advertised as 'Coatbridge's FAMILY Theatre . . . With TEMPERANCE bar adjacent'.

Although the Theatre Royal had held a cinematograph licence since 1910, its mixed diet of opera, melodrama, classic plays and variety continued until

Figure 11.2   Theatre Royal, Coatbridge (author collection).

1919, when faced with competition from cinemas, Buchanan decided finally to introduce cine-variety.

The Theatre Royal was again redecorated in 1920. This had to be done regularly as, quite apart from people smoking, the air in Coatbridge was so acrid that the theatre was frequently filled with smog, while the dirt from people's clothes quickly filthied the upholstery. When the Theatre Royal re-opened, as a part-time cinema, the *Advertiser* reported that 'the proscenium is now a thing of beauty once again and the stage arrangements are attractive and smart. The new street scene is a highly creditable rendition of Church Street in Coatbridge.' In 1922 the theatre was leased to the Stanley Rodgers Circuit, who ran provincial variety theatres scattered across northern England. James Louden was a local entrepreneur whose firm, Coatbridge Varieties Ltd, became the lessee in 1926. Drama was now abandoned completely in favour of low-cost pictures and variety shows. During the depression of the early 1930's he introduced a weekly talent show on Wednesdays, the winner being promised a week's engagement at the theatre. Friday was amateurs' night with 5s prizes for winning turns. Once a week, a big-name star was booked, usually from Glasgow, but the last variety show was given in May 1938, when Tommy Morgan and George West from the Pavilion appeared. The old theatre was then sold to the Harry Winocour Cinema Circuit, and to Green's (of Playhouse fame) in 1956. John Duddy, an Airdrie cinema projectionist, recalls a visit in the late 1950s:

> The Theatre Royal was the only cinema to usher its patrons up to the 'gods', which were not only terrifyingly steep, but creaky as well. It was listed as a 1,000 seater at the time, but on all occasions I visited, I never saw a seat! The audience sat on the raised steps of the floor, looking at a wee screen at their feet, through a wire mesh safety fence. To make things worse, you often had to face the side because of the shape of the balcony, or had a pillar to block the view. They crammed hundreds of kids into the dark, dirty interior. Although the paint was blackened by nicotine and the chandelier had gone, you could just make out painted panels around the screen and ceiling dome. I recall seeing Lon Chaney Snr in a re-issue of *The Unholy Three* there, billed as 'the man with a thousand faces'.

Largely unaltered since 1875, and totally unsuitable as a cinema, the Theatre Royal became the first casualty of the 1950s decline in attendances. It closed on 9 August 1958, amid rumours that it might become a dance hall. Instead it lay derelict until 1966, when it was demolished to enable road widening. Nowadays, the Jackson Street high-rise flats look down on where the Theatre Royal once stood in an area that has changed out of all recognition.

The Empire Theatre on Main Street opened in 1912. Without a change of name, it was sold to the Singleton Cinema Circuit around 1920. It became the Odeon from 1936 until closure and redevelopment in 1971.

AIRDRIE

Airdrie, Coatbridge's older neighbour, was a weaving village before it too was overrun by the iron and coal industries. Today, it has the only tangible remains of the once flourishing music-hall business in the Monklands in the much altered Rialto Bingo Club and amusement arcade in Hallcraig Street. The building actually started out as the town's Corn Exchange of 1856, designed by James Thomson. It has an attractive harled frontage on a corner with a pediment, flanked by chimneys and topped with the town crest. From the 1870s onwards, it housed shooting galleries, boxing booths and the side shows associated with a fairground on land behind. In 1908 it was completely rebuilt as the Hippodrome Theatre of Varieties, a small music hall with a single shallow balcony.

The **Hippodrome** is remembered by past generations of Airdrieonians for shows with the kilted tenor, J. M. Hamilton, who, brandishing a broadsword, took the theatre by storm with his rendering of 'McGregor's Gathering'. From

Figure 11.3   The Hippodrome, Airdrie (author collection).

further afield the great escapologist, Harry Houdini came to Airdrie. Indeed, so many folk wanted to see the great international entertainer on his visit in 1913 that having done a performance inside to a packed audience, he then performed in front of a crowd of 7,000 at the road junction in front of the theatre. Standing on the front steps, he was chained and handcuffed by the local police sergeant, but, as usual, quickly escaped from a variety of sacks and crates. Lastly, his famous 'Water Torture Chamber' was wheeled round and filled by the fire brigade. Of course, Houdini escaped yet again, amidst great cheers.

The Hippodrome closed for redecoration and the installation of central heating in June 1929 and re-opened as the Rialto with cine-variety on 30 September 1929. The theatre went over to films full time when the Second World War loomed ten years later. It has been a bingo hall since 1962.

Dating from 1911, the Pavilion Theatre in Graham Street was another variety house which ended up as an Odeon cinema. It was a basic brick shed with one level of seating (the 'balcony' was a few steps up from the stalls) and the stage was only 16 feet deep.

LARKHALL

Larkhall, a mining town south of Motherwell, had two music halls, despite a population of only 14,000. The Grand Central in Union Street, which opened in 1909, seated 1,000 and became a cinema in 1914. It was destroyed by fire in 1930, but amazingly, its rival, the **Empire** still stands in a largely unaltered state. It was a pioneering venture by George Urie Scott, a Glasgow cinema and theatre magnate. It was a typically sturdy brick hall with a small stage (no fly tower) and an ornate entrance portico. Inside, there was a single raked floor with wooden forms, a barrel-vaulted ceiling and pilastered side walls. There were two performances nightly with films shown on four nights from 1917. The Empire became a full-time cinema when 'talkie' equipment was fitted in 1930; live shows were dropped due to the popularity of talkies. Inevitably it is now a bingo hall and is a fascinating reminder of a lost era in entertainment.[1]

The type was common in smaller towns across Lanarkshire and those theatres and music halls that did not succumb to fire became cinemas before the First World War. The Pavilions in Wishaw and Mossend, the Empire in Shotts, the Olympia in Blantyre and the Alhambra in Carluke (destroyed by fire in 1935) all followed the pattern. In Bellshill, a town serving several mines, the **Bellshill Theatre** in the Main Street opened in 1904 with variety shows twice nightly. It became the Picture House in 1911 and the structure still survives, housing shops and a snooker club.

Figure 11.4 The Empire, Larkhall (author collection).

Figure 11.5   The Bellshill Theatre (author collection).

HAMILTON

The earliest permanent home for the presentation of concerts, melodrama and variety was the Victoria Hall in Quarry Street. It was located on the first and second floors of a substantial red-sandstone block, designed by local architect Andrew Downie in 1887. Comfort was not a primary concern for the capacity 1,500 patrons who sat on forms in the pit and wooden tip-up seats in the balcony. The single balcony was supported on slender iron columns and the shallow stage had no flies. It was leased to Rene Clayton, who came from a circus family. Having performed with equestrian acts all over the British Empire, he went into music-hall management and soon made friends with young and rising stars.

In 1908 E. H. Bostock bought the Victoria Hall and had it renovated as the Playhouse. Opened in 1909, it was Hamilton's first cinema and the emphasis was on 'educative productions'. It was not until 1 December 1947 that the Playhouse, rechristened the Granada Theatre, went back to live shows and for the next ten years, twice-nightly variety was presented.

The theatre was still cramped with inadequate facilities for both performers and audience. It closed in April 1958. Ironically, the ground floor was later converted to a television showroom – the medium that had darkened countless theatres. The auditorium of the former Playhouse has been floored over at balcony height to make a bedding warehouse; otherwise, it is still completely

Figure 11.6   The Hippodrome, Hamilton (author collection).

recognisable as an old-time music hall with some ornate light fittings intact and slender iron columns still holding up the floors.

Bostock's **Hippodrome** had already opened on 14 October 1907 in Townhead Street. It was a large predominantly wooden building with an English-style twin-towered facade which must have looked quaint among the dour sandstone terraces surrounding it. None the less, the *Lanarkshire Illustrated* was impressed by the theatre's appointments:

> The Hippodrome is a bright and airy building, brightly upholstered and exceedingly comfortable. The ceiling has been formed into panels containing a bold and effective design in shades of yellow, blue and crimson, on a cream ground. The walls are papered with Japanese paper, and the wood-work finished bright red and white, with ornamental door-caps, giving the building a rich, comfortable appearance. The corridors have been treated in tones of green and crimson; and the crush hall has been handsomely decorated and gilded with raised material in Louis XIV style . . . The Hippodrome in every part is healthy and well ventilated and is kept like a drawing room.

The interior had a circle and balcony, and the proscenium and stalls could be removed to make a ring suitable for circus performances. In 1941 the Hippodrome was sold to the Harry Winocour cinema circuit, with variety shows booked on three nights a week. In 1946 the very youthful Jimmy Logan made his debut there with his parents' troupe, the Fabulous Logans. He recalls:

> The old Hippodrome was one of the strangest theatres I have ever played. It was totally built of beautifully carved wood – the supports, the balconies, the ceiling – everything! It was also a bit cold and had seen better days, especially the dressing rooms. We had a good audience, though – Lanarkshire folk are always lively. It was booked by the famous Galt's Agency, whose offices were above the old Empire in Sauchiehall Street. Sadly a few weeks after we left, the Hippodrome went on fire.

Notwithstanding the *Lanarkshire Illustrated*'s claim when it opened that 'The arrangements against the outbreak of fire are such as to ensure perfect safety in all parts of the house,' Hamilton's magistrates had made several attempts to have the Hippodrome closed during the 1930s as it seemed inevitable that it would one day succumb to fire. These fears were realised on Burns Night 1946 when the theatre was reduced to a collapsed smouldering mass of corrugated iron sheeting, blackened timber and metal. Fortunately, it was empty at the time and its remains were quickly demolished.

MOTHERWELL

Motherwell, to the north of Hamilton, is a sprawling town whose reputation was founded on iron and, later, steel. The vast Ravenscraig and Dalzell works were the last remnants of these once mighty industries, but these too have been mothballed or demolished and the development of a one-way system and new shopping precinct has meant that very little of the town's original character remains. The old centre was around Brandon Street with its rows of two-storey buildings in red sandstone. Heavy industry was the heart of the local economy and there were huge populations to be entertained. Early variety performances were given in the local Working Men's Clubs, YMCAs or Orange Halls. In 1898 the town's first proper variety theatre opened at the top end of Barry Street, near to Brandon Street. The Alhambra was developed by a syndicate of local businessmen who had chosen their site carefully – it was at one of the principal intersections of the Lanarkshire tramway system. The Alhambra had a small, but flamboyant red-sandstone facade with brick and wood rear-quarters. Apart from some rudimentary plans and a couple of newspaper adverts, little can be found about the Alhambra. It became the Cinema as early as 1910 and was dismantled after a fire in 1934, being replaced by the much larger New Cinema. It too is long gone and the site is obscured by a new road lay-out.

The rival Pavilion, opened in 1900, stood not a hundred yards away at the foot of Brandon Street. This larger hall seated 1,200 and had a balcony with boxes. It became a cinema in 1913 when sold to the local Thomas Ormiston circuit. It later became a Gaumont, then the Majestic Ballroom from the autumn of 1959. A fire destroyed the predominantly wooden structure in 1963 and it was shortly demolished.[2]

The Empire Theatre at the corner of Camp Street and Parkhead Street had a more unusual history. It began in January 1911 as the Electric Theatre, rather banally designed but, for its time, an unusually large cinema which began with programmes of 'Cinematograph Pictures', followed by five variety turns. At Christmas 1916 it was sold to the Glasgow impresario Walter Thompson and the policy of showing the latest pictures with a live show continued until the advent of 'talkies'. Then, the big national cinema chains began to take all the latest pictures, so instead the Empire became a full-time variety theatre. During the summer when audiences dwindled and touring acts could not fill the cavernous interior, films returned and Christmas pantomimes were given every year from 1932. Mrs Mary Stephen, now in her seventies, remembers the Empire:

As a girl, I always thought the Empire was the poorer of the Motherwell theatres. My clearest memory is of Tommy Lorne, whom I thought hilarious. He did a sketch once of a village post office with Postmaster Lorne trying to give a customer a postage stamp. The request made Tommy search the office from top to bottom – even crawling over the floor, looking under the chair and table legs, all the time assuring his customer, with hysterical laughter from the audience, that he had seen one only the other day . . . In the thirties, all the big names visited – Joe O'Rourke, Tommy Morgan, Lex McLean and no show was complete without the Moxon Girls, a troupe of well-trained dancers who opened the shows. When you sat in the big, dingy theatre, and the music started and they came out in those super sparkling costumes – it was wonderful!

By the 1950s the Empire was past its best. As living standards and people's expectations grew, it could no longer attract the remaining big names. It closed in 1958 and was converted to a garage – a strangely appropriate use as the building had always resembled one. Later it was abandoned and for years lay derelict only a few metres away from the town's fine, modern civic centre.

The finest of Motherwell's many theatres, and possibly the finest provincial theatre in Scotland, was the delightful **New Century Theatre** in Windmillhill Street, which opened on 6 January 1902. Alec Cullen, who designed the New Century, was a local man, born in Craigneuk, who not only produced a group of four very fine theatres for the R. C. Buchanan chain, which controlled the New Century. His firm, Cullen, Lochead and Brown, was a leading exponent of art nouveau, and the New Century Theatre was one of the finest examples of the style. Built on the site of a row of demolished weavers' cottages, the new theatre had an elegantly proportioned symmetrical frontage in red sandstone. There were five separate entrances to the differently priced seating areas; above was a loggia of three bays capped with two imposing lanterns which shone invitingly down the street at night. The stalls and circle foyer had a brilliant white-marble floor with white wooden dados and statues of torch-bearing females at the foot of the stairways, which had crimson drapes and carpets. The auditorium seated 1,500 with two tiers and four boxes on either side of the proscenium. The *Motherwell Times* described the town's new wonder theatre at length, commenting on the use of upholstered tip-up seats, even for pit seats and on the use of electric lighting throughout.

> The dress circle is fully cantilevered and takes a wide sweep over the pit. The gallery follows the same line and a clear view of the stage is obtained, even from the back seats. High above the heads of the 'gods' is a beautifully decorated lantern. The decorations are sumptuously achieved in the style of Louis XIV; rich, yet characterised with artistic reserve. The gilt mouldings and ornaments, set off by crimson hangings and upholstery, form a combination of light and warmth which is most pleasing to the eye.

The opening night was a great event and, despite heavy rain, Brandon Street was blocked by the crowds. The Lanarkshire Tramway Company laid

Figure 11.7   The New Century Theatre, Motherwell (author collection).

on special services to bring patrons to and from the theatre, which opened with *Robinson Crusoe*. The *Motherwell Times* noted that 'although there was a little difficulty in getting things to work smoothly, the audience was very indulgent'.

The New Century became known for quality drama, musicals and lavishly costumed pantomimes. Many touring companies visited and, according to the pained messages written home by actors on picture postcards of the theatre, their greatest problem was finding suitable lodgings as their late hours did not appeal to 'better class' landladies! 'Living in squalor . . . leaking roof . . . no hot water . . . miserable town' wrote one London actress in 1918. The theatre was the scene of one grim tragedy during the matinee of the pantomime *The Babes in the Wood* in 1912. The large audience, mainly children, was engrossed in the play, but was suddenly startled to hear a middle-aged man in the gallery shouting 'This is mockery, but here is reality,' at the same time drawing a knife across his throat and expiring almost immediately. Suddenly, all was horror and confusion and the *Motherwell Times* thought it a miracle that no one was hurt in the stampede for the exits.

The theatre was immediately closed for redecoration and it re-opened as the Motherwell Theatre on 25 September 1913 – a cinema. Cinema shows were only a brief, and oddly unsuccessful, interlude and the theatre became the New Century again with drama and variety from 1915.

In November 1929 R. C. Buchanan sold the New Century theatre with three others to Scottish Cinema and Variety Theatres, a burgeoning cinema chain run by a Glasgow solicitor called John Maxwell. Maxwell was a staunch Liberal and had stood as the Motherwell candidate in the 1922 general election but despite a stirring rally at which David Lloyd George spoke, Maxwell was soundly beaten by the Communist, J. T. W. Newbold. The New Century Theatre became Motherwell's second Scottish Cinema and Variety Theatres cinema (Maxwell already ran La Scala), but was hardly ideal as it had too many seats with an angled view of the screen. It was closed and partially demolished in 1933 so that a radical reconstruction could take place. The site was excavated to a depth of twenty feet – right down to the boulder clay. Only one wall and part of the original facade remained and it was rebuilt as the Rex cinema in 1936 with 2,031 seats in a plain, modern auditorium. The internal modifications were necessary, but the partial cladding of the original frontage in brown and cream bricks was a mistake, especially as the remains of the original lanterns still stuck out of the top. The Rex closed in 1976 and after a spell of dereliction, the building became an amusement arcade and nightclub. It too failed and the building was finally demolished during the spring of 1995.

Today, Motherwell's entertainment is presented in the Motherwell Civic Theatre, in the modern civic centre complex of 1969, where variety favourites like Jimmy Logan, Dorothy Paul and Andy Cameron play to full houses. While the old entrepreneurs would not have been too surprised to find a hall holding over 1,800, they would have been amazed to find this venue has just 395 seats. It could never make a profit, but these ambitious showmen of old did not receive state subsidies.

However, they did leave a wonderful legacy of magnificent buildings, many of which will continue to entertain us well into the millennium.

NOTES

1. In Lanarkshire towns, most 'turns' were local singers and comics. Irish singing and dancing were popular. There were occasional visits by big stars from the Glasgow shows. In early days, some music-hall performers, most notably the hypnotist Dr Bodie, made extensive tours of these small theatres. Where none existed, the local public hall or Miners' Welfare Hall was used. Audiences were packed in and some brought their own supplies of drink concealed inside their coats. Many smoked and the atmosphere was reputedly foul smelling and stuffy.
2. See Allen Eyles, *Gaumont British Cinemas*.

GLOSSARY

Adam style the British neo-classical style of the late eighteenth century, evolved by Robert Adam (1728–92), which became fashionable again at the end of the nineteenth century.

architrave moulding round an arch or door frame.

art deco popular modern decorative style of the late 1920s and early 1930s derived from the 1925 Exposition des Arts Décoratifs in Paris and characterised by stylised angular shapes, Egyptian motifs and, later, streamlining.

art nouveau decorative style used across Europe from the turn of the century until the 1920s often using sinuous and stylised motifs derived from nature. Charles Rennie Mackintosh was its most famous Scottish exponent.

auditorium the part of a theatre occupied by the seated audience.

balustrade vertical supports forming stair handrail.

baroque architecture originating in Italy, the European style of the seventeenth and early-eighteenth centuries, it is characterised by exuberance, curvaceousness and over scaling.

bas-relief sculpture in low relief.

beaux arts style the classical style propounded by the École des Beaux Arts in Paris during the nineteenth century.

cantilever steel structure fastened to a wall at one end and used to support the weight of theatre balconies.

cartouche ornament, usually plaster when indoors, consisting of tablet surrounded by scrolls.

caryatid female figure used (or appearing) to support entablature.

coffering decoration of a ceiling or the underside of an arch, consisting of sunken squares with ornamental panels.

conch half-domed roof in the form of a sea shell.

corbel stone projection from a wall to support weight.

Corinthian order most ornate of the three Greek orders, having bell-shaped capitals with rows of acanthus leaves.

cupola a small dome crowning a roof or tower.

Doric order the oldest, sturdiest and simplest Greek order with unadorned capitals and columns without bases.

entablature the part of an order above the columns, consisting of the architrave, frieze and cornice.

faience coloured earthenware tiles or mouldings.

filigree delicate tracery ornamentation in low relief.

garland moulded plaster representation of a wreath of fruit and flowers.

Ionic order Greek order characterised by two lateral scrolls attached to the capital.

latticework fine open structure of plaster cross-lathes.

loggia a covered open arcade or balcony fronted by columns.

minaret slender turret connected to a mosque from which Moslems are called to prayer and frequently re-scaled as a motif for use in Victorian ornamentation.

mullion vertical bar dividing a window or separating window.

nautch girl voluptuous plaster representation of Indian dancing girl.

ogee S-shaped moulding.

pediment low pitched gable over an entrance or facade.

pilaster rectangular column projecting slightly from a wall.

portico entrance porch.

proscenium the opening around the stage or screen.

repertory theatre programming policy whereby a company or companies present a repertoire of classic and/or modern plays.

rococo style A lighter, more frivolous development of the baroque style, first popular from around 1740 to 1750.

slip narrow extension of balcony along side wall.

splay walls angled side walls of auditorium around the proscenium opening.

stadium-plan auditorium design with one level of raked seating.

steppings seating terraces on theatre tiers.

swags moulded plaster representation of drapes.

terrazzo patterns of marble or other chips set in concrete and polished off to form an ornate floor.

Travertine white or light-coloured soft marble, often with veined or pitted texture.

Tuscan order simple, unornamented order of Italian origin.

tympanum space forming the centre of a pediment.

Terms Describing the Tiers of a Theatre (from top to ground level)

gallery/balcony/gods the highest tier offering a basic level of comfort.

upper circle the second tier up from the stalls (omitted in smaller theatres).

dress circle the first tier up from the stalls traditionally offering a high level of comfort.

pit area of cramped cheap seats, usually benches to the rear of the lowest floor.

orchestra stalls comfortable seats on the lowest floor closest to the stage.

stalls the entire lowest level of seating in a theatre.

stage boxes vertically stacked boxes located either side of the proscenium.

BIBLIOGRAPHY

Books

Publication details have been supplied where available.

Angus, K., *A Scotch Play-House, Being the Historical Records of the Old Theatre Royal, Marischal Street, Aberdeen*, D. Wyllie and Son, Aberdeen, 1878.

Arnot, H., *The History of Edinburgh*, Edinburgh, 1830.

Atwell, D., *Cathedrals of the Movies*, Architectural Press, London, 1981.

Bannister, W., *James Bridie and his Theatre*, London, 1955.

Baxter, P., *The Drama in Perth*, Thos. Hunter and Sons, Perth, 1907.

Baynham, W., *The Glasgow Stage*, Glasgow, 1892.

Bostock, E. H., *Menageries, Circuses and Theatres*, London, 1927.

Boutcher, R., and W. G. Kemp, *The Theatre in Perth*, Perth, 1975.

Campbell, D., *A Brighter Sunshine*, Polygon, Edinburgh, 1983.

Cleland, James, *The Annals of Glasgow*, Glasgow, 1816.

Coveney, M., *The Citz*, Hern, London, 1990.

Cunnison, J., and J. B. S. Gilfillan, *The Third Statistical Account of Scotland: Vol V Glasgow*, Collins, Glasgow, 1964.

Denholm, J., *The History of the City of Glasgow and Suburbs*, Glasgow, 1798.

Devlin, V., *Kings, Queens and People's Palaces: An Oral History of the Scottish Variety Theatre 1920–1970*, Polygon, Edinburgh, 1991.

Dibdin, J. C., *The Annals of the Edinburgh Stage*, Richard Cameron, Edinburgh, 1888.

Eyles, A., *ABC: The First Name in Entertainment*, British Film Institute, London, 1994.

Eyles, A., *Gaumont British Cinemas*, British Film Institute, London, 1996.

Findlay, B., *A History of Scottish Theatre*, Polygon, Edinburgh, 1998.

Freer, W., *My Life and Memories*, Glasgow, 1929.

Glasgow Theatre Royal, collection of legal papers connected with the case of John Henry Alexander, lessee, Edinburgh, 1842.

Glasstone, V., *Victorian and Edwardian Theatres*, Lund Humphries, London, 1978.

Gourlay, J., and R. C. Saunders, *The Story of the Glasgow Citizens' Theatre, 1943–1948*, Glasgow, 1948.

Henderson's *Annals of Dunfermline*.

House, J., *Dunoon 1868–1968*, Glasgow, 1968.

House, J., *Glasgow Past and Present*, Henry Muir, Glasgow, 1966.

House, J., *I Belong to Glasgow*, Glasgow, 1978.

Hutchison, D., *Modern Scottish Theatre*, Glasgow, 1977.

Irving, G., *The Good Auld Days: The Story of Scotland's Entertainers from Music Hall to Television*, London, 1977.

Jackson, J., *The History of the Scottish Stage from its First Establishment to the Present Time*, Edinburgh, 1793.

Lindon, A. F., *Dunfermline Remembered: Between the Wars*, The Fife Press, Kirkcaldy, 1982.

Littlejohn, J. H., *The Scottish Music Hall 1880–1990*, G.C. Book Publishers, Wigtown, 1990.

McCarthy, S., *Hengler's Circus: A History and Celebration 1847–1924*, Third Eye Centre, Glasgow, 1984.

Mackintosh, I., and M. Sell, *Curtains!!!, or a New Life for Old Theatres*, John Offord, London, 1982.

Mackintosh, Old Stager (pseud.), *Stage Reminiscences of Celebrated Theatrical and Musical Performers, during the last Forty Years*, Glasgow, 1870.

McLaren Young, A., and A M. Doak (eds), *Glasgow at a Glance*, Collins, Glasgow, 1965.

Macmillan, J. E., *Know Your Perth Vol II*, Perth Advertiser, Perth, undated.

Mander, R., and J. Mitchenson, *The Theatres of London*, New English Library, London, 1975.

Miller, J., *The Magic Curtain: The Story of the Theatre in Inverness*, Friends of the Eden Court Theatre, Inverness, 1986.

Moore, John, *Ayr Gaiety*, Albyn Press Ltd, Edinburgh, 1976.

Morris, James, *Recollections of Ayr Theatricals from 1809*, Ayr Advertiser, 1872.

Morton, C., *Theatre Royal Dumfries 1792–1992*, Swains, Edinburgh, 1992.

Oakley, C. A., *Fifty Years at the Pictures*, Scottish Film Council of the BFI, Glasgow, 1946.

Oakley, C. A., *The Second City*, Blackie and Sons Ltd, Glasgow, 1946.

Paterson, T., *Citizens' Theatre, Gorbals: Its Story from the Beginning to the Present Day*, Glasgow, 1970.

Penny, George, *The Traditions of Perth*, Dewar, Sidey, Morrison, Peat and Drummond, 1836.

Pratt, J., *His Majesty's Theatre: A Short History*, Aberdeen District Council Library Services, 1992.

Rowell, G., *The Victorian Theatre 1792–1914*, Cambridge, 1978.

Sachs, E. O., *Modern Opera Houses and Theatres*.

Swan, J., *Select Views of Glasgow and its Environs*, Glasgow, 1828.

Thomas, B., *The Last Picture Shows: Edinburgh*, Moorfoot, Edinburgh, 1984.

Thomas, M., *Silver Screen in the Silver City: A History of Cinemas in Aberdeen 1896–1987*, Aberdeen University Press, Aberdeen, 1987.
Walker, B. (ed.), *Frank Matcham: Theatre Architect*, Belfast, 1985.
Worsdall, F., *The City That Disappeared*, Glasgow, 1982.

Newspapers and Periodicals

Aberdeen Press and Journal
Airdrie and Coatbridge Advertiser
Ayrshire Post
Bradenton Herald
Caledonian Mercury
Cinema Theatre Association Bulletin
Circle – The House Magazine of Circuits Management Association, no. 51, 1954
Daily Record
Dumfries and Galloway Courier
Dumfries Weekly Journal
Dundee Evening Telegraph
Dunfermline Journal
Dunfermline Press
Edinburgh Courant
Edinburgh Monthly Mirror
The Era
Evening Citizen
Edinburgh Evening News
Evening Times
Falkirk Herald
Fife Free Press
Glasgow Courier
Glasgow Eastern Standard
Glasgow Herald
Glasgow Journal
Glasgow Weekly Herald
Greenock Advertiser
Greenock Telegraph
Groome's Gazeteer
Illustrated London News
Inverness Advertiser
Inverness Courier
Kilmarnock Standard
Kilmarnock Standard Annual
Lanarkshire Illustrated
London Courier
Motherwell Times
Paisley and Renfrewshire Gazette

Perth Advertiser
Playgoer
The Scots Magazine
The Scotsman
Scottish Field
Scottish Music Hall Society Journal
Scottish Opera Magazine
The Stage
Stirling Observer
Sunday Post
Theatres Trust Newsletter

Essays (unpublished)

Boyd, Frank, 'The Drama in Dundee and District'.
Forbes, J. Macfarlane, 'A Century of Entertainment', Stirling Observer Centenary Number.
MacPhail, A., 'The Story of His Majesty's Theatre, Aberdeen'.
Sugden, D., with Arup Associates and John Wyckham Associates, 'Scottish Opera: Cost Study for the Conversion of the Theatre Royal, Glasgow'.

INDEX